HOLY WAR, UNHOLY VICTORY

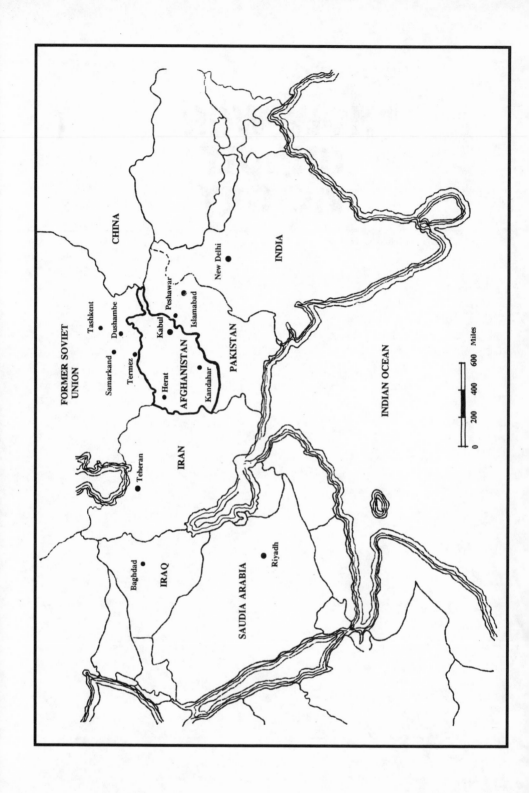

HOLY WAR, UNHOLY VICTORY

EYEWITNESS TO THE CIA'S SECRET WAR IN AFGHANISTAN

KURT LOHBECK

FOREWORD BY
DAN RATHER, CBS NEWS

REGNERY GATEWAY
Washington, D.C.

Library of Congress Cataloging-in-Publication Data
Lohbeck, Kurt.
Holy war, unholy victory : Eyewitness to the CIA's
Secret War in Afghanistan / Kurt
Lohbeck : foreword by Dan Rather.
p. cm.
Includes bibliographical references and index.
ISBN 0-89526-499-4 (acid-free paper)
1. Afghanistan—History—Soviet occupation, 1979–1989.
2. Afghanistan—History—1989– I. Title.
DS371.2.L635   1993
958.104′5—dc20   93-24344
CIP

Published in the United States by
Regnery Gateway, Inc.
1130 17th Street, NW
Washington, DC 20036

Distributed to the trade by
National Book Network
4720-A Boston Way
Lanham, MD 20706

Printed on acid-free paper.

Manufactured in the United States of America.

10 9 8 7 6 5 4 3 2 1

Dedication

When ongoing events in the world are no longer seen on our television screens we tend to believe they no longer exist. This is, of course, not true. A handful of dedicated, professional journalists remain to report events even when they no longer receive our focused attention. Associated Press reporter Sharon Herbaugh was a member of that handful of people. She was killed in a military helicopter crash in the spring of 1993 in the mountains of Afghanistan. She was the ninth Western journalist to die so that the world could witness what was happening in this remote country. They came from countries all over the world. This book is dedicated in memory of each of them.

Acknowledgements

I cannot give adequate credit to the courage of the many people caught in a capricious decade whose every day was an intense and dynamic adventure. Abdul Haq and the hundreds of other Afghan mujahaddin with whom I lived and worked must therefore be acknowledged by this book itself. Others need to be specifically mentioned: Din Mohammad, Abdul Qadir, Daud Arsalai, Khairullah Khan, Abdul Kabir, Hidyat Amin Arsala, Mohammed Gailani, Z'marai, Hamed Jaglan, Rahim Wardak, Ramatullah Safi, and Qazi Amin Wardak are on the top of a long list of dedicated people without whom this book could never have been.

Zubair Ali, Ismael Patel, Sahabzada Yaqoub Khan, Najmuddin Sheik, Ikramullah Jan, Shah Zaman, Masood Shah, are among the many Pakistanis who contributed so generously to my knowledge and my ability to function in their very different culture.

Numerous American, Pakistani, Afghan, Saudi, and British employees of their respective countries contributed to this book with the understanding they not be openly recognized. They fall under the category of "my secret phone number 74286." It is sufficient that they understand.

Steve Masty, Mike Malinowski, Marissa Lino, John Dixon, Richard Hoagland, Hank Cushing, Jae and Aisha, and Arnie Raphel kept me sane, or close enough.

I am also grateful for the encouragement and direct assistance of Hasan and Lisa Nouri, Robert Lohbeck, Susan Zabel, Izatullah

Mojadidi, Abdullah Etemadi, Said Ishaq, Omar Sawar, Paul and Michelle Britt, and Val Choslowsky. Special thanks are a pleasure to give to Patricia Bozell who made my ramblings into a book.

And Al Regnery who understands, as do I, that the torch must be passed on.

Contents

Foreword

BY

DAN RATHER

When I first walked through the Himalayas into Afghanistan, I had no idea what I was getting into. It was early 1980, just after the Soviet invasion. There were many harrowing experiences and close calls inside. I was lucky to make it out alive.

I came out knowing that Afghanistan had become one of the most dangerous places in the world and believing that it could develop into one of the most important battles of the Cold War.

Kurt Lohbeck was not with us that first time. "We" on that first trip in 1980 were a small team of CBS News regulars: Producer Andy Lack, Cameraman Mike Edwards, Soundman Peter O'Connor, and myself. Eden Naby, an American scholar and expert on all matters pertaining to Afghanistan, joined us as interpreter.

Lohbeck came later, after we had repeatedly urged—begged, really—CBS News to send *some*body to cover the war on a regular basis. After a couple of fits and starts with other outfits, Lohbeck in 1985 volunteered to go for CBS News and to stay. Various CBS News correspondents, producers, and camera crews had been and would continue to go into Afghanistan from time to time. But Lohbeck was assigned full-time to the war.

It might not have been his first choice—it wasn't mine—but he went as a "contract reporter/producer," with a contract to work regularly for CBS but not as a full-fledged staff employee. For him and for those of us at CBS News who believed in the story and its importance, it was the best we could do at the time and better than anyone else in the business was doing.

None of the other networks, and only a very few newspapers, magazines, or even wire services, was much interested in Afghanistan when the war first erupted and for quite a while afterward.

The very top of the U.S. government, including the White House and State Department, were downplaying the importance of the war. For one thing, they were convinced the Soviets would prevail. Some lower- and mid-level Central Intelligence Agency and Defense Intelligence people I knew had somewhat different views, a few quite different. But the top of the CIA apparently shared the White House and State Department assessment. Indeed, CIA leaders at the time were helping to shape the prevailing Washington view that the Soviets were bound to win in Afghanistan, probably quickly, and that it wasn't very important anyway. Plus there seemed to be at least a vague notion inside the CIA that given U.S. relations with Iran it might not be such a bad idea for the Soviets to have their way in Afghanistan, for a while at least. Fears of a second, Iran-style Islamic fundamentalist state—with its virulent anti-Americanism—and of an Islamic fundamentalist domino effect tipping over other states in the region made Soviet-bloc dominance look familiar and the lesser of evils. This was flawed reasoning and bad policy, but it reflected the view from the top in Washington at the time. And, I emphasize, most of these officials had no doubt of the Soviet Union's ability to dominate Afghanistan.

By the time Lohbeck agreed to be based in Pakistan and cover the war for CBS News from there, he believed us when we told him he might be covering one of the most important stories of his time. By that time, 1985, he had been in and around Afghanistan himself long enough to need no convincing.

He immersed himself in the story and lived it.

Out of his experience comes this book.

In it are his recollections, his impressions, his analysis of what happened and why in one of the least understood but most decisive battles of the Cold War. The Cold War, be it remembered, occupied half of the twentieth century and most of the world.

To understand why and how Afghanistan became such a pivotal battleground in the Cold War, the first thing to know and ponder is exactly where it is. Look at the map. This mysterious land of Central Asia is bounded on the north by what was, until recently, the USSR, on the east and south by Pakistan, in the northeast by China and India, on the west by Iran.

Its geographical location has made Afghanistan a crossroads of history.

Through it have flowed political and religious forces from Europe and Asia since the beginning of recorded history. Buddhism moved westward across Afghanistan from India and Islam eastward from Arabia long before the Christian armies of the British Empire plunged in. Alexander the Great came through it. So did Genghis Khan and Tamburlaine.

The many peoples in transit and in transition brewed one internal dispute after another, and influence at the crossroads was fiercely contested by the British and Russian imperialists in the nineteenth century, and after World War II by the USSR, Communist China, and the United States.

With Communist China's breakaway from the Soviets in the late 1950s and then with the rise of Islamic fundamentalism in Iran in the late 1970s, the USSR became increasingly concerned with trying to hold Afghanistan in its sphere of influence.

This it could not do. The failure of Moscow's puppet government and the Soviet army in Afghanistan helped to set in motion and then accelerate a whole series of shock waves, reassessments, and realignments inside the Soviet Union that contributed mightily to the fall of communism.

Because of this, many politicians of various persuasions and many intelligence organizations of various nationalities belatedly began to take credit for what happened in Afghanistan.

But the credit belongs almost entirely to those Afghans who fought the war. Whatever else one may or may not believe about them, they were brave, they were determined, they were persistent—and they did triumph.

Lohbeck spent a lot of time with them.

Along with every other journalist who covered firsthand this long, extraordinarily complex battle, Lohbeck made his mistakes and misjudgments, had his low points and his high ones.

He became an integral part of an effort that earned CBS News the right to say: When it came to the Afghanistan War, CBS got there early, kept on it with steadiness and constancy, and stayed late. Over the long haul—and it was a very long haul—nobody in journalism, print or broadcast, foreign or domestic, tried harder or succeeded more in covering the story.

And unlike some, including Kim Wimberger, who died on assignment for CBS News in Afghanistan, Lohbeck survived. He lived to tell about it and write about it.

This is his story.

Dan Rather
CBS News, New York

HOLY WAR, UNHOLY VICTORY

Prologue

The Golden Horde moved in a wave through Tian Shan past Pamir and into the region that is today called Afghanistan. Balkh was the cultural center of the area—Balkh, renowned throughout Central Asia, Persia, and Europe as a center of learning. Its library was reputed to contain over a half million works by scholars and historians, and its architecture was admired from places as distant as Florence. Although situated in the midst of a tribal society, its institutions were the basis of democratic government.

When the armies of the Lord of the Earth reached the outskirts of Balkh, they paused. The Great Genghis Khan saw no reason to destroy Balkh, but chose instead to infiltrate and administer from within. He struck an arrangement with the rulers of the city—he would install his nephew as governor of Balkh while the horde of the invincible Khan went southeast to subdue the warring tribes of the Pushtoons. The arrangement was readily accepted by the rulers of Balkh, who had heard tales of the utter destruction of Cathay by the Mongols. Thus it was that the young relative of the Lord of the Earth, the Scourge of the Mongols, the Khan of Khans, the Great Genghis Khan, took his place as governor of Balkh, while his uncle proceeded to the lower range of the Hindu Kush.

But the tribesmen proved to be a greater obstacle than the Golden Horde had expected. They would raid a regiment of the great army and then disappear into the shelter of the difficult and rugged mountains. The Great Khan had never encountered such audacity and prowess.

3

Meanwhile, in Balkh, the nephew, in the manner of younger offspring of great leaders, governed with tyrannical ruthlessness and demanded a subservience befitting the Great Khan. When the situation became intolerable, the citizenry of Balkh rose up *en masse*, as Afghans are wont to do, and killed him.

When word reached Genghis Khan, he was livid. How dare anyone question the absolute authority of his rule! Murder a governor he himself had installed, his own nephew! He disengaged from the tribesmen and assembled the Golden Horde on the plains of Jalalabad.

"Warriors of the steppes, heed my charge!" he bellowed. "It is my order and my command that we return to Balkh, that place of treachery. And you shall destroy it totally. You shall not rest until Balkh is no more. Not one brick shall remain connected to another, not one drop of blood shall continue to flow through one single vein. It is my command!"

Thus, the Golden Horde, with its thousands of horsemen, another thousand of foot soldiers, with tents, oxen, sheep, and all that accompanied the most terrifying army on earth, turned back to execute the order of the Lord of the Earth.

Execute the order they did. To this day, all that remains of the once proud city of Central Asia is a small segment of its high encircling wall. The wrath of the Great Genghis Khan had exacted its revenge.

When Balkh was no more, the Khan gathered the horde again. "You have once more carried out my command. And the world trembles before you. Your discipline makes you invincible. But before we continue, I must ask: Is there one among you who felt remorse while obeying my orders?"

The eyes of the bear-like man scanned the thousands assembled. There was not a sound, save the tears of the ground where so many had been slain. From left to right and back to the horizon he searched. Then, slowly, one banner was raised, and a lone Mongol warrior rode slowly to present himself before his lord and master. As he reached the rise where the Great Khan sat upon his steed, he threw himself prone on the ground.

"Tell me, tell your brethren, how you felt remorse," Khan commanded.

"Oh great Lord of the Earth, oh master of my life! When we received your order, we stormed the city as you desired," and the warrior shivered. "Upon entering the city, I came to a house with a great door. I smashed through the door and encountered a woman with a babe in her arms."

"And what did you do?" demanded the Great Khan.

"I ran her through with my sword."

"And then?" thundered the Mongol leader.

"And the babe fell to the ground. I placed my sword in its mouth, and the babe began to suckle the tip as if it were its mother's breast. At that moment, my Lord, I felt remorse."

"And what did you do?" quizzed the khan, with compassion or hatred, it was difficult to distinguish.

"Knowing the wrath of the Great Lord of the Earth, oh mighty Khan, I ran my sword through the babe."

"Mongol warrior, for this demonstration, you shall be raised above every member of the feared Golden Horde this very day!"

The soldier was hanged from a lonely tree as the horde rode away beneath him.

History, as it so often does, repeated itself in 1978 when the Soviet rulers infiltrated the government in Kabul and staged a coup to install their brother communist, Noor Mohammad Taraki, in power and thus capture Afghanistan and administer from within. The tribal descendants of those who had fought the Great Khan again revolted. To keep the prize, the Red Army of the Soviet Union invaded Afghanistan in December 1979. Five years later, well over a million Afghans had been slain by helicopter gunship, jet aircraft, artillery, and commando soldiers. The Red Army showed no mercy, no remorse.

The story of Balkh, in those years past, did not end with the destruction of the city. The tribesmen from the mountains continued to harass and attack, slashing and hacking away at the horde. It took years, but the tenacious Afghan tribesmen fought a holy war to rid their country of the invader, and eventually they succeeded. The mighty Genghis Khan returned to the northern steppes of Asia without the banner of Afghanistan on his lance.

Similarly, centuries later, and nearly a decade after the largest army on earth, the Red Army of the Soviet Union, entered Afghanistan, it began to withdraw, but not in victory. The tribesmen of the mountains of Afghanistan, calling themselves the mujahaddin (holy warriors), chipped away at the Soviet intruders like furious hornets. And the mighty Red Army returned to its homeland without the banner of Afghanistan on its lance.

This book is the Afghans' story. It is the story of battles and intrigues, of friends and foes, of heroes and traitors. It is the story of people who take the last rites of Islam before going into battle, for they are already dead and will remain so until they are killed and their souls are loosed. Or until they free their homeland. It is called *Jihad*, a Holy War; there is no other way to describe it.

Those who die while participating in *Jihad* are called *shaheedan*, or martyrs. In the past decade, over one million people have become *shaheedan*. This book is written in their memory.

CHAPTER 1

Weaving a Tangled Web

"You should say what you mean," the March Hare went on.
"I do," Alice hastily replied: "at least—at least I mean
what I say—that's the same thing, you know."
"Not the same thing a bit!" said the Hatter.

—LEWIS CARROLL, 1832–1898

On August 17, 1988, an American-built C-130 military transport airplane of the Pakistani air force took off from Bahawalpur, Pakistan. Among its passengers were Pakistani President Zia ul-Haq and eight of the top generals in his army. At the last minute, another passenger went on board—the American ambassador to Pakistan, Arnold Raphel. Minutes into the flight the plane began to bob and weave in the air; then, abruptly, it nosedived and slammed straight into the ground. All aboard were killed. The plane, it was later determined, had been sabotaged. This would prove to be one of the most significant events in the entire Afghan War.

On August 20, just three days later, Secretary of State George Schultz arrived in Islamabad for the funeral of Zia ul-Haq. Accompanying him was Raphel's successor, Robert Oakley. The unprecedented speed of the appointment clearly signaled the importance of the office. The ambassador was instructed to coor-

7

dinate U.S. involvement in the Afghan War that was taking place just across Pakistan's northern border.

Robert Bigger Oakley, ambassador and plenipotentiary of the United States to Pakistan, had not received his appointment by virtue of a large campaign donation to the president. He was a veteran of American covert activities. Oakley came to the job directly from his position as strategist on the staff of the National Security Council in the White House. Prior to that, he had been assistant secretary of state for counterterrorism. A tall, thin, lanky Texan, he knew his way around the labyrinthine world of intelligence operations.

The United States Embassy in Islamabad, Pakistan, had been burned to the ground by a ruthless mob of Muslim extremists in 1979. They were protesting rumors that the U.S. was behind the violence that had taken place in the Holy City of Mecca during the pilgrimage of Haj. On that occasion, hundreds had been killed in the holiest city of Saudi Arabia when Iranian Shiia Muslims attempted to take control of the Grand Mosque.

The new American embassy was built on the outskirts of Pakistan's capital city of Islamabad in an area called "the diplomatic enclave." It was a red brick fort, surrounded by a ten-foot high wall topped with concertina wire (razor-sharp barbed wire). Inside the walls but separate from the main embassy building was a luxurious split-level home known as "the residence," the ambassador's plush residence.

I was first introduced to Bob Oakley by former Ambassador Gerald Helman in Washington in 1985. Helman was deeply involved in the State Department's operations in support of the Afghan War. Oakley was then assistant secretary of state.

When the plane carrying President Zia and Ambassador Raphel crashed, I was on the outskirts of Kabul with the mujahaddin commander Abdul Haq. We listened to a short-wave radio broadcast of the Voice of America as it announced Oakley's appointment. Abdul had met Oakley in Washington. Since I was returning to Pakistan the next day, Abdul Haq asked me if I would deliver a note to the new American ambassador, a simple message welcoming him to his new assignment and wishing him well.

I returned to Pakistan the next day and called Oakley two days later. He invited me to the residence for a drink. When I reintroduced myself, he said, "I know who you are; the State Department is familiar with your reputation." I gave him Abdul's note and he seemed to appreciate the gesture, remarking that Abdul Haq was considered one of the top commanders of the Afghan mujahaddin. He ruminated a bit on the embassy staff's resentment of his quick appointment. Arnie Raphel had been a very popular man, making it difficult for anyone to replace him. But, he said, he intended to shake things up.

Moving on to a discussion of the situation inside Afghanistan, I mentioned the havoc that Gulbaddin Hekmatyar, a fanatic resistance leader, was causing. Gulbaddin had gained a reputation for doing battle against more mujahaddin groups than against the communist Afghan regime. He was virulently anti-American and supported the extremist Pan-Islam movement. I spoke of the concern of numerous other mujahaddin leaders concerning Gulbaddin's growing power among the refugee population, which was a direct result of American largesse—the United States and Pakistan were Gulbaddin's primary sources of money and supplies. Oakley assured me that the situation would change.

A year later, in the fall of 1989, Ambassador Oakley held a media background briefing at his residence. He was accompanied by Terry Flaumer, a State Department specialist on the Afghan War, and William Lenderking of the United States Information Service (USIS) office in Islamabad, who would get nervous and fidgety if Oakley was asked a direct question on Afghanistan. Approximately twenty Western journalists attended.

The Soviet army had withdrawn from Afghanistan in February 1989. But the anticipated collapse of the regime in Kabul had not taken place, primarily because the Resistance had no alternative government ready to take power. The principal cause of this debacle was the obstinate opposition of Gulbaddin Hekmatyar to the six other mujahaddin parties.

Gulbaddin, contrary to published reports and State Department briefings, did not have a highly effective fighting force inside Afghanistan, but he did have a lot of money and a huge supply of weaponry. His tactics were to buy support among other resistance groups and, it was said, to have those who opposed him assassinated.

At the background briefing in his home, Oakley was asked by a British reporter why the United States was providing so much money and support to Gulbaddin, particularly since Gulbaddin fingered the U.S. as the number one evil to the Islamic world.

Oakley stated unequivocally that American support of Gulbaddin had been stopped completely. Still, Flaumer insisted, humanitarian assistance, such as food, was being given to refugees aligned with Gulbaddin.

For the next several days, news stories around the world reported that "Western diplomatic sources" had confirmed that Gulbaddin had been cut off from American supplies. Several mujahaddin leaders were quoted as being optimistic of a sensible solution to the war if Gulbaddin, the proverbial "dog in the manger," were indeed removed. Gulbaddin, for his part, was quoted as saying that the Americans could not cut him off from supplies because they had never given him anything in the first place.

About a week later, I was awakened around two o'clock in the morning by aircraft flying low over my house. I lived about a half mile from the Peshawar airport, which was closed at night—except for an occasional military flight—because there were no radar or other instruments for night landings and takeoffs. On this particular night, it sounded as if a large plane were circling every few minutes. Going to my front yard to investigate, I could see large aircraft on landing patterns for the Peshawar airport. Several planes were flying low overhead.

I got into my car and drove down the road to the fence at the back of the airport. Through the fence, I could see several large, dark green, military transport aircraft, with engines running, on a tarmac on the military side of the airfield. Pakistanis wearing the baggy *shalwar kameez* dress of the subcontinent were unloading large boxes to put into trucks. Western men in trousers and jackets, some wearing baseball caps, were directing the operation. One of these men looked familiar—I had seen him in the bar of the American Club at the U.S. Embassy. The planes, clearly visible in the moonlight, had no markings. Conspicuously missing on their tails was the green and white crescent and star of the Pakistan air force.

As each plane was unloaded, it taxied to the runway and took off—at least six, perhaps more, as I watched through the fence. After about an hour, the convoy of fifty or so Bedford trucks left through a back gate in the fence surrounding the airport and proceeded down the road past me. The last truck was followed by a Pakistani army jeep.

I got into my car and followed the convoy. At about four o'clock in the morning, the long trail of trucks, loaded with what was obviously arms and ammunition, wound its way through the deserted streets of Peshawar and onto the road to Warsak, a village close to the Afghan border.

Close to an hour later, the convoy came to a large encampment surrounded by a tall fence. It was the training camp of Gulbaddin Hekmatyar. I had been there several times for interviews or other events staged by him. I pulled off the road, walked up a hill, and watched as the trucks were unloaded into underground bunkers inside the compound. From my vantage point, I could clearly see what was being unloaded—rocket launchers, boxes I recognized as the type containing rocket-propelled grenades, 107 mm shells, and thousands of small arms ammunition. I was dumbfounded. Only a week before, the United States ambassador had stated, point-blank, that no more military supplies would be delivered to the fanatically anti-American, antidemocratic extremist, Gulbaddin Hekmatyar.

Several questions sprang to mind. What would I do with this information? How would I get the story out? And why? Why would the American intelligence services continue to support the one man who was preventing an auspicious end to this brutal and devastating war?

Certainly, the on-going "covert" weapons supply had been a long-held open secret in Pakistan. American, Saudi, Egyptian, and others would deliver weapons, ammunition, and other logistical materials to the Pakistani military intelligence service (ISI) either by ship at the port of Karachi or by aircraft to a number of military airfields. These materials would be stored in Pakistani arms depots for distribution to various mujahaddin commanders. But the operation this night to all appearances came directly from Western, obviously American, intelligence services to Gulbaddin Hekmatyar.

Had the ambassador lied? Or was the covert operation going on without his knowledge?

The next evening I ran into the U.S. consul general to Peshawar, Mike Malinowski, and asked him directly, "If the ambassador and the embassy are publicly saying that Gulbaddin has been cut off, why is a convoy of several dozen trucks delivering weapons to him at this time?"

Malinowski, one of the most competent observers of the mujahaddin and the war, answered candidly, "Well, Gulbaddin is the most effective fighting force in Afghanistan; he's the only one who can defeat the regime."

I was flabbergasted. For over two years, Malinowski had been one of the foremost American officials in Pakistan to denounce and warn against the ruthless fanaticism of Gulbaddin. Now he was practically endorsing him.

For the remainder of 1989, the embassy, consular offices, and USIS put the "spin" on the Afghan story: Gulbaddin *was* the Resistance. Which was quite simply not true. Gulbaddin had no effective fighting organization. He had not a single commander with any military reputation for fighting the Soviets or the Afghan regime. He had made alliances with top regime military figures. And he had killed numerous other mujahaddin commanders. Yet the United States government and the covert agencies were doing their best to convert that lie into reality.

At the time, I was in my seventh year of covering and reporting the Afghan War, most recently as the reporter/producer for CBS News. My first trip to Pakistan, and into Afghanistan with the mujahaddin, had been as a freelance television documentary producer in 1983, then the only American journalist regularly to travel inside Afghanistan with the mujahaddin.

Originally, prior to 1983, I had no intention of coming to this remote country known as the "roof of the world." But I was living in Washington when the Soviets shot down a Korean airliner, killing over a 160 passengers, and anti-Soviet demonstrations sprang up around the world, including Washington.

Following a day of protests, a large group of friends went to Desireé, a private club, to celebrate the turnout. Most of them were young Republican activists enjoying Ronald Reagan's Washington. There I met a young woman who explained that she was helping a group set up an organization to lobby official Washington to support the Afghan resistance fighters. Anne Hurd told me that the hardest job was publicizing the plight of the Afghans who were resisting the invasion of the Soviet army. Network television, she said, had devoted only ten minutes of airtime in the first year of the Resistance. I asked why only ten minutes? She said that everyone was afraid to go into the remote mountain country and face the Soviet army. And, she added wryly, the Soviets were not providing tours for journalists.

Within two weeks, Anne and I had formed an independent television documentary company to go into Afghanistan and cover the war. We hoped to get this remote but important conflict on the television screens—a tactic vital to any cause.

Over the course of the next nine years, I would learn that the Soviets were not the only ones that objected to unbiased reporting of the Afghan War. The CIA, if for other reasons, was right alongside them.

CHAPTER 2

In the Eyes of the Beholders

It was long ago in my life as a reporter that I decided that facts must never get in the way of truth.

—JAMES CAMERON, 1911–1985

I spent most of the next eight years covering the war in Afghanistan from Asia as well as Washington. I was the only American journalist to cover the war full time, living in Pakistan and traveling inside by crossing over the highest mountains in the "roof of the world." I watched the Afghan mujahaddin as they fought the army of the Soviet Union, and I met, and was involved with, all the players as the conflict unfolded, both in Afghanistan and in Washington. The war would come deeply to involve the United States. How did it start? After lengthy interviews and conversations with the people concerned around the world, I have been able to reconstruct what happened on that bleak December night in 1979.

Christmas Eve, 1979, was crispy cold and clear in Kabul. The mountains ringing the city were covered with snow, but the city itself was only brushed with its traces. A heavy snowfall was overdue. Western diplomats and other visitors to the Afghan capital gathered at the Intercontinental Hotel for a party.

"The State Department had ordered the evacuation of all

dependents in August," recalled one diplomat. "So there weren't a lot of us to celebrate." But there was much talk.

Michael Malinowski, a junior foreign service officer, vividly remembers the evacuation. "They sent my wife and our household belongings by air, because the government could not secure the overland trip to Peshawar, Pakistan."[1]

"Our operations around the country," interjected mujahaddin leader Haji Din Mohammad, "were extending into Kabul itself. Three or four months and Hafizullah Amin's government would have collapsed."[2]

"I remember in September," Malinowski continued, "I was talking with Vassily Safronchek of the Soviet Embassy, and I goaded him by saying things were not very secure. Safronchek responded, 'Very soon you will see strong changes in that regard; you will be pleased.' "[3]

"I talked to the fellow [Hafizullah Amin] on the phone in mid-December," said Pakistani President Zia ul-Haq. "It was my impression the chap wanted to pull away from the Soviets, but didn't know how to accomplish it."[4]

"I was the Afghan chargé d'affaire in Moscow," Majid Mangal recalled. "They summoned our president to a meeting with Brezhnev. At the meeting, they pulled out a document for us to sign. They said it was a 'friendship treaty.' They would not give me an opportunity to read it. The president was not interested in reading it; he just signed it. Then Brezhnev signed it, and we all had a glass of vodka to celebrate. It was that simple."[5]

The diplomats at the Intercon on Christmas Eve were not thinking of "friendship treaties" or phone calls between presidents of neighboring countries. In fact, several of them overcelebrated and had to book rooms in the hotel for the night.

By midnight the din of engines was overwhelming. "What the hell is happening?" shouted Malinowski. What was happening was an invasion by the Soviet army. The Antonov transport planes, an exact replica of the American Hercules in design and structure, were landing and taking off at the rate of "one each minute," according to Malinowski.

The planes disgorged several thousand infantry soldiers and

hundreds of tanks, trucks, and jeeps. MI-6 and MI-8 helicopters brought in several thousand more commando troops. The Christmas celebrants looked on, stunned, from the hilltop hotel.

Minutes before the first Antonov hit the runway, a KGB assault team stormed the Presidential Palace in the Darulaman section of the capital. Led by Colonel Boyarinov, the commandant of KGB Department 8, Special Operations from Balasika, they cut down the outside guards with AK74 sniper rifles, Kalikovs. Colonel Boyarinov and three men burst into a sitting room where President Amin was entertaining a young lady. A bartender, mixing drinks on the side of the room, was later thought to have made sure that the president would be in this particular room at this particular time. The theory will never be verified, for the first fusillade of bullets cut him in two. After quickly dispatching the other two occupants of the room, Colonel Boyarinov drove to the airport, climbed aboard one of the departing Antonovs, and returned to Moscow.[6]

The KGB had done its job; the rest was up to the army.

East of Kabul in Nangahar Province, a young commander of a small group of anticommunist guerrillas watched the planes landing in Jalalabad. From reports, he learned that hundreds of tanks were tearing down the road from Kabul. Twenty-one-year-old Abdul Haq remembers telling his men, "Now our job has begun."[7]

The next morning, Radio Kabul interrupted a music program with a special bulletin. It was not revealed that the program originated in Tashkent, capital of the Soviet Republic of Uzbekistan. Babrak Karmal was introduced, although he was already well known to the Afghan population, most recently as their ambassador to Czechoslovakia. Prior to this, he had been deputy prime minister and one of the organizers of the Parcham (banner) faction of the Communist party.

Babrak calmly told the people of Afghanistan that he was their new president. He did not waste their time by attempting to define under what legal process this had occurred. He then explained that, as president, he had requested their brothers in the Soviet Union to assist in providing peace and security to the country. The brothers had responded by sending a "limited contingent" of soldiers. By the time the broadcast ended, the limited contingent was approaching eighty thousand men and the requisite support supplies.

In the Situation Room of the White House in Washington, D.C., President Jimmy Carter was livid. Neither Secretary of State Cyrus Vance nor the director of Central Intelligence, Admiral Stansfield Turner, had accurately predicted the events, although Turner pointed out that they had sent numerous reports of Soviet troop buildups and unusual movements in the Tashkent sector to the National Security Council (NSC) staff. In fact, the president himself had expressed his concern publicly. But the American hostage crisis in Tehran had strongly overshadowed developments in Afghanistan.[8]

Carter knew he had to react quickly and dramatically. The right wing of the Republican party was gearing up for an assault on White House foreign policy. He ordered that options be presented to him by December 26.

On December 26, nearly forty-eight hours after the first troop transport planes landed in Kabul, Soviet radio announced: "THIS IS RADIO MOSCOW, BROADCASTING TO GREAT BRITAIN AND IRELAND. THE SOVIET NATIONAL DAILY PRAVDA HAS COMMENTED ON THE DEVELOPMENT OF THE EVENTS IN AFGHANISTAN. THEY SAID THAT A LIMITED NUMBER OF TROOPS WAS SENT TO AFGHANISTAN AND THESE TROOPS ARE TO PROVIDE SECURITY TO THE FRIENDLY AND PEACE-LOVING PEOPLE OF AFGHANISTAN."[9]

The president of the United States addressed the nation on December 27, 1979. "The implications of the Soviet invasion of Afghanistan could pose a more serious threat to the peace since the Second World War." He went on to express his dismay at the Soviet action, saying Brezhnev had "deceived him." And, finally, he announced the cancellation of American wheat sales to the USSR and the withdrawal of the American team to the Moscow Olympics in 1980, calling upon American allies to do the same.[10]

By this time, the cities of Jalalabad and Gandahar had been

secured, according to Red Army dispatches intercepted by Western intelligence offices in Islamabad and New Delhi.

In Riyadh, Saudi Arabia, the three sons (of dozens) of the late King Abdul Aziz ibn Saud who ruled the country were worried. Crown Prince and Prime Minister Fahd ibn Abdulaziz (although King Khalid was the titular ruler, Fahd ran the day-to-day affairs of the government; Khalid died in June 1981 and Fahd ascended to the throne), Prince Abdullah ibn Abdulaziz, deputy prime minister and commander of the National Guard, and Defense Minister Prince Sultan ibn Abdulaziz were convinced the Soviet move into Afghanistan was only a prelude to direct Soviet involvement in Iran.[11]

Saudi intelligence was well aware that Dr. Najib, the Afghan ambassador to Iran, was a protegé of KGB Chief Yuri Andropov. They had received reliable reports that Najib had been given $24 million by the KGB to increase Tudah party activities and further destabilize the chaotic situation in Tehran.

The Saudi royal family decided to contact Pakistani General Abdul Acktar Rahman Khan, Zia confidante and director general of Inter-Services Intelligence (ISI), to compare notes. Prince Bandar ibn Sultan, the son of the defense minister, who was being groomed for a bigger role within the government, was assigned to scout various governments, including the United States, to help further their own destabilization program in Afghanistan.[12]

General Acktar was highly receptive to the Saudi initiative. The Soviet invasion was a real and present threat to the delicate stability of Pakistan. With President Zia's strong backing, he reorganized the ISI and provided much expertise and logistics to the Afghan Resistance. For years, ever since the Socialist Mohammad Daoud's coup in 1973, Pakistani intelligence had been behind the Islamic resistance in Afghanistan. Ali Bhutto, wary of Daoud's friendship with India, had also provided considerable support.

Pakistan also enlisted Chinese aid for the Resistance in the form of weapons and ammunition; the Saudis would pay the bills. And since the Egyptians had warehouses full of Soviet weaponry, King Fahd was easily able to convince Anwar Sadat to join the cause. Ostracized by the Arab community since signing the Camp David accords, Sadat grabbed this opportunity to respond to an Arab request for assistance.

In Washington, CIA Director Turner balked. He was being asked to have CIA-sponsored operations and weapons kill Soviet soldiers. But National Security Advisor Zbigniew Brzezinski won the argument by pointing out that this time the Soviets had gone too far. They had to be stopped. And he assured President Carter that this was exactly the type of hard-line policy that he needed going into the 1980 political season.[13] The CIA put up $100 million. The Saudi's agreed to match U.S. expenditures dollar for dollar. The war was on.

CHAPTER 3

Past is Prologue

Those who cannot remember the past are condemned to repeat it.

—GEORGE SANTAYANA, 1863–1952

From September to mid-November 1983 I planned and organized my trip to Afghanistan. I talked with "experts" at the State Department and met and interviewed old Afghan hands, those who had lived there in the 1950s and 1960s, as well as people who had become involved in lobbying or support efforts since the Soviet invasion. One of the most helpful was Brigadier Mohammad Nawaz Choudary, the Pakistani defense attaché in Washington. He educated me on the history of Pakistan's relations with Afghanistan and briefed me on its assistance to the anticommunist resistance fighters—the mujahaddin.

Researching the events that led to the 1979 Soviet invasion, I discovered that history does indeed repeat itself, or at the least, that nations do not give up their goals simply because they have failed to achieve them in the past. It became obvious that the Soviets' current strategic goals did not differ from those of the czars in the past. The craving of the Russians for the mountain kingdom had started well over a century ago.

All Soviet schoolchildren, particularly military students and cadets at the Frunze Institute, look at the world differently from their Western counterparts. Their maps of the world and of Eurasia are downsideup, with India at the top and Russia centered at the bottom.[1] When viewed from this perspective, Afghanistan is the natural gateway through the mountain barriers to China, India, and Iran. To the Russians, taking Afghanistan is the most logical way of surrounding their neighbors. With either friendly states or client states in Syria, South Yemen, India, Burma, North Korea, and Vietnam, the move to Afghanistan would help complete the circles around the Persian Gulf and China itself.

Although some analysts and political commentators attributed the Soviet invasion of Afghanistan to a desire for warm water ports or as a strategic move to the Straits of Hormutz, the drive into Afghanistan was also an end unto itself. A look at the downsideup map makes that obvious.

British India was able to keep the ever-encroaching empire, first Russian and then Soviet, at bay until the end of World War II, when Britain no longer had the power or political will to maintain its control over the subcontinent.

As for Afghanistan, in 1933, nineteen-year-old Zahir Shah ascended the throne after the assassination of his father, King Nadir Shah. The uncles of Zahir Shah ruled Afghanistan as regents for the young king for twenty years, until 1953. (It was considered an unusual and good sign that they did not kill young Mohammad Zahir and name one of themselves king.[2]) They ruled the tribal kingdom of the Hindu Kush loosely, maintaining power through ever-changing coalitions of tribes. Their foreign policy was distinctly pro-Western, with a watchful eye on the Soviets to the north.

Asia was not an important concern of the United States when it emerged from World War II as a world power. Afghanistan, in particular, was not even on the horizon of American interests until early 1944 when Major General Patrick J. Hurley made an official visit to Kabul as President Franklin D. Roosevelt's personal representative. Roosevelt had clearly stated that the United States wanted to keep Britain as a first-class power. But, with equal firmness, the U.S. opposed any form of imperialism and, moreover, wished to prevent Britain and the Soviet Union from

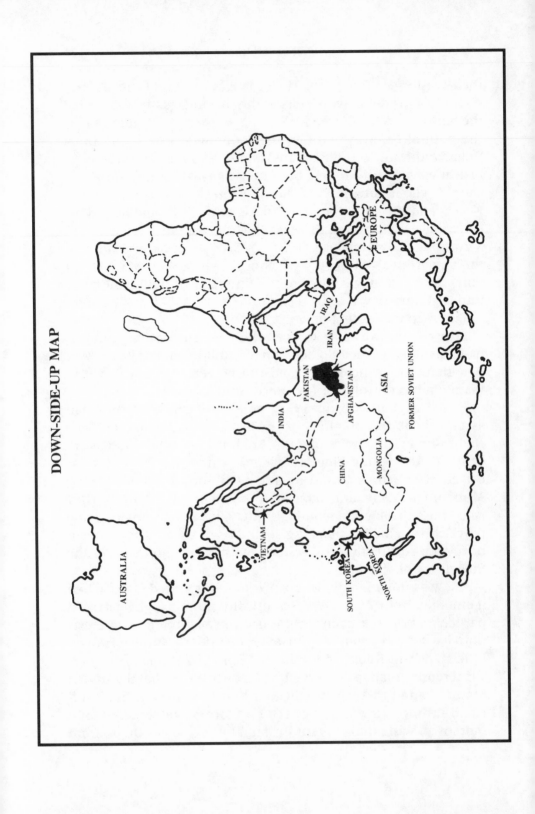

DOWN-SIDE-UP MAP

hogging the spoils of war. America had learned from experience: after World War I, the victorious powers had cut the United States out of postwar policies.

General Hurley carried a mandate as the personal representative of the American president to tour the Middle East and the India-Burma-China theater to "observe and recommend" on the situation there to the president. His directive called for him to "extend your observations as far as Karachi." In this context, Hurley decided to take a look at Afghanistan.

Ignored in the first few years of the war, with the exception of some German feelers (see chapter 30), Afghanistan drew the attention of the United States after China had been isolated by the Japanese invasion. Hurley's mission to Kabul was twofold: first, to investigate the possibility of oil; and second, to investigate whether Afghanistan could become a land route into the Sin-Kiang Province of China—this because as matters stood supplies to China and Chiang Kai-shek could only be delivered by air via the dangerous "Hump Route" over the Himalayas.

On December 28, 1943, Patrick Hurley was invited to Afghanistan as the guest of King Zahir Shah. Hurley flew to Peshawar, in the Northwest Frontier Province of British India, on the first leg of his trip to the mountain kingdom. Foreigners were generally not welcome in Afghanistan; Hurley, however, had not only been invited, he had also been given permission to fly over Afghan territory. This signified the high regard the Afghan rulers had for his mission.

The British in Peshawar were alarmed by the American visit to Kabul. They considered Afghanistan their playground, off limits to the Americans, and so, in due course, a series of British-inspired mishaps occurred to thwart Hurley's trip. First, the plane in which he was to fly over the mountains to Kabul was declared unfit to land on the Kabul air strip; then the British airfield officials "lost" the key to the gasoline pump and could not furnish fuel for the flight; and, following that delay, ominous weather reports from Kabul were withheld from the Americans so that they had to turn back when they were within a tantalizing twenty miles of the Afghan capital. The next day, a repeat: the

Americans, again close to the capital, had to return to Peshawar because of engine trouble that had developed during the flight.

Finally, in disgust, General Hurley and his party of four officers and four enlisted men left Peshawar by automobile and drove through the Khyber Pass, leaving instructions for a plane to be sent to Kabul on January 12 for their return to India. On January 8, 1944, much to the chagrin of the British, Hurley arrived in the kingdom of Afghanistan.

During the five days of his stay, the red carpet was rolled out for the representative of the American president. Afghanistan, he soon learned, was a rugged and primitive country with no railroads, few roads, and little means of communication. Natural resources were not underdeveloped, they were undeveloped. The Afghans explained to Hurley that only thus could Afghanistan avert becoming a victim of the imperialistic greed of the British or Russians. In contrast, they seemed to regard the United States, proponent of the Atlantic Charter and the Declaration on Iran, as a potential friend who would help them develop, protect them from neighbors, and not exploit their country.

The American military attaché in Kabul wrote to the War Department: "The favorable impact of General Hurley's visit to Kabul was very marked. Psychologically it was exceedingly well timed because while Turkey, Iran, Iraq, Egypt, etc. had either shared or participated in the Teheran Conference, Afghanistan had been left out entirely. Afghans were eager for some notice from the United States although they were too proud to invite it. Moreover, it afforded Afghanistan a direct channel to the United States which is now looked to as the arbitrator of Afghan-Russian and Afghan-British relations. Politically the effects of General Hurley's visit tended to strengthen the rule of the present regime."[3]

Hurley cabled Roosevelt: "Since leaving Afghanistan I have confirmed the impression I received there which is that neither Russia nor Britain has the confidence of the Afghanistan Government. All the members of the Government, including the King, expressed their complete confidence in you. The fact that the United States government has no imperialistic designs may be regarded as the chief reason why it is trusted by Afghanistan. The King himself is also familiar with the principles advocated by you. He expressed himself as being in complete accord and anxious to follow your leadership."[4]

That leadership never developed, although the Afghan government continually held out a friendly hand to the United States. The Afghans hoped to be able to develop their country in the postwar years with American investment and assistance.[5] Among the enterprises that developed with American aid was the project in Helmand City that became known as "Little America."[6] Mohammad Amman, a strong supporter of American technology, was one of its directors. Years later, three of his children became important figures in the Resistance against the Soviets: Din Mohammad, Abdul Qadir, and Abdul Haq.[7]

With the death of President Roosevelt in early 1945, the sights of American foreign policy were directed elsewhere. President Harry S Truman came to office almost totally ignorant of Roosevelt's plans for postwar Asia. And Averell Harriman, U.S. ambassador to the Soviet Union and a product of the State Department, seemed principally concerned with implementing the Yalta agreement and protecting Soviet interests in Asia.

It was not until 1949 that a small loan was given to Afghanistan through the Export-Import Bank.[8] The United States, however, ignored Afghan pleas for military aid to strengthen their internal and external defenses despite Afghan fears of a Soviet invasion now that the British had left India.[9] And, indeed, the Soviets were focusing their attention on Afghanistan, and beyond. In a speech to the United Nations in 1951, Soviet Foreign Minister V. M. Molotov stated that the future of the Soviet Union "lies south of Baku." While the statement was intended to reassure Europe, it had the opposite effect in Kabul.

When Pakistan was created following the British withdrawal from the subcontinent, the issue of Pushtunistan emerged. This red herring issue was devised by the Indian politicians of the Congress party in an attempt to keep Pakistan from being carved out of India.[10] The northern border of Pakistan was arbitrarily marked off at the Durand Line, which line was drawn according to the natural flow of water. The mountain streams flowing northwesterly and into the Kabul river designated Afghanistan; where the water flowed southerly and into the Indus river was Pakistan.

Perhaps also intended by the British, the line ran right through the middle of the ancestral lands of the Pushtoons, the large tribal group of people that populate 80 percent of Afghanistan and most of the Northwest Frontier Province (NWFP) of Pakistan. British tactics had always been to divide and conquer. The subcontinent was now divided along ethnic and/or religious lines. The people of the NWFP, the Pushtoons, were closely linked, socially and politically, with their tribal cousins in Afghanistan.

The foremost leader of the Pushtunistan movement in Pakistan was Khan Abdul Ghaffar Khan, a close associate of Mahatma Ghandi in the struggle for Indian independence. Ghaffar Khan's "Red Shirts" (currently known in Pakistan as the Awami National party) did not support the independence of Pakistan from India, but after Pakistan became a reality, they led the fight to establish a separate Pushtunistan.

The Pushtunistan issue boiled for several years, threatening war between Pakistan and Afghanistan. Pakistan was at the time of major importance to the designs of the new American secretary of state, John Foster Dulles, who wanted to encircle the Soviet Union with countries militarily allied with the United States. The new country began to emerge as a strategic ally (exemplified by its allowing U-2 flights from Pakistan's Peshawar Air Base, one of which resulted in Francis Gary Powers being shot down over the Soviet Union).[11] President Dwight D. Eisenhower, in consequence, refused repeated Afghan requests for military aid and instead told the Afghans to settle the Pushtunistan issue.

The Soviets took full advantage of the Pushtunistan problem by openly supporting Ghaffar Khan's attempt to break up the new federations of Pakistan. In 1955, Afghan Prime Minister Mohammad Daoud, a cousin of King Zahir Shah, decided to accept the Soviet offers of military and developmental assistance. Soviet leaders Khrushchev and Bulganin subsequently paid an official five-day visit to Afghanistan—in sharp contrast to Eisenhower's two-hour stop at the Kabul airport, en route to New Delhi.

Mohammad Daoud had taken power as prime minister in what was largely a family dispute. He replaced the king's uncles, who had served as regents for twenty years, but did not have the pro-American inclinations held by most of the royal family.

Daoud moved swiftly to accept Soviet involvement in several areas. Afghan military officers were sent to the Soviet Union for training, and the Soviets began a road-building program and constructed several power-generating dams. Soviet advisors in every area of expertise began pouring into Afghanistan.

Rather than countering these moves, Dulles mistakenly decided that Afghanistan was of no strategic importance.

By 1963, the Afghan border with Pakistan had been closed for two years, creating economic problems, and the royal family, fed up with Daoud's mismanagement and growing dependence on the Soviets, removed him as prime minister. Afghanistan took the opportunity to begin an experiment with democracy. The new constitution created a constitutional monarchy and an elected Parliament. And King Zahir Shah personally inserted a clause that prevented members of the royal family from holding public office.

These moves were implemented without pressure or assistance from the United States. In fact, Leo Poullada, a State Department official concerned with Afghanistan, wrote, "It was in America's security interest to know what the Afghan Communists were up to, and to support and encourage the democratic political development of Afghanistan—but again, American diplomacy failed to rise to the occasion. A measure of this failure is the fact that in every year of the democratic experiment, American economic aid declined."[12]

The Afghan communists, though few in number, became quite active during the new democratic period. Subsidized by the Soviets, they worked vigorously to undermine the new government. There were two factions in the Afghan Communist party (People's Democratic party for Afghanistan, or PDPA): the Khalqi (masses) group led by Nur Mohammad Taraki, and the Parcham (banner) group directed by Babrak Karmal. Although several members had run for office, only four were elected to the new Parliament—Babrak Karmal, Nur Ahmad Nur, Anahita Rat-ebzad,[13] and Fezan al-Haq. Babrak used this forum to condemn and denounce the king and the government openly.

Babrak also began organizing students in Kabul. One of his key agents and instigators was a young medical student named Najib (Najib would replace Babrak as president of the puppet regime in 1986). Street demonstrations and riots led by the young Najib became commonplace in Kabul. In later years, it was revealed by defectors such as Majid Mangal that these activities were directed in detail by the KGB from the Soviet Embassy.[14]

While Babrak and the Parchamis were agitating publicly, Tar-aki was craftily building up the rival Khalqi faction within the military. Key officers sent to the Soviet Union for training were sought by the KGB for special training, and all became secret members of the PDPA Khalq.

Student activism in these years was not confined to the communist cause. Various antimonarchist and religious political movements were emerging, the latter encouraged and supported by the Muslim Brotherhood movement,[15] which was centered in the *madrassas* (Islamic schools) of Cairo, Egypt. Professor Bur-hanuddin Rabbani of the Islamic Law Faculty at Kabul University was one of the most influential founders of the student organization. Among the most vocal and active of the student members were Gulbaddin Hekmatyar, Din Mohammad, Ahmed Shah Masood, and Qazi Amin.[16]

Afghanistan is an Islamic country. Even the communists had to pretend to be practicing Muslims in order to garner support among the people. But it is also the Southern California of Islam, not to be compared with the fanaticism of Khomeini's Iran or the rigidity of Saudi Arabia. With deep tribal traditions governing social intercourse and the pride and almost disdainful attitude with which Afghans view all foreigners, they never allowed Islam to oppress them. On the contrary, Islam was a way of life which offered freedom and contentment to the average Afghan.

Tribal and regional in their social and political patterns, the people of Afghanistan were united nationally by two traditions—the monarchy and Islam. The king, a member of the Mohammadzai tribe which had ruled Afganistan for generations, was not considered immortal, but Islam was eternal and could never be replaced.

In 1973, the king was overthrown. Economic conditions in the country deteriorated, aggravated by a severe famine caused by drought—ideal conditions for communist agitators. They began to work on Mohammad Daoud, who had been sulking since his removal as prime minister ten years before. During this period, he had also became enamored of socialism, swayed by his new friends in the Maoist organization, the Shola-i-Jawid.[17]

CHAPTER 4

Lack of Vigilance

Asia is not going to be civilized after the methods of the West.
There is too much Asia and she is too old.

—RUDYARD KIPLING, 1865–1936

Political unrest foreshadowed the beginning of the end—the overthrow of the king of Afghanistan in 1973. One of the warring factions was the Maoist Shola, which drew its membership primarily from the academia of Kabul and the laboring poor. Their public meetings were frequently disrupted by the Islamic Student Society, which received guidance and leadership from several faculty members at Kabul University, including Burhanuddin Rabbani, Abdul Rasul Sayaaf, and Sibgratullah Mojadidi. At one such rally, violence erupted and at least one member of the Shola was killed, with several more hospitalized. Some of the Islamic students, among them Gulbaddin Hekmatyar, were arrested and charged with the killing.[1]

Pressured from the Left and the Right, Zahir Shah vacillated. Ten years earlier, during student demonstrations against the monarchy, Army Chief of Staff General Sardar Abdul Wali sent troops who opened fire on the crowd, killing seven. The king and General Abdul Wali knew that such a show of force this time around might well incite open rebellion.

The solution to the political unrest in Kabul was hammered out at a family council. General Abdul Wali, now Zahir Shah's son-in-law, advised the king to absent himself until tempers cooled, to travel to Europe, ostensibly for medical treatment.[2] Zahir Shah went to London in July 1973.

On the night of July 17, 1973, as the Afghan king was dining with the Queen Mother in London, troops from the Pul-i-Charki garrison took control of the palace in Kabul. With the help of Babrak Karmal and his fellow Parchamis in the army, Mohammad Daoud grabbed the reins of government and, in a radio broadcast, declared the creation of the "first Republic of Afghanistan." As cousin to the king, and also as a Mohammadzai, Daoud declared himself president. While there was token resistance from the Kabul police force, the coup was achieved with relative ease. (The population of Kabul, for the most part, regarded the change of power as just another family affair.)

The communists, particularly Noor Mohammad Taraki and Babrak Karmal, were ecstatic. They viewed Daoud's coup as a prelude to a full communist takeover. (Babrak's assistance to Daoud was a due bill, for which payment could be called at the right time.)

Daoud, for his part, told confidantes that he was not concerned about the communists, because they were not experienced in leadership and their atheism would in any case never be acceptable to Islamic Afghanistan. Of more concern were the rightist Islamists, who he felt would drag the country back to the Middle Ages.

The Islamic Society leaders, however, decided that Daoud was preparing the way for a communist revolution and decided to take measures against him. Three options surfaced. Rabbani contended that they should organize themselves and fight Daoud in Parliament by winning over the electorate. Another faction led by Gulbaddin, although he was in jail at the time, wanted to take up arms and overthrow the government. Maluvi Younis Khalis—an Islamic scholar from Nangahar Province, who was working in the Ministry of Information and had established a reputation as an antileftist writer and journalist—advocated both measures.[3]

With Daoud as president, Khalis returned to Nangahar Province, formed the Hezb-Tawa-Bin, a small regional party, and began a weekly newsletter edited by Professor Gulham Niazi. This group became the forerunner of the first guerrilla resistance operation.

In Kabul, the Islamic Student Society intensified its efforts. The core group included Qazi Amin, Ahmed Shah Masood, Din Mohammad, Ahmed Shah, Habibullah Rachman, Abdul Rachman Niazi, and, of course, Gulbaddin Hekmatyar, who was released from jail by Daoud in an act of amnesty.

Soon a number of street clashes erupted between the communist student groups, led by Najib and Hashmet, and the Islamic Students. In one near riot, Gulbaddin was badly wounded and Din Mohammad's head severely burned when the communists set his beard on fire. Following this incident, the group decided to attempt a coup against Daoud.[4]

As they plotted to take control of the palace and a few key military installations in the city, Maluvi Khalis interrupted them: "Who are you going to install to head the government? Who will run each ministry? And who will take command of the army?" This was greeted with general laughter, and the questions were brushed aside. They had not planned that far ahead.

The day before the attack on the palace, Daoud was tipped off. Police and soldiers began rounding up the leaders of the society. Sayaaf was captured and jailed, but Mojadidi was in Libya at the time and could not be apprehended when the order for his arrest was issued. The remainder fled the city—some to Pakistan, others to the mountains of Nangahar or Paktia provinces.

For the next year, those who had escaped remained underground as they put together the beginnings of a guerrilla operation. Zulfikar Ali Bhutto, prime minister of Pakistan, when he saw that Daoud was fanning the fires of Pushtunistan, provided assistance in the way of arms and refuge in the tribal areas of Pakistan bordering Afghanistan. Daoud was also aiding Gaffar Khan and his Red Shirts in the Peshawar area, which incensed Bhutto all the more.

The Islamists, now an insurgency group, began to stage hit-and-run operations on government installations, mostly in Paktia and Nangahar provinces. At one point, the group, the new revolutionaries, numbered only fifty men. By 1974, it had grown to about three hundred men.

During their first year underground, they had two significant successes. One band of only twenty men captured Methar Lam, the provincial capital of Laghman, and held it for two days before the army moved in. And in Paktia Province, Maitullah Khan launched an attack on an army garrison in Urgun, inflicting casualties and capturing a significant amount of weapons and ammunition.

For the next three years, the guerrilla group grew in size and strength. Apart from contributions by wealthy Muslims in various parts of the Islamic world and token arms and money from the Pakistani government of Bhutto, they captured most of their supplies by raiding government outposts and convoys. Food and logistic support were offered by villagers as the resistance bands moved through the countryside establishing hideouts in the mountains. Their tactics were remarkably similar to Indian bands in the Old West of the United States with their hit-and-run attacks on the cavalry. And the Afghan army frequently met the same fate as had General George Custer.

In Kabul and, to a lesser extent, in Jalalabad, Khost, Mazar-i-Sharif, and other cities, the communists, led by Noor Mohammad Taraki, continued to organize. Taraki concentrated on the military, with Babrak working the streets and the campuses. Both were regular visitors to the Soviet Embassy. Years later, Majid Mangal, a former chargé d'affaires in Moscow, told me in an interview that Yuri Andropov, then a high-ranking KGB official, set up an entire section to oversee and support the increasingly militant Afghan communists.

Under Daoud's second regime, the Soviet government greatly stepped up its involvement in Afghanistan. In an attempt to stem the ever-increasing Soviet domination of the country, Daoud turned to the shah of Iran, who responded by increasing Iran's economic support to the nation. Many of the declared communists and other leftists were removed from government, but Taraki's cells within the military had become too powerful for Daoud to control.

In late 1977, a younger brother of Islamic student leader Din Mohammad was working with the underground in Kabul City on sabotage operations and on plans for a coup. Although still a teenager, he had already used several aliases while assisting the anticommunist guerrillas. Years later he would become known throughout the country, and beyond, by his final *nom-de-guerre*, Abdul Haq.

In 1977, Abdul Haq learned that Daoud's agents were seeking to arrest him under his given name, Humiyun Arsala. He had loaned a pistol to a friend and failed to notice when it was returned that the magazine clip had been removed. That afternoon, as he boarded a bus in an attempt to escape the city to Paktia Province, the vehicle was surrounded by dozens of police. When a police colonel told him he was under arrest, Abdul Haq pulled his pistol, aimed it at the colonel, and pulled the trigger. It failed to fire, and the police grabbed him.

The police held him in a nearby office awaiting a security truck to transport him to the Interior Ministry. While there, Abdul Haq realized he had a list of nearly fifty names of officers who supported the underground, and he threw the list into a heater. The officers tried to salvage the piece of paper, but it had burst into flames. Abdul Haq relaxed; whatever happened to him was of no consequence. He was sentenced to death and placed in prison to await execution.

On April 17, 1978, a Kabul labor leader, Mir Akbar Khaibar, a prominent member of the Parcham faction of the PDPA, was assassinated. Most believed he had been killed by a group within the Khalqi faction. The PDPA nevertheless organized mass protest demonstrations and accused the regime of ordering Khaibar's murder. After a week of violent protests, Daoud cracked down. He ordered the arrest of the PDPA leadership, including Taraki and his deputy, Hafizullah Amin. On April 26, Taraki was led blindfolded and handcuffed to the cellblock holding Abdul Haq.

Several of the prison's security agents had been previously recruited by Hafizullah Amin into the Khalq. Upon his arrest, he was allowed to send a message to Qader Watanjar and other key Khalqi members of the army and air force. The coded messages ordered the Khalqi cells in the military to stage a coup, which the KGB had planned in meticulous detail just two weeks before (according to Oleg Gordievsky, former KGB colonel, in his book *KGB: The Inside Story*). Khalqi officers took control of each of the major military headquarters and ordered troops loyal to them to storm the Darulaman Palace. Daoud and his family were murdered in a hail of machine-gun fire while attempting to hide inside the palace, and several thousand people were killed throughout the city. With Daoud dead, Qader Watanjar formed a Revolutionary Council to run the government. Abdul Haq watched as Taraki was led out of the prison. He had been under arrest for less than twenty-four hours.

Three days later, Noor Mohammad Taraki was named president and prime minister, Babrak Karmal was appointed first deputy prime minister, and Amin deputy prime minister and foreign minister. It was the month of April, which corresponds to the Islamic month of "Saur." The "Great Saur Revolution" was the beginning of over a decade of genocide and destruction.

Under Taraki, Babrak, and Amin, a ruthless restructuring of Afghanistan began. Huge blocks of land were confiscated and distributed to the peasants, but these refused to accept the government gifts of land. Calling such seizures "un-Islamic," most of the farm workers left their villages to join the underground resistance. Thousands of businessmen, scholars, religious leaders, and landowners were arrested and summarily executed. Amin soon established a reputation as a butcher, frequently supervising over or personally assisting in the mass executions.

Meanwhile, Abdul Haq's family arranged for a high court judge to review his case, and he was moved to the new Pul-i-Charki prison, where he and the family members of Daoud who had survived the coup were incarcerated. Still under construction, the prison had no sanitary facilities, no food, no water. Every necessity had to be brought in.

Each day, prison guards would take prisoners out to be executed. After several months, it was Abdul Haq's turn. He gave his watch, radio, and money to friends in the cellblock, and, blindfolded, he was led away. But instead of being executed, he was taken to the Security Department of the Interior Ministry. His family had "arranged" his release with a huge amount of money. At 2:00 A.M. he arrived at the house of his mother, who until then had refused to believe that he was finally safe.

Abdul went immediately to Peshawar, Pakistan, and from there to the mountains of Paktia Province in Afghanistan, where he worked with Maulvi Jalaluddin Haqani and others in organizing the Paktia Front. In September of 1978, he went to Nangahar Province and began guerrilla operations in and around Jalalabad with a party led by Younis Khalis.

The religious leaders of the country had by now declared that the resistance against the communists should be regarded as a *Jihad*—a Holy War—and that the underground members were "mujahaddin," or holy warriors. In Islam, to die in *Jihad* is to become a martyr or *shaheed*. A *shaheed* goes directly to paradise in the kingdom of Allah. In 1978, Afghanistan had a population of approximately 15 million people. In the next ten years, over 1.5 million of them would become *shaheedan*.

CHAPTER 5

Infiltration

Assassination has never changed the history of the world.

—BENJAMIN DISRAELI, 1804–1881

The Carter administration's reaction to the communist coup is easily described. It never happened. No official statements were issued decrying the loss of thousands of lives of Afghans during the coup, no presidential voice rang out against the murderous purges that instantly swept the country. Silence reigned.

On the day of the coup, Secretary of State Cyrus Vance was in Moscow praising the Soviets, and Leonid Brezhnev in particular, for their cooperation on the SALT treaty to limit nuclear arms.[1] A new ambassador, Adolph "Spike" Dubs, an experienced member of the State Department in Soviet affairs, was sent to Kabul. No denunciation of the communist coup followed. Washington had conceded the legitimacy of a Soviet puppet regime.

During the summer and fall of 1978, the brutality of the new regime reached staggering dimensions. One of Taraki's two deputy prime ministers, Hafizullah Amin, was responsible for the most frightful acts of terrorism and torture. Mass arrests took place around the country, and the Pul-i-Charki prison filled rapidly with political prisoners. To keep the Afghan army in line, Soviet advisors were attached to every unit.[2] By the end of the year, an estimated ten thousand Soviet military personnel were in the country "to help stabilize" the situation. Soon, the fragile unity between the two factions of the Afghan Communist party began to shatter. Most leading Parchami figures were sent into semi-exile as ambassadors to communist countries—Babrak to Czechoslovakia, Najib to Iran.

Meanwhile, President Taraki, the Khalqi leader, signed hundreds of treaties and agreements with the Soviet government. Among these was the infamous "Friendship Treaty" which contained a provision allowing the Afghan government to "request" Soviet military aid if required. This clause would be frequently cited by the Soviets in upcoming years to justify their invasion and occupation of Afghanistan. All the treaties, of course, were declared great victories by the Afghan government.[3]

Tens of thousands flocked to join the resistance groups in the mountains, while protests and uprisings sprang up across the country; and finally, inevitably, a massacre took place in the village of Kerala in Kunar Province. Nearly all of the able-bodied men of Kerala were living in mountain camps of the mujahaddin when Khalqi troops led by Soviet advisors surrounded the village and demanded that the "bandits" be turned over to them. When the women, the elderly, and the children were unable to comply, the troops moved in. Over 1,100 people were slaughtered, their corpses left in the open to rot as a warning to others to cooperate with the new masters.

But the people reacted quite differently; "Kerala" became a rallying point and a battle cry for the mujahaddin. Bloodier and more destructive acts of terrorism followed, but Kerala symbolized the declaration of war—of *Jihad.*

The tribal code of the Pushtoon people has three mandates by which the Afghans live: Honor, Hospitality, and Revenge. The honor of these strong and vibrant people is legendary. And their hospitality knows no bounds. Now, however, the time had come for the third demand. The Afghan communists and their Soviet comrades would begin to experience Afghan revenge.

In response to anticommunist demonstrations in the ancient city of Herat, the regime's air force led by Soviet pilots began carpet-bombing the city, leaving little more than rubble, with

thirty thousand of the city's civilians dead. Such terror and tragedy brought the overwhelming majority of Afghans to a state of
open rebellion. The regime was losing control of the country; the
Resistance was gaining strength each month.

In February 1979, a strange incident occurred in the center
of the city of Kabul. The American ambassador, "Spike" Dubs,
was traveling from the embassy to a meeting at the Foreign
Ministry, when his car was brought to a stop and surrounded
by heavily armed gunmen. Dubs was taken at gunpoint to a
room in the Kabul Hotel. The kidnappers claimed to be dissidents.[4] (Babakakhel, a Kabul police officer at the scene, told me
years later that at least one of the "dissidents" was an Eastern
European—a Czechoslovakian, he thought. The officer said that
none of the gunmen was Afghan and "they spoke very bad
Farsi.")

The police surrounded the hotel and placed several officers in
the corridor outside the room in which the ambassador was
being held. Mike Malinowski, an officer from the American Embassy, arrived at the hotel ready to negotiate for Dubs' release. A
police deputy chief telephoned directly to Deputy Prime Minister
Amin and, shortly thereafter, four KGB agents arrived, ostensibly
to advise the police on rescuing the American ambassador.
Within minutes of their arrival, the agents ordered the police to
storm the room under open fire. A grenade was hurled into the
room, killing the kidnappers as well as Ambassador Dubs. One of
the police officers at the scene, who later joined the mujahaddin,
told me he had no doubts that the ambassador had been killed by
the KGB agents who directed the attack. But in a later conversation, Malinowski, who was in the hallway, was unclear about the
exact chain of events.[5]

As before, there was no strong protest from President Carter or
Secretary of State Cyrus Vance other than to deplore what had
occurred. The State Department refused to release their reports
or cables concerning the murder of an American envoy. Dubs,
however, was not replaced, and the embassy's affairs were conducted from that time forward by a chargé d'affaires.

Refugees were pouring into neighboring Pakistan. By the spring of 1979, they numbered almost half a million. With tens of thousands of additional mujahaddin operating from tribal areas on the Afghan border, Pakistan was hard pressed to care for them all.

General Zia ul-Haq was in control of Pakistan, having ousted Bhutto in a coup. When Bhutto was tried and subsequently executed on a trumped-up charge of conspiracy to murder, President Carter stopped American aid to Pakistan. Carter's policy of human rights was once again at odds with the strategic interests of the front-line anticommunist states bordering the Soviet empire. Observers—in and out of the administration—were stating that the strategic interests of the United States and its Western allies were seriously threatened by the Soviet influence creeping closer and closer to the oil fields of the Persian Gulf.[6] Pakistan was in a particularly precarious position. It was squeezed between its bitter enemy, India, to the south and the troublesome communist regime to the north. Only Iran lay between Afghanistan and the Straits of Hormutz. Yet even there, the lynchpin of security in the region, the shah of Iran held precarious rule. When his turn came to be ousted in a coup, Carter's human rights policy would again be used in justification.

The summer of 1979 saw Afghanistan engulfed by a sea of death and destruction. The numbers reaching Western media from refugees and diplomatic reports were so high that most dismissed them as exaggerations.

Taraki and the Soviets, however, were worried. The coup had failed to bring about control of the country. Following an official state visit in early September with "brother" Fidel Castro in Havana, Taraki traveled to Moscow where he met with KGB Chairman Yuri Andropov. Taraki was told that Hafizullah Amin's excesses were the primary cause of instability, and he was ordered to eliminate him.[7]

On September 14, 1979, Amin heard of the plot (though not of the planned assassination) against him and, accompanied by his personal guards, he confronted Taraki in his palace office. The announcement of Taraki's death came two days later, along with

Amin's assumption of the presidential office. Distrusting various other Khalqis associated with Taraki, Amin took over the posts of foreign minister and minister of defense as well.[8]

The Soviets were furious. Spurned by Moscow, Amin vainly tried to get rid of the extensive KGB control over the vital sections of his government. Feelings of isolation and frustration convinced Amin to seek other allies. He turned to General Zia in Islamabad, with whom he regularly conversed, and even made overtures to the Americans. But they were not interested. According to his few confidantes, this particularly upset him. Despite his reputation as the butcher of Kabul, he truly believed, in his paranoid state, that his leftist American friends from his years at Columbia University would rally to his support.[9]

Soviet military officers then revealed to Amin that the KGB wanted to assassinate him. Claiming that they despised the KGB, they assured him of their protection. In order to "protect" Amin, the number of Soviet "advisors" increased dramatically in October and November 1979. On the thin excuse of "winterizing military vehicles," batteries and other vital parts were removed by Soviet soldiers from Afghan tanks, APCs, jeeps, and trucks. By early December, Afghan military units in and around Kabul were practically immobilized.[10]

By the last week of December, all was quiet as far as the Afghan military was concerned—uneasy, perhaps, but quiet. The Westerners in the Afghan capital were preparing for a subdued celebration of the Christian feastday. Although Christmas Eve is not celebrated in Kabul, and it is certainly not an Islamic holiday, December 24, 1979, will not be soon forgotten in Islamic Afghanistan.

Reaction

"If everybody minded their own business," the Dutchess said in a hoarse growl, "the world would go round a deal faster than it does."

—Lewis Carroll, 1832–1898

Having traveled to many countries around the world and experienced various diverse cultures, I have come to realize how little other peoples understand the fundamentals of the American political system. Only the British appear genuinely to comprehend our free electoral process and independent media.

I have spoken with presidents, prime ministers, and political leaders who cannot seem to grasp the concept of a truly free political system—even those who have lived and been educated in the United States. Aware of the degree of control, or at the very least, the strong influence their governments have over politics and media, they cannot seem to grasp that one of the most powerful nations in the world does not control these areas of power.

In retrospect, this was the underlying cause of a major miscalculation by the Soviets in December 1979. At that time, American Embassy personnel were being held hostage in Tehran as the United States wrung its hands; the Carter administration had been passive spectators to the active ongoing resistances to Soviet-backed insurgencies in Nicaragua, Angola, and Mozambique; Carter policies had abandoned anticommunist figures such as Somoza, Zia ul-Haq, and Shah Reza Pavlavi; and the administration had accepted without so much as a whimper the communist coup in Afghanistan.

Given this supine attitude by the United States, Leonid Brezhnev and his comrades in the Kremlin concluded that the reaction would be equally spineless when the Soviet army invaded Afghanistan. The Islamic countries, of course, would make speeches in the United Nations. And Pakistan would cry foul. But when the initial finger wagging ended, it would be accepted as a *fait accompli.*

But, this time—Christmas Eve, 1979—the Soviets completely misread the American political situation. The media were bludgeoning Carter daily with the Iranian crisis, and both of the Republican frontrunners, Ronald Reagan and George Bush, were hammering him on his indecisive foreign policy. Furthermore, what Carter considered one of his major achievements in foreign policy, the SALT II treaty, was headed for trouble in the Senate in the upcoming election year. Closer to home, although Cyrus Vance ruled the roost at the State Department, Zbigniew Brzezinski, the national security advisor, had daily access to the president's ear. And Brzezinski, a Polish refugee who hated the Soviet expansionist empire, saw the Afghan invasion as an opportunity, in his words, "to finally sow shit in their backyard."[1]

Disregarding CIA and Pentagon estimates that "the Resistance had no chance against the largest army in the world and would be overrun in a matter of weeks," Carter reacted explosively.[2] On December 28, 1979, he wrote an uncharacteristically strong letter to Brezhnev demanding the immediate withdrawal of the Soviet army from Afghanistan.[3]

Brezhnev's reply—that the Soviet Union had been invited into Afghanistan and was only performing its international duty—further infuriated the American president. Branding Brezhnev a liar, Carter stated, "This action by the Soviets has made a more dramatic change in my own opinion of what the Soviets' ultimate goals are than anything they've done in the previous time I've been in office."[4]

Now, perhaps for the first time, American strategic analysts took a look at the map of Eurasia downsideup. And things began to move.

Carter increased the initial sanctions against the Soviet Union. He halted cultural exchanges and put a stop to opening new consulates in the U.S. and the USSR. Stringent trade restrictions were imposed and an Occidental Petroleum contract trading minerals and chemicals was canceled. And he announced—although belatedly—the creation of a Rapid Deployment Force to defend the oil fields of the Persian Gulf.[5]

On another front, Defense Secretary Harold Brown was sent to Beijing to discuss the situation with the Chinese leadership. He found the Chinese ready to commit to active opposition of the invasion. They had already announced that relations with the Soviet Union could not be normalized until the Soviets had withdrawn completely from Afghanistan. In addition, they began, not exactly covertly, to funnel weapons to the mujahaddin through Pakistan, with whom they had a long-standing relationship.[6] A deal was cut, later greatly expanded by the CIA's William Casey, for the Americans to help finance the Chinese efforts on behalf of the Afghan Resistance.

In the political arena, Carter faced serious challenges. Not only was the loss of Iran being credited (or debited) to him, but he was receiving a daily barrage of criticism for the continuing plight of the fifty-five Americans being held hostage in Iran. In Nicaragua, Carter's man, Daniel Ortega, had shown himself to be a miniature Fidel Castro, not the democratic reformer the liberals had been touting. And now, with the Soviet invasion of Afghanistan, Carter could be blamed for allowing the Soviet Union to spread its tentacles into the most valuable real estate on earth—the oil fields of the Persian Gulf. The Soviets were threatening American strategic interests; the plight of the Afghans was secondary. Time was running out on Carter's political career.

Brzezinski traveled to Pakistan to meet with General Zia. Although long part of America's strategic network, Pakistan's relations with the Carter administration were strained. Carter obviously needed Zia ul-Haq if he were to react in any tangible way to the Afghan invasion, but Zia was an adept politician. And he had much to mull over. He needed Western support to maintain his tenuous control over Pakistan, but, then again, he feared such support would reignite hostilities with India and he knew that his military could not defend against such an eventuality.[7] Zia was therefore determined that Pakistan develop its own nuclear weapons program as a deterrent to Indira Ghandi's military might, but Carter stood in the way; he was the foremost proponent of nuclear nonproliferation.

Brzezinski was the perfect envoy to send to Zia. The two men were among the few in the world's political hierarchy who believed that merely halting Soviet expansion would be insufficient; it must be sharply curtailed. Furthermore, they agreed that Afghanistan was the place to begin.

In a well-publicized visit to the Khyber Pass, Brzezinski stood at the last Pakistani army outpost on the frontier of Afghanistan and looked down upon Soviet border guards on the international border at Torkham. Taking up a rifle belonging to a member of the famed Khyber Scouts Regiment, he pointed the rifle northward. The symbolism was clear. It was time to begin shooting back.

The mujahaddin began receiving arms and ammunition from the Chinese, Egyptians, Libyans, and Pakistanis. Money was provided by the Saudis, the Americans, and, to a lesser extent, the British. The muj stepped up their campaign against the Soviet occupiers with remarkable success. With guerrilla tactics honed over the centuries, they were able to keep the Soviet infantry, for the most part, pinned down. Soviet jet bombers destroyed towns and villages, but they could not wipe out the mujahaddin, who darted in and out of their mountain hideouts, always just out of reach.

Meanwhile, in Kabul, the KGB remodeled the Afghan Secret Police after its own design. The quasi-military organization was renamed the KhAD (a Farsi acronym for "State Security"), and Najib was brought back to head it. Najib was referred to variously

as "the bull," because of his massive build, by those who didn't
know him well (the diplomatic corps), and "the cow," because he
was big and stupid, by those who did (his former fellow students).

Mass arrests, tortures, and executions became commonplace
under Najib. But Babrak Karmal, the new president, tried to
dissociate himself from the horror by presenting an amiable
image of himself. He wished to be viewed as an affable politician
trying to save Afghanistan from the dark ages, into which, he
warned, the radical bandits in the mountains were taking the
country. Judging by the additional refugees—1 million—in 1980
that fled Afghanistan, he was not very convincing. By 1983,
those numbers would exceed 6 million—over one-third of the
prewar population.

The mass exodus was the result of Soviet military policy—
terror campaigns aimed to drive out those most likely to resist.
The mass of refugees soon burdened Pakistan and Iran, the countries chiefly in opposition to the occupation. In addition, a staggering number of people were killed. By the end of 1980, nearly
a million were slain as an example to those who remained—
neither resist nor give shelter to those who do resist.

Years later, with the accepted death toll in excess of 1.5 million
and the refugee count of 6.5 million, a high-ranking State Department officer explained to me that the Soviets had softened
their tactics. As proof, he cited the decrease in the number of new
refugees and the number of reports of mass murders. It did not
occur to him that, outside the main Afghan cities, there was
nobody left to kill or flee.

The USSR and Karmal's communist government continued to
sign trade and economic agreements, drawing Afghanistan still
further under Soviet domination. One such agreement ceded the
Wakhan Corridor to the Soviet Union. (This narrow strip of land
was designed by the British, at the time of the partition of India,
to prevent Pakistan from having a common border with the
Soviet Union.) This giveaway increased China's nervousness.
With control of the Wakhan, the Soviets had easy access into the
underbelly of China through the Karakoram Pass in the Hindu

Kush mountains on China's southeastern border and direct access into Pakistani territory, undoing the British reason for drawing the border as they did.

To nobody's surprise, Carter lost the 1980 elections. He was replaced by Ronald Reagan in a landslide vote. One of the key Reagan figures was William Casey, whose background included serving in Bill Donovan's OSS during World War II. Casey also believed that Soviet expansionism should be countered, not only in Afghanistan, but in Nicaragua, Angola, and Ethiopia. President Ronald Reagan appointed Casey director of Central Intelligence (DCI). As DCI, Casey wasted no time declaring and prosecuting a worldwide war against the Soviet Union, and more directly, his agency's counterpart—the KGB.

CHAPTER 7

Peace Through Strength

Of the four wars in my lifetime, none came about because the U.S. was too strong.

—Ronald Reagan, b, 1911

William Casey was the national campaign manager for the Reagan presidential campaign of 1980. His influence on Ronald Reagan became obvious as the campaign progressed: the campaign's emphasis on foreign policy, particularly the desire to confront the Soviet empire, departed sharply from that of Reagan's presidential run in 1976. Many campaign insiders credited Casey with having won the Republican nomination for Reagan—a feat they felt Casey's predecessor, John Sears, could not have achieved.

Before the 1980 landslide had fully settled, Casey went to work with the transition team to prepare the Reagan administration to hit the ground running on Inauguration Day. At first, Casey thought he would like to be secretary of state. But the political pressures on a presidential transition team are a thousand times greater than those faced in a campaign. In order to revamp the foreign policy agenda of the Carter administration, Reagan needed a brusque, but articulate, commander in charge of State. Casey had the ability, but he was anything but articulate. The job went to General Al Haig. More than one biographer of Casey attributed this choice to Nancy Reagan.[1] She thought that Haig looked and sounded like a secretary of state, whereas

Casey's speech, mannerisms, and appearance would do nothing to project "Ronnie's" image.

But Casey had earned a reward. And the Republican right wing did not want him bogged down in a domestic policy job, such as running the Securities and Exchange Commission as he had in the Nixon administration. In the end, Bill Casey was given the post of DCI, and unlike his predecessors, he would receive cabinet rank. As head of the supersecret Central Intelligence Agency, his mumbling speech and distracting mannerisms would not cause any public relations problems. Given his background at the OSS, his confirmation was expected to sail through. It did.

Casey later revealed that he had had some hesitations in accepting what he considered an insufficiently important job. But upon assuming command at the agency's Langley, Virginia, headquarters, he took to the job like a duck to water.

Reagan and Casey over the years had developed a close and easy rapport. Having conversed with both men, I find it difficult to conceptualize the two of them in a deep discussion over policy matters. True, Casey had a brilliant mind that could grasp details and an uncanny ability to predict the reactions of others. But if Ronald Reagan was the "Great Communicator," Casey was frequently the "Great Mumbler." It may, of course, have been a facade. At times, Casey could articulate his thoughts with crystal clarity; at others, his sentences made no sense whatsoever. During his confirmation hearings, Senator Biden asked him to move the microphone closer so that he could be understood. Casey responded with a gleam in his eye, "It's in my lap now!" Intentional or not, he used this ability, or lack of it, to his advantage.

Casey envisioned his job as having a twofold purpose: first, to restructure the agency and lift it out of the despondency caused by the unending investigations and purges of the 1970s; and second, to confront what he saw as the caldron of evil in the world—the expansionist Soviet Union. In that regard, he became the foremost adherent of the slogan of the first Reagan administration: "PEACE THROUGH STRENGTH."

Casey accomplished his primary goals rapidly. He rebuilt the agency and, in the process, lifted the morale and renewed the sense of purpose of its thousands of employees—overt and covert. Together with Secretary of State Al Haig and Defense Secretary Caspar Weinberger, Casey was able to focus on the task of confronting what the new president publicly declared to be the "evil empire."

Halfway around the world, Casey's counterpart was himself prepared to pursue an all-out, worldwide, covert war. Yuri Andropov was chairman of the Committee for State Security (*Komitiet Gosudarstviennoi Biezopasnosti*—KGB). Though sinister in appearance, Andropov was unique among the Soviet leadership: he was an intellectual. And he shrewdly implanted a benign image of himself by such simple ploys as publicizing the fact that he listened to Western music. In reality, his worldwide terrorist and expansionist operations gave Stalin's old MKVD a run for its money. Andropov fashioned the KGB into a more sophisticated—and dangerous—agency than ever before.

Andropov first came to Western notice in Hungary, where he was in charge of suppressing the uprising in 1954—a task he accomplished with brute force. As he worked his way up through the labyrinth bureaucracy of the KGB, he nurtured the careers of several younger protegés. Among them was a young party *apparatchek* named Mikhail Sergiavitch Gorbachev.

In 1981, Casey and Andropov were sworn adversaries. The Brezhnev Doctrine, which supported any and all Marxist liberation movements, was in full operation around the globe. Cuba and Nicaragua were directing insurgencies in El Salvador, Peru, and Columbia. Africa was in turmoil: in Ethiopia, Mozambique, and Angola, the Marxist governments were fighting to suppress anticommunist rebels; in South Africa, the ANC—closely tied to the South African Communist party—was making headway. Elsewhere, Iran was unstable, and Afghanistan was occupied by Soviet troops.

The Soviet Union's expansion under Andropov and Brezhnev had been abetted by American domestic politics. Jimmy Carter's CIA chief, Admiral Stansfield Turner, had fired over eight hundred people in covert operations, and the Church Committee of the U.S. Senate, ostensibly to correct excesses of the CIA, had for all practical purposes emasculated what was left of it. Until Ronald Reagan arrived in Washington, Andropov had been playing solitaire.

During the first few months of the Reagan administration, attention was publicly focused on Central America and on the general problem of terrorists. Al Haig released special reports and photographs, supplied by the CIA, of weapons being smuggled into El Salvador, and data showing that the KGB was involved in training terrorists were made public. But for two years, little information emanated from the White House, State Department, or the CIA regarding Afghanistan. The covert operations, that is, remained covert.

One of Casey's first foreign visits, however, was to Pakistan. In Islamabad he renewed his acquaintance with General Acktar Abdul Rahman Khan, known as General Acktar. They became good and trusted friends. Casey convinced Acktar that the United States would stay the course in supporting the anticommunist Resistance in Afghanistan, and as the battle was taking place in Acktar and Zia's backyard, they would be allowed to call the shots. As Casey told me later, "Those fellows knew the players, and we had a mutual goal." Casey's reliance on the Pakistanis overlooked the fact that Pakistani goals for Afghanistan differed from those of the Afghans themselves, a fact that would cause many serious problems over the years.

In response, Zia successfully argued that India was a real threat to Pakistan. Zia reasoned that the Soviets might induce India to create trouble on Pakistan's southern border in retaliation for the Pakistanis' assistance to the Afghan Resistance. Casey promised Zia and Acktar that the Reagan administration would lift the sanctions imposed by Carter and that, furthermore, the United States would upgrade Pakistan's military. This was demonstrated by a quickly approved sale of forty top-of-the-line F-16 fighter bombers.

During his tenure at the CIA, Casey would make over half a dozen trips to Pakistan to coordinate with Acktar. Each time, he visited mujahaddin training camps located in Pakistani army bases. Casey, in fact, considered himself the commander-in-chief of the war against the Soviet army in Afghanistan.[2] He assembled a team of what he considered top-notch subcommanders, some Pakistani, others American. Within two years the CIA station operating from Islamabad became the largest agency operation in the world outside of Langley headquarters.[3]

Conspicuously absent from the high command of this extensive covert operation were the Afghans. Their participation was considered unnecessary, since they were viewed as mere cannon fodder for American and Pakistani objectives. The explanation of the goals of the Resistance—their reasons for sacrificing their lives—was left to foreign politicians.

Harmony between the United States and Pakistan continued throughout the Soviet occupation of Afghanistan. As Ambassador Arnold Raphel told me in 1988 in an interview, the U.S. and Pakistan "were in lockstep on Afghanistan." But not with Afghanistan, or at least not with the mujahaddin, who had significant differences with the Pakistanis.

At about this time, Casey received a windfall from an unexpected ally in his attempts to finance the covert operations in Afghanistan. Texas Congressman Charles Wilson, a member of the powerful Appropriations Subcommittee of the House Armed Services Committee and the House Intelligence Committee, had become a devotee of the mujahaddin because, he said, he wanted to repay the Soviets for Vietnam: "I wanted to hurt them. I wanted them to count bodybags going back to Moscow," Wilson said unabashedly.[4]

Wilson became the number one crusader for the mujahaddin in Congress. "I went to the leadership of the committee and the leadership of the House," he told me on several occasions. "I was willing to trade my political soul for the Afghans. I told them they could have my vote on whatever they wanted, as long as they supported me on the Afghans." The political tradeoff worked. Every time the CIA requested an appropriation for the operations in Afghanistan, Wilson doubled it. Casey was delighted.

The agency began treating Wilson like royalty. Its most extravagant gesture came about when a brigadier general (*the names of covert CIA operatives in the United States and abroad are not used in this book; it is a violation of U.S. law*) gave Wilson what was purported to be the firing tube from the first Stinger anti-aircraft missile used to bring down the first Soviet aircraft in Afghanistan.

Casey placed Deputy Director of Operations (DDO) John McMahon in charge of the Afghan War. McMahon proved to be a reluctant chief. He openly questioned whether an American covert operation should take part in killing Soviet soldiers. He also strongly resisted providing the Afghans with any sophisticated weaponry, fearing such items would end up being used by Islamic terrorists in Libya, Iran, or Lebanon. A situation developed that saw Casey considering the Afghan War a priority, while the individual he put in charge of covert aid downplayed its significance.

People close to McMahon told me that he prided himself on understanding the peoples and cultures with whom he dealt. But in regards to the Afghans, he widely missed the mark. For example, in his biography on Casey, Joseph Persico quotes McMahon, following a visit to the mujahaddin in Pakistan, referring to the seven Afghan resistance parties as "eight different tribes" and calling Younas Khalis a "tribal chief," whereas, as the DDO of the CIA should have known, the different parties were not divided by tribe, and Khalis, a key man, was definitely *not* a tribal chief. Such ignorance concerning the Afghans may well explain why the CIA granted Pakistan's ISI so much operational control over American-supplied assistance.

In any event, one fact stands out: Casey incontestably considered the Afghan War a priority. He clearly recognized that the Soviets were attempting to surround the oil fields of the Gulf and understood how important the occupation of Afghanistan was to this effort.

CIA operatives went on a worldwide arms-buying binge, purchasing Soviet-style weaponry that would be compatible with arms captured by the mujahaddin. Egypt was enlisted to manufacture rockets and launchers, and Pakistan eased the shipments through the port of Karachi. Other allies were pressured to help bear the cost; Margaret Thatcher was eager to help and France kicked in, as did the Japanese.

Islamic countries aided their own, too. Libya's Mummar Khadafi and Iraq's Saddam Hussein sent money and arms, primarily in support of Hekmatyar, a promoter of their version of Pan-Islam. And Iran gave assistance to the smaller groups of Afghan Shias.

Several countries would not, or legally could not, provide lethal assistance. Casey therefore asked them to assist with the massive aid required to care for the millions of refugees in Pakistan. The burden had become too great for Pakistan to absorb; by 1983 the refugees cost Pakistan over $1 million per day.[5]

By 1983, Casey had built up an impressive military opposition to the Soviet occupation of Afghanistan. Arms were pouring into the mujahaddin camps, and provisions for the refugees were being supplied under the direction of the United Nations High Commissioner for Refugees, paid for by the United States, Britain, France, Germany, Switzerland, and others.

Yuri Andropov was quick to respond—he turned up the heat. Terrorist bombings began to rock the Pakistani city of Peshawar, killing hundreds of innocent Pakistanis and refugees. Soviet planes then aimed their bombs at mujahaddin safe areas inside of Pakistan, and Soviet envoys increased their arm-twisting of Zia ul-Haq in an attempt to force him to back off from assisting the mujahaddin.

In 1983, Soviet-sponsored operations in other parts of the world kicked into high gear: El Salvador became a free fire zone— helicopters and more sophisticated armaments were provided the Sandinistas in Nicaragua—and Angola flared into a full-fledged civil war, as did Ethiopia. Bill Casey and Ronald Reagan strove desperately to strengthen the resistance in each situation.

On September 3, an event occurred which plunged the reputation of the Soviet Union worldwide. A Korean jetliner, Flight 007 from Alaska, was shot down with a missile fired from a MiG jet fighter near the Soviet island of Sakhalin. Many of the doomed passengers were Americans, including conservative Republican Congressman Larry McDonald. These events, described earlier, led indirectly to my first trip to war-torn Afghanistan.

CHAPTER 8

East is East

When visiting foreign lands, one must remember you are the foreigner.

—ARTHUR CHAPMAN, 1873–1935

I arrived with my crew—Pete Heinlein, Anne, and Al Lohbeck, more about whom later—in Islamabad, Pakistan, in early November 1983. The scene at the airport was right out of the pages of Rudyard Kipling. Emerging from Immigration and Customs, we encountered over a thousand people, dozens of whom grabbed, pulled, pushed, and clamored over our luggage, while dozens more hustled taxis and cars. Wading our way through the chaos, we found a van painted with the Holiday Inn logo—the only Western-style hotel in Pakistan's capital city.

The five-mile drive into the city had all the characteristics of a roller coaster ride. We careened down the highway, dodging sheep, cows, and people, and watched helplessly as the oncoming traffic filled any available space in the onslaught of vehicles without regard to lane or direction. The sounds, sights, and smells were distinctly Asian, unlike anything in the West.

Whitewashed on the side of a hill alongside the road were huge signs which read: FAITH, UNITY, DISCIPLINE. It was the motto of General Zia ul-Haq's government.

The first official Pakistani I talked with was a prim, proper, and very erudite gentleman named Zubair Ali. Zubair was the director of the External Publicity Wing of the Information Ministry. His office was in a dark complex in an administration building. All the lights were off, which was true of most government offices, because of the poor power facilities in the country.

Zubair immediately offered us cups of sweet green tea, different but very good. We thought it was a kind gesture until we learned that drinking green tea was what south-central Asians did most of the time. If you had six appointments in a morning, you would drink a minimum of twelve cups of green tea. There is no polite way to refuse, not that a refusal would have done much good anyhow.

Zubair was the only man in the offices wearing a Western suit. All the others, like most Pakistanis and all but a handful of Afghans, wore the loose fitting *shalwar kameez*, much like pajamas (which, incidentally, is the Farsi word for the outfit), with its billowing pants and long shirt reaching below the knees. Zubair explained that he had lived in self-imposed exile in London and had become accustomed to Western clothes, which was unfortunate, because the *shalwar kameez* had recently been declared the national dress by General Zia. And General Zia's declarations had a way of prevailing over law or personal choice.

Personally, Zubair was bitterly opposed to the dictatorship of Zia. Asked why he worked in Zia's government, Zubair replied that Zia needed him. Zubair had been the national television news anchor prior to Zia's coup, and Zia found it to his advantage to keep the popular Zubair around.

Now, he asked, why was he blessed with the visit of an American journalist? I explained that I wanted to do a documentary on the Afghan mujahaddin. They had received very little coverage in the States, and I felt the underreported story was important and deserved better treatment. "Ah, yes," Zubair sighed, "the mujahaddin. Of course, we have nothing whatsoever to do with them, Afghanistan being a sovereign country and all. The Soviets, don't you know, would slap our wrists if we gave any assistance to foreign journalists in this regard. I'm afraid this government cannot help you. In fact, as an official of the Information Ministry, I must forbid you to proceed any further. What you must do is go to Peshawar, where my subordinate, Mr. Azim Afridi, will give you all of the assistance required."

So went my introduction to the Pakistani policy of "wink and nod." On the face of it, they had denied any access to the Afghans. In reality, they wanted the story reported as much as the Afghans did. Thus, after an official refusal, they would bend over backward to help.

I kept in regular contact with Zubair Ali, who, over the years, helped me greatly in learning about Pakistani culture and the political scene. He went on to become the minister of information in Pakistan's London Embassy until his retirement in 1989. His replacement, Ismael Patel, became an even closer friend, who more than once assisted me in accomplishing the impossible within the multitiered and unworkable bureaucracy. Patel rose to become President Gulham Ishaq Khan's most valued personal assistant following the death of Zia.

The culture shock of our arrival in Islamabad turned out to be minor compared with our trip and introduction to Peshawar. The hundred-mile journey across the Punjab and into the Northwest Frontier was a journey back in time. I would describe it in our subsequent documentary as "having to set your watch back— back about two hundred years."

Although we passed through sparse arable land, people dotted the landscape, wandering aimlessly or simply standing by the roadside. Some herded sheep, goats, or water buffalo, but there was no sense of purpose or of diligence. It was different in the towns, where the bazaars were beehives of human activity and the vehicles were both fascinating and terrifying—brightly decorated buses and Bedford trucks careening down the highway at breakneck speed.

Arriving in Peshawar for the first time is an assault on the senses. The cacophony of noise is deafening; drivers use their air horns in place of brakes. Dozens of motorized rickshaws weave in and out of traffic, their beeping horns vying with the bleats and yaps of horses, goats, and dogs. This blends with the sounds of the bazaar, the thousands of people talking, walking, and shouting. Your nostrils are under attack as well by diesel exhaust,

curry cooking on open fires, hundreds of animals and their remnants, and the stink of open sewers.

Then there were the people, the fully veiled women, covered
from head to toe in a tent-like garment of a variety of colors—
white, blue, yellow, pink. Many of the men wore wide, large
turbans, again in a variety of colors. Unlike Islamabad, all men
wore some type of headgear, and all wore the *shalwar kameezes*.

We checked into Dean's Hotel. It had been built at the turn of
the century to house British officials and officers visiting the
border outpost. Peshawar was the final post in the Northwest
Frontier Province (NWFP) of the British Empire in India. Surrounded by a high wall, the hotel had single rows of buildings,
with a reception area and dining room in the central building,
and a large garden spread across the front. Each accommodation
consisted of three rooms—sitting room, bedroom and dressing
room, and bath. The staff was suspicious of us, as, apparently, it
was of all Western guests. In those days, not many Westerners
ventured to Peshawar. In later years, there would be a deluge.

I quickly became "Mr. Kurt." Last names, or family names,
have little relevance in most Islamic countries. In fact, most
people do not have family names as such. In Afghanistan, people
are given a single Islamic name, although a few, in an attempt to
westernize their names, add their tribal affiliation. I would have
fun reading major Pakistani newspapers when VIPs from the
United States or Europe would visit. When General Norman
Schwarzkopf came to Islamabad in 1989, the media referred to
him as "General Norman"; British Foreign Secretary Douglas
Hurd was heralded with the headline "MR. DOUGLAS CALLS UPON
PRESIDENT ISHAQ."

Azim Afridi's office was darker and danker than Zubair's. To
reach it, we had to wind our way down a narrow lane away from
the center of the city and walk through a courtyard surrounded
by private residences until we finally reached a group of small,
dirty offices.

Over green tea, I explained my mission and gave him the
introduction provided by Zubair. After telephoning Zubair, Azim
explained that as a member of the Afridi tribe, which was located

in the area around the Khyber Pass, he paid little attention to the federal government. The tribal areas of Pakistan, he said, were autonomous, with their own system of governing. Although an employee of Zia's federal government, he was first of all an Afridi. He explained this, he told us, because the Afridis had a habit of kidnapping foreigners in their territory and holding them for ransom to the government. However, because we had the good fortune to be his guests, we would be safe. Afridis were nothing if not respectful of guests. Besides, he assured us, kidnap victims were always treated well. On the other hand, we should be wary of other Pushtoon tribes, because they often killed people.

Over the years, we heard the same yarn, with a twist, from all the other tribal people; they warned us to beware of the dangerous Afridis. The writings of Kipling and Winston Churchill (from his years in the NWFP) began to make consummate sense.

Azim introduced us to two men. The first, Aziz, told us matter-of-factly that he was an intelligence officer assigned to keep track of foreigners. This, I would learn, was a never-ending job of two Pakistani agencies—the military Inter-Services Intelligence (ISI) and the Intelligence Bureau (IB). Telephones in Peshawar were tapped to ludicrous degrees; sometimes there were so many clicks on the lines that it became impossible to complete a call; at others the tappers could be heard coversing or laughing at something overheard. Aziz added that he should never be contacted directly through his office. If needed, we were to reach him through his "secret phone number 74286."

The Pakistani police were organized along the lines created by the British over a period of 150 years. Their intelligence operation was the Special Branch, which worked closely with the IB. Special Branch officers would trail foreigners relentlessly and take enough photographs to keep the Fuji film company happy. In the strictly conservative culture of Pakistan, where there was no such thing as male-female dating, the police and spooks were dumbfounded by Western lifestyles. One IB officer showed me photos of two Britishers walking down the street, a young man and woman. It semed innocent enough, but to this conservative

Muslim, it was near pornography. The officer thought she must be a prostitute.

The second man introduced to us by Azim was named Shah Zaman. He would be our guide to the refugee camps and provide us with introductions to the mujahaddin.

Shah Zaman told us that most Pakistanis, particularly those in the NWFP, looked upon Afghans as cousins and brothers: cousins by blood and brothers by religion. It was the obligation of Pakistan to aid and assist their fellow Muslims in their time of need. Nevertheless, the burden of 3.5 million refugees on Pakistan soil was heavy.

Shah Zaman took us to refugee camps where we filmed thousands of Afghan refugees crammed into rabbit warrens. These people from the open valleys and tall mountains of a spacious country were jammed together, receiving handouts of bulk rice, wheat, and kerosene. It was pitiful. Yet, something about the Afghans struck immediately. These were not forlorn people. They were alive, their eyes vibrant. They laughed and joked, despite the horror stories we heard about conditions in their homeland. They were a proud and dignified people, easily differentiated from the Pakistanis.

Talking with them, we heard identical stories. At first, we wondered whether they had been drilled to give a Pakistani version of reality, but after meeting hundreds, and over the years thousands, we knew we were hearing the truth. The Soviets had destroyed their country, bombed their villages, killed their brothers, sisters, mothers, fathers, cousins. They would fight until the invaders were driven out. How could they fight a superpower? "With the help of Almighty Allah. We will be victorious, *Inshallah* (by the will of God)." And to a man, and woman, they would fight to the last Afghan if necessary. Not as American or Western puppets, but because it was their duty and their tradition. The honor of the Afghans was under attack, and there was no greater evil. God was on their side; the communists had no god. They never doubted the outcome.

In those days, we questioned how a primitive, simple people could possibly combat the army of the Soviet Union. In time, their resolve not only convinced us, but, eventually, convinced the Soviets.

In short order, Shah Zaman arranged for us to meet one of the seven leaders of the Afghan mujahaddin. He explained that the few Western journalists who had come to Peshawar had always met a representative from one of two parties (NIFA or Jamiat) because they spoke very good English. But he was taking us to a party which he personally thought did the best fighting inside of Afghanistan. It turned out to be a most significant choice for me. Shah Zaman took us to one of the most imposing men I have ever met, or will ever meet—Younas Khalis. This toughened mujahaddin leader was asked to take me to the war in Afghanistan.

CHAPTER 9

Citizen Soldiers

History shows that there are no invincible armies.

—JOSEF STALIN, 1879–1953

Shah Zaman had given us a basic course on the Who's Who of the mujahaddin. At this time, there were seven different parties— four parties were called "fundamentalist" and three "moderate" by Western diplomats and the few journalists who had made trips to cover the war.

The four "fundamentalist" parties and their leaders were:

1. Jamiat-i-Islami, led by Burhanuddin Rabbani, comprised primarily of Tajiks from the far north of Afghanistan. Their most renowned commander was Ahmed Shah Masood of the Pan-jsher Valley. Rabbani was a religious professor at Kabul University and an early member of the Ikhwan ul-Muslimi (Muslim Brotherhood).

2. Ittehad Islami, led by Abdur Rab Rasul Sayyaf, one of the smallest parties, but with a reputation for fighting hard against the Soviets. Sayyaf, also of the Ikhwan, was released from jail in Kabul by Hafizullah Amin. He went to Peshawar, where he was elected to an alliance of the different mujahaddin groups. With the large sums of money given by Arab supporters, Sayyaf formed his own party. With no natural constituency, he purchased commanders and tenuous loyalty from tribal groups.

3. Hezb-i-Islami, led by Gulbaddin Hekmatyar, the most fanatic of the parties, subscribed to the theory of Pan-Islam. This,

the most anti-Western group, was the favorite of the Pakistani military establishment. Gulbaddin, also a member of the Ikhwan, had close connections with the PDPA in the 1960s. He was the most divisive of the mujahaddin leaders and has been charged with killing a number of mujahaddin commanders from each of the other six parties.

4. Hezb-i-Islami, led by Younas Khalis, the most military and least political of the parties. It had the same name as Gulbaddin's party, because the original group had separated into two early on in the war. (In the beginning of the Resistance, the groups were not divided by parties. The division came about primarily with the distribution of weaponry and assistance from the West and Pakistan. Egos were blown out of proportion and led to much unfortunate and unnecessary squabbling among the leaders.) The Hezb-i-Khalis was made up of farmers, villagers, and mostly rural tribesmen who looked upon Khalis as a dedicated anticommunist. Khalis was the only leader to take part in military operations; he spent half his time on the battlefields in the early years of the war.

The "moderate" leaders and groups were:

1. Pir Sayed Gailani - NIFA (an English acronym for National Islamic Front for Afghanistan - in Pushtu, MAHAZ). Gailani was a spiritual leader of the mystical Qadirya Sufi sect of Islam. He traced his lineage directly back to the Holy Prophet Mohammed. Gailani and most of his followers were royalists—supporters of the exiled King Zahir Shah. For the most part, NIFA was comprised of the upper middle class and former military officers.

2. Professor Sibgratullah Mojadidi - Afghan National Liberation Front, the smallest of the parties. Mojadidi was one of the first Islamic protesters in the 1960s. As a religious leader, Mojadidi was highly respected, but he did not have a significant military operation. However, he played a conciliatory role between the parties, particularly in the first years of the war.

3. Mohammad Nabi Mohammadi - Harakat-i-Inqilab-i-Islami —a theologian and member of Parliament in the late 1960s and early 1970s. He was backed by several Pushtoon tribes and

middle-class business people from the Helmand and Kandahar areas.

One clear morning, Shah Zaman came to the hotel to pick us up. He had arranged for our group to meet Khalis. We drove to the outskirts of Peshawar and turned onto a narrow dirt lane. Coming to a house surrounded by a wall with several jeeps parked outside, we saw several young Afghans milling about—armed with Kalashnikov machine guns. They escorted us to the back room of the house. A single light bulb hung from a wire in a room that held a small desk and various chairs. Several Afghans were squatting on the floor against a wall. We sat down to wait for Khalis.

The first sight of Maulvi Younas Khalis was startling. About five foot nine inches, in his sixties (in 1983), he was strong, with chiseled features. Wearing a white turban and seemingly simple *kameez*, the first thing we noticed was Khalis's beard. It was flame red. His eyes, bright and intelligent, glimmered with humor. But you would not want to upset him. He wore a bandoleer and a pistol strapped across his chest. By the looks of him, Khalis could have done battle with Ghengis Khan.

With Shah Zaman translating, I explained our mission. I said I wanted to go into Afghanistan with his men and make a film for a television documentary. When (if) we came back, I wanted to interview him on camera. Afterwards would be better because the experience would have taught me what to ask. The imposing figure looked us over carefully and made a quick assessment. He nodded. One of his commanders, Abdul Haq, would make the arrangements. He stood up and left the room with his entourage.

After he had gone, one of the men leaning against the wall introduced himself as Abdul Haq. A short, slightly rounded young man with curly hair, and the only Afghan without headgear, he looked like John Belushi. But it was obvious that this man was strong—physically and mentally. And he thought we were funny, really funny. Later he told us he had wondered, that afternoon, what in God's name had brought these soft Westerners to a real war. It was the first of a thousand times he would laugh at us. I, in turn, would marvel at the impact this man would have on my life—and, more importantly, on the future of his country. That afternoon, however, he was just a twenty-five-year-old, slightly overweight Afghan.

We returned to the hotel somewhat subdued. These people were fighting a guerrilla war against the largest army on earth. It was one thing to discuss going halfway around the world to cover a remote and bloody war. It was quite another to commit to traveling with these primitive tribesmen as they went off to fight with the men and machines that marched and rolled down Red Square each May Day. My thoughts began to focus on bullets, helicopters, bombs, battle injuries, and, yes, death. Oh well, we had come this far; no reason to stop now.

Pete Heinlein, my cameraman, thought I was crazy. That was not the time to tell him I agreed. Pete had worked as a reporter when I was a television news director in El Paso and had recently been in the newsroom at Voice of America. He had jumped at the chance to take a vacation from VOA and rub up against the Soviet army. He would later become VOA's correspondent assigned to New Delhi.

Anne and Al Lohbeck (my uncle) made up the rest of the crew. Al was an electrician/musician. I asked him along because I thought it might be prudent to have family around for the adventure. I had naively believed that Al could hang around a bar and play the piano while I traipsed across the mountains. I had overlooked the fact that Islamic Pakistan had no bars, and Peshawar no pianos.

The next morning we heard a motorcycle roar up the street in front of the hotel. Going out to investigate, we saw Abdul Haq in a pilot's jacket skid to a halt in front of our door. He bounced into the sitting room and promptly ordered tea. He said he knew we wouldn't be polite enough to offer, but never mind, he would order for us too.

Pete and I had made serious preparations for our trip. We had gone to an army surplus store in Washington and stocked up on clothing as advised by Andy Eiva, an Afghan lobbyist. Eiva described the knee-deep snow and the need for camouflage, so we bought field jackets, pants, gloves, heavy boots, and ski masks. When Abdul Haq asked us about our provisions, we proudly displayed our genuine U.S. army gear. Abdul Haq began to wheeze, then giggle, and came just short of rolling on the floor. The Afghans wore *shalwar kameezes* when they went home to fight. This stuff would make us stick out like a sore thumb. Not only that, but it was the funniest getup he had ever seen. Eight years later, he would still bust a gut remembering.

Abdul Haq spoke broken, but understandable, English. Every week, he would add several words to his vocabulary. Primarily because of us, he developed a distinctly American accent, unlike the clipped British inflections of most Pakistanis. In the first couple of years, when I used a sound byte from Abdul Haq, I would have to chyron his words over the screen. After that, it was no more required than if he had grown up in Missouri.

Abdul Haq took us to the bazaar to get us properly outfitted. We bought *shalwar kameezes*, blankets for jackets (it was difficult to learn to use a blanket as an item of apparel, but we did, and it works), and Chitrali hats, the rolled beret-type hat worn by Afghans who do not wear turbans. Back at the hotel, he told us to be ready by evening; he had a surprise for us. He warned us to have our camera ready.

About nine o'clock in the evening, Abdul Haq came to the hotel, this time in a jeep. We all climbed in, squeezed in the camera gear, and took off. Abdul Haq drove like a pilot in a jet aircraft on the final feet of a runway. He made the Pakistani look like slow motion drivers. He wound his way through the streets and pulled into the house where we had met Younas Khalis. This time, we were served tea and food—Kabuli rice and mutton, with mutton kabobs. Afghan food is delicious, not with burning curry like Indian-Pakistani cuisine, but with simmered, stewed, and subtle flavors.

After dinner he brought out the surprise—a young, Soviet soldier about twenty-three years old, a prisoner of the Khalis group of mujahaddin. An intelligent, blue-eyed Afghan named Kabir translated from the Russian. I would ask questions in English, Abdul Haq would translate them into Pushtu for Kabir, and Kabir would ask the question in Russian for the boy. And back again. Awkward, but adequate. My questions were formulated to encourage him to tell his story.

It was a device I would use frequently in Afghanistan. Traveling and living with indigenous bands of guerrillas fighting an occupying superpower was in many ways a reversal of the reportage from Vietnam during the war. Reporting on the mujahaddin gave us some understanding of the situation the Soviet soldiers were experiencing in Afghanistan.

His name was Vladislov Naumov and he was from Volgograd. So far so good. We were fascinated and a bit confused. Vladislov was open but intimidated. Captured only a few days earlier, here he was before four Americans with a video camera. He must have thought we were part of the CIA, which Soviet propaganda had told him was directing all phases of the war.

Naumov was a mechanic working on the boats on the Volga river when he was drafted and sent to Tajikistan for infantry and armor training. After only two months, he was sent to join an army unit in Afghanistan. Life as a draftee was miserable, he said. Officers and senior noncommissioned officers routinely beat the lower-ranking soldiers. Drug use and alcoholism were rampant. Soldiers would steal weapons, boots—anything of value—and sell them to the Afghans for hashish and heroin. Caught attempting to steal a pistol from an officer, he escaped rather than face the brutal punishment.

He told us about the "zampolit" (political officers) who held mandatory weekly classes in Marxist indoctrination for every Soviet soldier. And about the atrocities against civilians which were routine in Soviet military maneuvers. He had witnessed soldiers driving tanks over women, and then laughing. Major Churbanov of the KGB, he said, had ordered women and old men killed in a Panjsher valley village for providing food to their husbands and sons in the mujahaddin.

Life in the Red Army, as described by Naumov, was far worse than in any Western prison. I asked what would happen if he went back. "Zastrieliat!" he said, grimacing. "They would shoot me!"

Returning to the hotel, we knew we had an exclusive and

powerful story. It was the first television interview with a Soviet POW since World War II. In it, he condemned the Soviet actions in Afghanistan with the fervor of a convert. I would later be interviewed on NBC's "Today Show," where they showed portions of Vladislov's interview in the dimly lit mujahaddin office. John Palmer, who conducted the NBC interview, was particularly struck by the brutality of Soviet officers to their men.

In the upcoming years, I would interview and get to know several Soviet POWs captured by the mujahaddin, but none ever evoked the emotion of that first interview.

That story had a happy ending. Vladislov and two other boys, Sergei Plotkin and Vadim Busov, worked and fought alongside Khalis mujahaddin in numerous military operations. The boys were helpful to the muj in repairing captured weapons and instructing them on probable Soviet operations. Two years after meeting Vladislov, I was instrumental in helping to get the three boys to Canada. When he arrived in Toronto, Vladislov opened an office for the Khalis mujahaddin and spoke on all possible occasions on Soviet conduct in Afghanistan. All three men were successful immigrants to the West—not, unfortunately, always the case, as will be discussed later.

The next day, Abdul Haq made arrangements for Pete and me to go to Afghanistan. We would travel in Nangarhar Province to the outskirts of Jalalabad. We told him we did not want a military operation put together solely for our benefit. "Don't worry," he responded. "It is what we do, every day, every place. I don't know what the operation will be. Maybe attack a convoy, maybe attack a post. We take advantage of whatever opportunity there is. This war is not for your benefit. You will leave tomorrow; be ready."

I had come to trust Abdul Haq. I knew he would provide for us as well as he could. Nevertheless, none of us got much sleep that night. When Abdul Haq arrived in his jeep very early the next morning, we were not ready. He told us he had expected as much and proceeded to jettison over half of the equipment we planned to take. Dressed in *shalwar kameezes*, but retaining our heavy boots, we loaded the camera, recorder, and gear into the jeep. We drove out of Dean's Hotel and headed into the unknown.

CHAPTER 10

Sweet Revenge

For a war to be just, three things are necessary: public
agreement, just cause, right motive.

—THOMAS AQUINAS, 1225–1274

At the Khalis office in Peshawar we were introduced to Haqim, a large, broad-shouldered man with a deep resonant voice and a friendly disposition. Like many village fighters, Haqim was physically a powerful man. He was older than most of the muj I had met so far, perhaps forty. Age is difficult to determine with Afghans. Some are weatherbeaten and appear prematurely aged by wind and sand. Others seem to thrive on the hardship of outdoor life and look much younger than their age.

Haqim was a father figure to the few men under his command. He operated in Nangarhar Province, in the region from Kama to Cheknower, just west of Jalalabad. His younger brother, Nooragha, was the district commander of the Khalis organization for the area stretching from Jalalabad to the Pakistani border.

The plan was to cross into Afghanistan with Haqim and three others. We would walk across the country to a safe area and there join a larger force under the command of Nooragha.

We left Peshawar in a jeep, six of us and the heavy television gear crammed tight. A few miles outside the city, we encountered a police checkpost at the border of the Tribal Area, land of the Afridis, and the entrance to the famed Khyber Pass. The mujahaddin vehicle breezed through. As the years went on, smuggling journalists past these checkpoints became more and more difficult for the mujahaddin, but early on, the police and tribal militias were not on the lookout for foreigners.

We drove across barren country with only low scrub to alleviate the monotony. Suddenly the road started to climb, winding and twisting up into the mountains. As we entered one of the most famous landmarks in the world, the view was breathtaking. The highway's winding switchbacks snaked through the Khyber, while here and there, we spotted a scattering of adobe houses, each with its two-story tower and surrounding wall. We saw few people. On each mountaintop stood stone military outposts. Originally constructed by the British over a century ago to protect the narrow pass, they continued to serve that same purpose for the militia.

We found the scenery and the history it evoked spellbinding. The muj were uninterested; they were concentrating on the job ahead.

We passed two huge forts, obviously constructed by the British, now used as active military installations by the Pakistanis. Another reminder of the history of the Khyber Pass were the regimental crests that had been painted onto cliff faces. The pictures depicted British and Indian units which, at one time or another, had defended the pass. Driving through three or four tribal villages, we noted that once again each home was built like a minifort with high walls and guard posts. These people were apparently accustomed to defending themselves.

Reaching the summit of the pass, we came upon the town of Landhi Kotal. It was the last bazaar, or town, before the Afghan border. In both Afghanistan and Pakistan, rural towns are called bazaars, which is what they are. Usually, the towns are more trading posts than residential centers. Most of the people who shop or barter at the bazaars live in far-flung areas.

Landhi Kotal consisted of two streets lined with shops selling everything from tires and electronic equipment to cloth, food, and you name it. It was also the center for smuggled goods coming from the north that will be clandestinely distributed in Pakistan and further south in India, among them opium and hashish. Throughout the 1980s, Landhi Kotal also acted as an arms depot for all the mujahaddin parties.

We pulled off the main road and drove through huge steel gates in the wall of a fortress-like house. In the courtyard thousands of boxes of ammunition were piled in stacks nearly eight feet high. Several rocket launchers were lying on the ground alongside piles of RPGs (rocket propelled grenades). We entered a room and sat on the *toshaks* (cushions) ringing the floor. Hanging from nails on the wall were several dozen Kalashnikov submachine guns. The Afghan in charge, a supply sergeant of sorts, served us green tea. He welcomed us proudly to his war with a friendly, toothless grin. With the exception of the modern weapons, the scene could have sprung from the ancient past— tribal Afghans sitting on cushions spread over a dirt floor drinking tea and discussing past and upcoming battles.

Every Afghan wore a blanket, most of thin cotton, but a few of wool. While it took me years to get used to wrapping these blankets around my shoulders and arms, they are indispensable to the Afghans. They keep out the cold, rain, and other elements, of course, but they also serve as camouflage, being mostly off-green or beige in color—many a time a group of muj would blend into the rocks on a mountainside wrapped in the blankets. The blankets are used as tablecloths when spread on a dirt floor or on the open ground, and, doubled up, serve as prayer rugs five times a day. They also frequently become backpacks, holding large amounts of equipment, food, or other supplies.

We spent about two hours at the mujahaddin depot in Landhi Kotal. Here Haqim and the others picked up weapons—Haqim a 9 mm pistol and a Kalashnikov; the others either Kalashnikovs or RPGs. We got into the jeep and headed out. We rode northeast from the Khyber on a little traveled dirt track, not really a road, that went straight up, and up, to the summit area of a towering mountain. When we crossed the summit and started down, Haqim boomed in his vibrant voice, "Welcome to Afghanistan, thank you veddy much!"

As we started back down, the trail stopped; it was gone. The jeep began to rattle down and down over loose gravel at an angle that would be difficult to walk, much less drive. Khalil, our driver, was happily and carelessly going full speed—straight down. On the positive side, an incredible panorama spread out before us—a beautiful valley unspoiled by humans, with a large river wending its way three thousand feet below. Nature displayed her beauties in their pristine splendor. On the northern horizon were snowcapped mountains. Alongside the river, the landscape was dotted with adobe-like houses. As we got closer to the bottom, we could make out sheep grazing in the foothills. We had arrived in the mysterious mountain kingdom made famous by the likes of Curzon, Churchill, Handyside, and Kipling.

"*Shuravie* post," said Haqim, pointing off into the distance. Our untrained eyes could see nothing, but we understood "*Shuravie,*" the Pushtu word for Soviet. Of a sudden, the war had become real. Haqim and the muj seemed unconcerned—the post might well have been a hundred kilometers distant instead of five. We reached the bottom of the mountain.

Driving alongside the riverbank we came to a complex of two or three houses within a single wall. An elderly man came out to greet us. Seeing Haqim and the three muj, he hugged them and began the routine Afghan greeting: "Peace-be-unto-you-how-are-you-how-is-your-health-you-are-well?" which spurts out in a rush of sounds. The responses issue simultaneously: "And-unto-you-peace-I-am-fine-I-am-well-thank-you." Then a repeat, but in reverse. Each Afghan hugs and shakes hands. If twenty people are in a room and the twenty-first enters, he greets the room with, "Peace be unto you (*Salaam alai-kum*)," and then proceeds to shake hands with everyone in the room, whether he has never met any of them, or has left them ten minutes earlier.

The man invited us inside and into a guest room. Most such complexes have a simple room set aside for guests. They have several *charpoys* (cots with woven twine stretched across wooden frames) around the walls and, usually, an open pit fireplace in the center of the room for cooking and warmth. Without chimneys, the upper half of the rooms are frequently filled with smoke. This evening was the first of hundreds of choking experiences.

Our host brought a long narrow strip of oilcloth and spread it on the floor. The six of us and about six male members of the household sat cross-legged on the floor. A young boy put an oval flat of unleavened bread (called *nan*) in front of each of us, much like placemats, except that these placemats were edible—steaming, warm, and fresh. This was followed by several heaping platters of rice and a few dishes of a spinach-type vegetable. Inside each platter of rice were hunks of well-cooked mutton. There were no utensils.

A few years later, an Afghan told me of a time when, in Kabul, he and some friends had lunched with students from a European school for diplomatic children. The man laughed recalling how the European children brought their own forks and spoons, because they didn't know how to eat with their hands. Their lack of education continued to amuse him. On this November night in 1983, I began to further my education. But after almost nine years, I still have not perfected the ability to squeeze a wad of rice into the size of a golf ball and flip it into my mouth with my thumb.

After dinner, all scraps and leftovers were pushed to the center of the oilcloth, which was rolled up and hauled away. The dinner was followed with green tea and war stories.

We resumed our trip before dawn the next morning, this time on foot since our jeep had returned to Pakistan. The muj carried most of our equipment as if it were made of light foam. One young man, Ambrullah, placed one of our bags with heavy batteries, weighing almost one hundred pounds, on his head and pranced towards the river. The camera and heavy recorder were wrapped in separate blankets and carried as backpacks. Each of the muj, in addition, carried a weapon.

We walked a couple of miles until we came to where the Kabul river cuts sharply eastward, skirting the mountains of the Khyber Pass, before arcing southward and into Pakistan to join the Indus. It was a wide, raging river. Believing we were meant to wade or swim across, I became alarmed. Our equipment would be ruined if it got wet. For once, my fears were allayed; Haqim assured me we were waiting for a boat.

Fifteen minutes later, the boat arrived from upriver. It consisted of two cowhides sewn together and filled with air, like balloons with legs pointing outward. Strips of wood were lain over the bloated carcasses to form a platform of sorts. We crossed three at a time, and in half an hour had all reached the other bank, dry as a bone. The mujahaddin navy was doing its part in the war against MiG aircraft.

We walked for two more hours, until we came to a small village resembling a Hopi Indian pueblo, nestled in the foothills of a mountain range. The Afghans in this area near the village of Kama were of the Shinwari Pushtoon tribe. Women, with scarves covering their hair and wrapped in front just underneath their eyes, were carrying clay pots of water from a well to the village. We saw no children and only two old men. Haqim explained that the village was often attacked by the *Shuravei* and the children had been taken to refugee camps in Pakistan for safety. The men were with the mujahaddin. The women stayed behind to provide food and information to passing groups of muj.

In the center of the village, Haqim removed a couple of adobe bricks near a water well to reveal a deep hole in the ground—an ammunitions cache. Taking several small boxes of bullets, he passed them out to each of his men. Then he said, *"Arakat"*— Let's go.

We headed up the mountain. Afghanistan has two sizes, huge and towering. This one was merely huge, probably 3,500 feet from the village to the summit. Walking straight up or straight down had no visible effect on the speed of our Afghan hosts. They climbed steadily, neither too fast, nor too slowly. Had they been alone, they would not have stopped. But the higher and more steeply we climbed, the more frequently I needed to rest. Once we finally reached the top, another spectacular view burst before us: to the south a wall of high mountains forming the border with Pakistan, to the northwest the Nangarhar plains leading to the valley near Jalalabad, to the northeast increasingly tall snowcapped mountains, reaching beyond the clouds. There were no roads, no electric lines, no vehicles, no signs at all of the twentieth century.

Below us was another village of perhaps twenty houses, each encircled by the ubiquitous wall. Wisps of smoke rose as the evening meals were prepared. We were three thousand feet above them, but Haqim wanted to get there before dark closed in. Ambrullah, with the heavy bag still on his head, was singing at the top of his voice, "We understand this lesson." It was the only English phrase he remembered from some far distant classroom. It became our greeting to each other for the rest of the journey. Each morning, he would smile and we would say to each other, "We understand this lesson." Now, I was the student learning the ways of people who had not changed in centuries.

Reaching the bottom of the mountain, we waited in a clump of trees alongside a stream, perhaps half a mile from the village. It was dusk. Haqim sent one of the men ahead to the village. Cut off from quick escape to Pakistan, he was now as cautious and alert as a deer. The Afghan and Soviet armies regularly patrolled this area. We would wait for the latest information.

It was dark by the time the man returned. A Soviet army patrol had been to the village that afternoon; they were be-lieved to have camped a few miles down the valley. Haqim decided to move after a quick respite. We entered the village through the stable area; the guest room was in a corner of the stable. We were tired (at least, I was tired; the muj would probably never admit it) and hungry. A few handfuls of rice and *nan* were warming and refreshing. As soon as the sun set, it started to get cold. We left the village an hour later, walking single file, with about three yards between us. Our movement would be difficult to spot. Even at three yards it was not easy to see the man in front of you. We walked silently for over three hours. Twice we saw campfires to our left, probably army en-campments, Haqim later explained.

The metal clacking of a gun bolt being snapped cracked through the night's silence. My stomach sprang to my throat as each man froze in place. Shouting in Pushtu split the air. We heard several cartridges loudly chambered into guns on our right and to the front of us. Haqim, next to me, pulled his pistol and crouched down. I saw a nearby tree and dove for its base.

I could see nothing, but I could feel my heartbeat and thought I could hear it. The stillness was broken by yelling and then an argument between two people. Haqim, still wary and alert, got up and walked towards the commotion. After much loud conversation, we began again to move forward. In the area just ahead, I saw several Afghans, guns at the ready, staring down at us as we passed.

Further down the trail, Haqim explained that we had stumbled across a group of Jamiat mujahaddin bedded down for the night. Not knowing who we were, they challenged us before permitting us to pass.

As the years passed, stories proliferated of muj groups fighting each other. But rarely were the Khalis involved. They were universally respected and had no particular political axe to grind. Gulbaddin Hekmatyar's people, however, were almost always implicated in these fratricidal battles. Fighting and killing were most common between the Gulbaddin and Jamiat groups.

It took a while for the tension and excitement of the incident to pass. Although nothing had actually occurred, the stark reality of men with guns taught a powerful lesson—to relax and daydream at war was suicidal. Sixth, seventh, and eighth senses had to be developed.

We reached the large village of Cheknower well after midnight. Once again, we waited outside the village while Khalil scouted ahead. With the all clear, we entered; inside a dusty, bugridden guest room, I fell asleep instantly.

In the morning, my feet were blistered and bloody. The heavy boots had been a mistake, one I would not make again. They were only impediments in that terrain. Afghanistan is the rockiest country on earth, its mountains and valleys carpeted by small loose stones. The country, seismically among the most active anywhere, is rocked by frequent earthquakes of great magnitude, which shatter the mountains and boulders as if they were stacks of glass sheets pounded by a great weight.

The villagers of Cheknower brought us fresh *malta* (oranges). They were heaven-sent. We waited in the Cheknower area for three days, changing houses each night for security reasons. Haqim did not want anyone to know where the two foreigners were staying. It was not easy to know whom to trust in a large village.

The village showed evidence of recent bombing. Some of the men took us to a spot where a school and several houses lay in ruins. But the main portion of the village was intact, and some one thousand people lived there and went about their business. The next time I passed through Cheknower, two years later, not a single building remained. It was a ghost town, in ruins.

On the third day, a tall young Afghan with hair to his shoulders and a long beard came into the guest room where we were staying. All Afghans have beards, but his was down to his chest, like a picture from old Bible stories. This was Commander Nooragha, Haqim's younger brother. He had come to take us to an operation he had underway.

The men with Nooragha were a different breed from those I had met up to that time. They had shoulder-length hair and a coldness about them. Although always friendly and with a great sense of humor, they were deadly serious about their business. These were men who lived in and for battle, lived each day as if it were their last.

By this time, we had spoken with many Afghans—old men in villages, young men at war, and commanders with a deep sense of purpose. They all told the same story. The foreigners, the Soviets, had come uninvited into their country and had begun to destroy it. The intruders demolished the Afghans' homes, raped their women, killed their families, and scorned their religion. The Afghans did not hesitate to fight back. Many had to rely on old Enfield rifles to counter the enemy's helicopters and tanks, but they would never stop fighting—not until the Soviets were driven out. To a man they agreed it would be accomplished, if not by themselves, then by their sons, or grandsons. Later, when asked about their determination on the CBS "Morning News" show, I reported: "At first, I thought such statements were two bits worth of rhetoric, but after being with them and living with them for several years—I believe them."

"*Arakat!*"—this time from Nooragha. It was time for the action. With his twenty-five men, our group now numbered over thirty. Single file, we headed out of the village and into a marshy plain. The flat land was covered with high grass, the ground slightly soggy from backwater seeping out of irrigated fields. I remarked haphazardly to Pete that Rommel or Patton would love this place, "It's tank country." Within five minutes we heard the unmistakable sound—the mechanized rumble of tanks. Nooragha heard it before we did. Two muj, placed ahead of us as lookouts, reported that the tanks were headed away to our right, not in our direction. We continued walking until we met another wide and fast-moving river, the Kunar.

We came to a crossing point where a wire cable was stretched across the river. A raft connected to the cable was ferrying muj back and forth. It was a busy place, here in the middle of nowhere. Our group of thirty-one was waiting to cross north, while another couple of dozen were headed south. Greetings were exchanged, with the requisite hugs and handshakes. The process took forever and the noise level was in the upper decibels. They must have figured tanks could not hear above their engines.

By midafternoon, we reached an orchard, row upon row of *malta*. Nooragha explained it was a state garden controlled by the Soviets. His men picked several kilos of fruit and loaded them into our blankets, and we continued to a group of trees in a small depression. A village lay just ahead. Here, Nooragha informed us, was a government administration building protected by soldiers. This was our target.

For the past two days, he had been moving men and weapons to surround the complex. Pete and I would move up to a small walled area by the garden a mere hundred yards from the army encampment and government buildings. We would film the action through a hole in the wall surrounding the garden.

We moved stealthily, in a crouch, across the distance to the secluded area. Inside the wall we were able to relax a bit and set up our camera. A turret-mounted Dashika heavy machine gun was pointing through a small hole in the wall. Through the hole we could see the post, a small fort with guard towers. Soldiers were hanging around on top of the wall, which suggested there were walkways on the inside of the complex.

The plan was for Nooragha to signal the attack with a burst of machine gun fire. But before the prearranged time, someone on the other side of the post fired. All hell broke loose. Rockets and grenades came whizzing over our heads and exploded in the far corner of our garden, and gunfire from all sides ripped into the post. The machine gun at our placement was fired until the barrel grew red with the heat.

I got the bright idea that we could get a great shot of the machine gun firing if we were on the other side of the wall and shooting our pictures back. Pete thought I was crazy, but he came along anyway. We got a great shot. So, unfortunately, did the enemy. After a few minutes of superb filming and bullets screaming by our heads, we scrambled back behind the wall.

One of the Afghans, who had been sent along as our interpreter, was lying in a fetal position in an irrigation ditch. He was terrified. He had been a schoolteacher and this was his first trip to *Jihad*. Probably his last, as well. Until that moment, he had been useless as an interpreter, having seemingly forgotten any English he had ever known. Now he said in clear English, "We go now?"

We stayed in the garden for about an hour until dusk began to create heavy shadows. Then Nooragha indicated it was time to go back to Cheknower, an hour away. Nooragha, Haqim, and their men were from these villages and knew every inch of the terrain, which was one reason they could run circles around the invading Soviets. But somehow, we promptly got lost.

We tramped through corn fields, through mud from recently irrigated fields, through corn fields once again. After wandering in circles for three hours, Haqim admitted he had no idea where we were. We stopped to get our bearings. The sky was magnificent. There was no moon, but the stars were beyond description. With no electric lights or pollution, there was no visual interference, and the billions of stars sparkled in incomparable brilliance.

That's when we saw a sight that drove home the contrast between the sophisticated West and primitive Afghanistan. In a field a group of tribesmen roamed, people whose way of life had not changed in centuries. Above them, crossing the billions of stars, streaked a bright light—the space shuttle. We had heard of its launching the previous day on our short-wave radio. The contrast in technology was incredible. We tried to explain a space shuttle; it was impossible.

We eventually reached Cheknower. The tension fell off us like layers of clothing. We had just been through our first battle of the Afghan War. It had been small, yet two of the muj had been killed and several wounded. They did not know, as yet, the damage on the other side. We were safe for the moment, however, and even the muj increased their normal banter.

The guest room was the worst yet. It was filled with piles of sticks for firewood and covered with soot. Pete asked our interpreter, Sher Ali, the one phrase he had understood throughout the trip: "Where is the toilet?" The usual response had been to point to a large bush, or a low retaining wall of an irrigated field. This time, Sher Ali broke us up when he said in his best English yet, "This whole place is a toilet."

For the return trip, Haqim found a donkey for me. My feet were useless. We headed back by a different route, crossing even higher mountains with panoramic views that no camera could catch.

The first noticeable sign that we had entered Pakistan was the sight of electric lights and concrete buildings. Next came the paved roads and vehicles. After our ten-day experience, Pakistan seemed like civilization, Peshawar almost cosmopolitan.

We had made it. We had become a part of the small group of foreigners who had sneaked inside occupied Afghanistan. We had it on videotape. Now we had to get people to explain, on camera, what we had seen.

Pete and I felt pretty good. We probably strutted a bit, until, that is, Abdul Haq showed up at Dean's. "That was nothing. Maybe next time you'll see something dangerous." One of Abdul Haq's new duties in life was to keep me from "having too much pride."

CHAPTER 11

David vs. Goliath

It is better to have a lion at the head of an army of sheep than a sheep at the head of an army of lions.

—DANIEL DEFOE, 1661–1731

I interviewed Younas Khalis in the courtyard of his party's office, with Shah Zaman translating. I needed the videotaped interview to wrap up my documentary before returning to Washington. When we first sat down, I thought Khalis was fingering his prayer beads—what Westerners frequently call "worry beads" since Muslims seem always to be fidgeting with them. But as my eyes roamed from his white turban down his red beard, bandoleer, and pistol, to his hands, I noticed he was playing with two pistol bullets. He was rolling them over his fingers, much as a riverboat gambler exercised his fingers with silver dollars.

Khalis explained what was going on in Afghanistan—the war of the mujahaddin, the contest between David and Goliath—using the simple formula of a schoolteacher: "We have no choice but to fight. They, the Soviets, are trying to steal our country. They are godless people, who cannot win. Bands of mujahaddin will continue to go into our country and, God willing, we will prevail. In Afghanistan, everything and everybody is the mujahaddin. The rocks are mujahaddin; the trees and the birds are mujahaddin. Every man, woman, and child of

81

Afghanistan will not rest until these infidels are driven out of our land. We do not fight for honor or glory or political power. We fight to rid our land of this sickness. If we give our lives for this struggle, we will be rewarded in heaven. But the Soviets did not invade Afghanistan just to make *us* communists. We are fighting them on behalf of the entire world. We do not need manpower. We will survive without help. But if the other countries of the world, if the West, want to help, we will accept it. We will not extend our hands to them, but if they want to help—we are fighting their fight."

He was succinct and to the point, as always. He could be stubborn and bullheaded, but he never wavered from his purpose. Time and again over the years, when the other mujahaddin groups would bog down with distracting squabbles, Khalis was there to refocus their aim, their sole reason for existence—to push the communists out of Afghanistan.

In public statements or meetings with the media, Khalis could be aggravating, but this too was in character. At one news conference, he read a statement about a political decision he had made. When he had finished, the journalists shoved and shouted to get their questions in. Khalis silenced the uproar tersely. "I have read my statement. I was formerly a journalist and therefore I have anticipated all possible questions and included the answers in my statement. There can be no other questions. Thank you." With that he got up and left the room. End of statement, end of news conference. The media never loved him. Yet every Afghan respected his demeanor.

That evening Abdul Haq had us over to his house for dinner. Like the average Afghan household, his was full of people, fifty or so, including a dozen small children. He explained that it was impossible to turn away relatives or close family friends who had been forced to flee their homes with only the belongings they could carry. These people would stay until they could find their own places in the refugee camps. The turnover was constant. With a laugh he said he loved going to *Jihad*. "War is quieter."

Born in Nangarhar Province, Abdul Haq spent the first period of the war fighting there with the Khalis mujahaddin. But he soon decided that the Resistance had to take the war to the capital city—to Kabul, the heart of the country. History had shown that control of Kabul was essential to control of Afghanistan. The communist regime and the Soviets must feel the fire of the Resistance.

He went to Khalis and asked for supplies to start operations in and around Kabul. Khalis said that it was too dangerous and that, in any case, Abdul Haq was too emotional and young for the project. Abdul Haq was not so easily put off; he argued that since Nangarhar was now controlled by the mujahaddin, with trained commanders in all the districts around Jalalabad, it was time to dig deep into enemy territory, to hit the center. But Khalis was adamant. So was Abdul Haq. He would do it with or without help.

Abdul Haq launched his plan. He gave a number of guns to a friend, a taxi driver called Qadar. Hiding the guns in the taxi, Qadar drove into the city to await the arrival of Abdul Haq. But a few days later he was captured by the secret police (KhAD) and executed. Upon hearing the news, Abdul Haq, with only three other friends, left on foot for Kabul.

The journey through the mountains from Pakistan to Tezin, on the outskirts of Kabul, took three days. The men hid out in the home of a close friend, Faisal. While there, Abdul Haq convinced Faisal that they must begin operations in the city. Together, the five men set out for the city. In the evening, they paused in the hills overlooking the lights of Kabul. This was where the Soviets and their puppets must be hit. Once inside the city, they were befriended, given food and a place to rest, and inundated with information about government activities.

In a few weeks, Abdul Haq's band grew. He decided to headquarter the group in Paghman, a suburb of Kabul close to military centers—and to the mountains, which could provide refuge. Enlisting the support of muj from the Paghman area, they began to assault agents of the communist government.

In the early months, the group was supplied solely by what they could capture and what the sympathetic residents of the area and the city could provide. Soon, the group's attacks on the Soviets and the regime's army began to get public notice, so much so that, one night, as they were listening to the radio, they heard the BBC announce that "13,000 resistance fighters" were operating in the Paghman area. That particular night, Abdul Haq's group numbered exactly eighteen men. Yet their impact was such that the government was forced to exaggerate the size of the group or risk being completely humiliated in the eyes of the population.

On one operation against a military outpost, Abdul Haq was wounded—shrapnel to the head. Back in Pakistan for medical treatment, he argued his cause further and finally convinced Khalis and other leading figures of the Resistance to support his cause, the Kabul Front.

Returning to Kabul, Abdul Haq began to enlarge and strengthen his network in the city, creating cells of covert members under his command, starting with friends, relatives, and people known to be strongly antiregime. They began to infiltrate all phases of life in Kabul. The network grew; cells sprang up inside the government bureaucracy and finally inside the army itself, including the Defense Ministry. Groups were organized among students and businessmen and throughout the bazaars. Special cells were developed for information and operations across the city. Each cell was separate and unknown to the others for its own protection. Abdul Haq kept everything concerning the network secret, allowing only three of his most trusted confidants to serve as links between the different cells.

When I met Abdul Haq in 1983, the commander of the Kabul Front was already gaining a reputation as the most damaging thorn in the side of the occupying Soviet forces. He had the sparkle and vitality of a man in his twenties with the authority and analytical mind of a person much older. Although he resented having to waste his time on trivial conversation, he always had the patience to listen to his followers. His solicitude was repaid. Time and again I saw the devotion and confidence the Kabul Front men had for Abdul Haq. Their loyalty was total.

"The Soviets didn't come to my country to capture me or just my country," he told me in my first taped interview of him. "They came this way for many reasons. First, they want the warm waters; they don't have warm waters for their navy. Second, they want the oil and the gas from the Gulf. They have built this huge pipe, pipe for the gas which they sell to Europe. They will just turn off the oil and the gas. Europe cannot function without these things."

Did he need help from the outside world? "The Soviets have tanks and helicopters and jet airplanes. We have nothing, a few guns. We are not fighting just for Afghanistan or for the region; we are fighting for the whole world. If they want to help, they are just helping themselves. If they don't, we will still fight."

What was his opinion of the Soviet army? "They are good when they are with their tanks or with their helicopters. When they get just a few meters away from their tanks, from their helicopters, they are like nothing, no problem. You see, everybody has lost a mother or father, a sister, brother, uncles, children. We will fight until only one Afghan is left. Then they could just have a desert."

I imagined General Boris Gromov, commander of the Soviet forces in Afghanistan, sitting in the Chilsatoon Palace in Kabul. His uniform was resplendent, a match for his surroundings. His men were discontented, suffering in camps in an alien country. Abdul Haq, on the other hand, wearing an old *shalwar kameez*, was sitting on the floor in a rundown house. His men were devoted—devoted to Afghanistan, to Islam, and to him. General Gromov had met his match.

On the flight out of Pakistan, our minds were overflowing with images and events of the weeks past. Afghanistan, its people and its plight, were as addictive as any narcotic. These people, against tremendous odds and with such terrible suffering, maintained a spirit that could no longer be ignored. Their story must be told, and we were going to tell it. Looking out the window of the airplane, we knew we would return. Later, Rob Schultheis, in an article for the *Washington Post* Magazine, asked why I kept going back inside Afghanistan. The answer was easy: "When you go into that beautiful country, into those mountains, you leave a part of your soul. I have to keep returning in order to visit myself."

CHAPTER 12

Helping Hands—
Overt and Covert

It was as helpful as throwing a drowning man both ends of a rope.
— ARTHUR BAER, 1897–1975

Upon our return to Washington, several things had to be done simultaneously. I needed to edit and finish our documentary. And I needed to discover what Washington was doing officially in respect to the Afghanistan War.

I put together a rough cut of our documentary, entitled "Beyond the Khyber Pass." It relied heavily on Khalis and Abdul Haq's portrayals of Afghanistan's resistance and included pictures of refugee camps and Pakistani officials describing the plight of the exiles. My life had become consumed by these people and their country.

I went to events held by the Afghan community in the Washington area who were equally embroiled in the tragedy taking place in their homeland. Numerous men had brought their families to the safety of the United States, only to return themselves and join the *Jihad*.

As word of my trip circulated in Washington, people from the State Department began to seek me out, eager for first-hand accounts from inside Afghanistan. But while they mouthed the political rhetoric of the White House, namely support for the

Resistance, I did not meet a single person in those days who gave the Afghans a snowball's chance in hell of survival, much less victory. On the other hand, the USSR invasion of Afghanistan had given the diplomats leverage in dealing with the Soviets. No official contact was ever made without the inclusion of American protests over Afghanistan.

There were, of course, the exceptions, those who strongly disagreed with the general policy of "bloodying the Soviet nose despite the inevitability of defeat." A young woman, Desiree Milliken, was in charge of the Afghan desk at the State Department. She, for one, thought more should be done to support the mujahaddin. But her arguments, rooted for the most part in the Afghans' fight against foreign invaders in the historic past, were not given much credence. One senior State Department official described Milliken to me as a "true believer," a sure kiss of death in that nonideological department.

The State Department's party line was expressed by its senior spokesman on Afghanistan, Robert Peck, who candidly described the government's official estimation of the Resistance: "They can never defeat the Soviet Union, but what they can do is keep the pressure on and hope for some diplomatic achievement."[1]

Most of the career foreign service officers I spoke with regarding Afghanistan were miffed, moreover, that State was not the lead American agency "on the Afghan problem." Bill Casey and the CIA had taken the initiative, and thereby control, of American dealings with the Afghans. The Defense Department was called upon for technical and logistic support, but Casey was unconvinced of the dedication of his own deputy, John McMahon, much less the State Department, to the cause. In one respect he was correct; most of the planners at State thought the CIA's Afghan adventure was doomed to defeat. They appeared to accept the Brezhnev Doctrine as invincible. The sheer guts and determination of the Afghan people had earned universal admiration, but as one diplomat said, "It's like being a fan of the Cleveland Indians—why get your hopes up?"

The assistant secretary of state for Near Eastern Affairs, Richard

Murphy, was the seniormost official dealing with the Afghan question on a day-to-day basis, and Charles Dunbar and Robert Peck were assigned to "his shop." Murphy had spent a great deal of his career dealing with Arab nations. In the beginning, Afghanistan had been mistakenly lumped with the Arabs, disaffecting both Arabs and Afghans. Always polite, the Arab diplomats treated Murphy with formal cordiality, but privately one Arab ambassador told me, "Richard Murphy is typical of State Department elitists. He is proud of his superficial knowledge of Arabs. He drinks his coffee in the prescribed Arab manner, but he is distrustful, even fearful, of Islam. And he does not understand Islam as our way of life. Episcopalians have their religion on Sunday morning and their politics the rest of the time. Muslims cannot separate the two." The ambassador's message was clear: he understood the people at the State Department, and he knew they did not understand him.

The CIA was not in the business of providing humanitarian aid, but the human suffering of the Afghans was overwhelming. In Pakistan alone, the 3.5 million refugees were a logistic and economic nightmare. Besides, if their families were not fed, how could the Afghan men go off to war? The administration had lined up several countries to assist with this burden—primarily the UK, Sweden, Germany, and France. Gerald Helman, former U.S. ambassador to the United Nations Mission in Geneva, was one of the lead people at the State Department to coordinate worldwide humanitarian efforts for the Afghans. Working more for the CIA than the State Department, Helman brought the aid program under the umbrella of the United Nations. It became the largest operation undertaken by the UN bureaucracy.

United Nations involvement also brought some strange people to the program, which was essentially an anticommunist effort. The head of the Swedish Committee's Pakistani operation, for example, was an avowed Marxist.[2] And one of the highest-ranking UN officials to come to Pakistan in an overseer role was Martin Barber, the Britisher who, after touring Pol Pot's torture cells in Cambodia, commended the Pol Pot regime for "making great humanitarian strides."[3]

Concerning the efforts of other nations, the French organization Medicin Sans Frontier (MSF—Doctors Without Borders)
was the first aid operation of any consequence to set up operations out of Peshawar. The French had enjoyed a long-standing
relationship with Afghanistan before the war. The struggle of the
mujahaddin, and the difficulties faced by the country itself,
moved many Frenchmen and women to volunteer. Dr. Juliet
Fornot, for example, made several trips to the north of Afghanistan to treat and vaccinate villagers in the Pansjher valley.
This region was controlled by the mujahaddin, namely Jamiat
Commander Ahmed Shah Masood.

Masood spoke French, as did some of his subcommanders.
This, more than any other reason, brought French aid and
French journalists to Masood and the Pansjher valley. The resulting French news reports and publicity for MSF—the French are
adept at generating publicity for themselves—promoted Masood
as Joan of Arc and El Cid rolled into one. The legend of Masood
became such that many observers, and even diplomats, thought
he was the commander of the entire Resistance instead of the
foremost Tajik commander in a nation overwhelmingly populated by Pushtoons. The overblown hype contained a risk for the
Resistance; should something happen to him, it would be viewed
as a death blow to the movement. All this aside, many of the
French can be numbered among the brave, unselfish, and competent people who braved all to help the Afghans.

The British also got into the humanitarian business for the
Afghans in the early stages of the war. British journalist John
Fullerton, one of the first to travel with and write about the
mujahaddin, came to Peshawar with his wife, Romy. When they
divorced, John moved to Hong Kong, but Romy stayed on to
start an operation called Afghan Aid UK. She found political and
initial financial support from Viscount Lord Robert Cranbourne,
a member of Parliament. Lord Cranbourne was the stereotype of
an upper-crust, public school Britisher. On one occasion, he
appeared before the U.S. Congress Special Joint Task Force on
Afghanistan. Sweeping into a hearing room of the Russell Senate
Office Building, Viscount Lord Robert Cranbourne twirled his

full-length cape around his chair before seating himself to testify on his aid efforts.

Romy Fullerton's Afghan Aid began with work projects for refugees but it soon encompassed everything from medical to agricultural aid, in addition to offering a hostel for British journalists. When Romy returned to England, several directors took over the operation. Afghan Aid received considerable British government funding in addition to massive amounts of money from USAID (United States Agency for International Development). Several people involved with the organization were known to have connections with MI-6, later SIS, the British Intelligence Service. Afghan Aid, like its French counterpart, furnished much of its support to Masood in the far north of Afghanistan. This bothered the other Resistance parties more than the link with intelligence.

Another foreign group, the Swedish Committee, ran a large medical aid program inside of Afghanistan as well as several assistance projects in the refugee camps. It grew to be one of the largest foreign operations to build an administrative bureaucracy in Peshawar. And, like the others with large offices and many employees, it was difficult to pinpoint where the millions of dollars their budgets claimed were expended inside Afghanistan actually went. The country was in ruins, travel was hazardous, and Westerners were targeted by the Soviets and the regime. Moreover, in the eight years I traveled throughout the country, I saw very little evidence of Western humanitarian aid operations, with the exception of the far north. Reporting as much did not endear me to the do-gooder crowd.

The Swiss, to their credit, had a viable operation that worked through the International Committee of the Red Cross (ICRC). The ICRC had large hospitals for Afghans in Peshawar and Quetta, Pakistan. They treated the war wounded, fitting amputees with prosthetics, and did other meritorious work.

In 1983, very little visible aid was being given to the refugees and practically none inside Afghanistan. Five years later, the aid business had grown to monster proportions, with 90 percent of the funding for all of the foreign aid groups coming from the

United States, funneled through the UN or USAID. It was both irritating and amusing to hear the anti-Americanism of many of these Europeans, while they scurried to get every last possible penny from U.S. grants.

This community, which grew to almost two thousand people, in many instances avoided dealing with the Afghans, whom they considered too primitive to be able to run their own affairs. As for the war itself, it was dismissed as an American ploy to use surrogates to fight the Soviets.

In short, the early aid workers came out of genuine concern for and interest in the Afghans; the latter crop became a business and a bureaucracy in the name of humanitarianism.

In the early years, when Ambassador Helman, USAID, and the CIA began distributing large sums of money to these various European organizations, the question stood out starkly: Where were the Americans? Only two small private groups, without government funding, could be found. On being asked, Helman told me that it was their policy to keep a low profile of American involvement in any aspect of the war. When I asked to whom the low profile was being presented, he smiled. The Soviets were well aware, of course, of the covert military aid and the funding of the other operations. As U.S. Senator Chris Dodd later said in a minidocumentary I produced, "I don't see any problem helping the Afghans. And I don't think it should be covert. These people have a problem; they've been invaded. The only people we are trying to keep this secret from are the American people—the Soviets know what we're doing." And so it continued throughout the war—the covert military aid was public knowledge, the humanitarian aid was almost deep cover. It made no sense.

The distribution of humanitarian aid and the covert operations of the CIA frequently became so intertwined that it was difficult to separate them. One example concerned the American mules shipped to Afghanistan. The mujahaddin had to carry their armaments, ammunition, and supplies into Afghanistan, and since the roads were controlled by the Soviets, it was necessary to transport such supplies by horse, donkey, and mule over hundreds of foot tracks across the mountains. The dangerous treks and the diminishing number of pack animals added to the mujahaddin's problems as the war intensified.

Some bright person (many took credit) came up with the idea of sending American mules to the war, and soon planeloads of them were shipped from Texas and Tennessee to Pakistan on flights coordinated by the U.S. military. These planes brought humanitarian as well as military consignments, while the return flights were often used to transport wounded Afghans to American hospitals. The mules, once in Pakistan, were added to the regular Afghan pack animals under the supervision of USAID, even though they were part of a CIA project. The tale is not over. The American mules were accustomed to life in corrals and pastures; carrying several hundred pounds of weapons across the highest mountains in the world did not go over well with them. And although they were better than nothing, most of the mujahaddin did not think much of them. To top it off, the Americans running the project had no idea what they were really doing. When I told a top USAID official that the Afghans were encountering problems with the pampered American mules, he said, seriously, "Sure there are problems, but the second generation of these mules will work out just fine." And so with many of the other covert schemes to help the Afghans.

While American aid organizations were not encouraged to join the Afghan effort, American fundraising and lobbying groups got into the act with both feet.

The self-proclaimed watchdog of the "liberal media," Reed Irvine, organized the Committee for a Free Afghanistan, and Andy Eiva started a letterhead organization called the Afghan-American Federation. They competed for the same donor dollars and used the same handful of congressmen who were active on the issue on their letterheads. Every time a newspaper or television network would run one of the infrequent Afghan news items, both groups would take credit for having "placed the story." If an Afghan politician or commander would visit Washington, they would elbow each other for the honor of "hosting" the visit.

The Committee for a Free Afghanistan was, in fact, helpful in finding doctors and hospitals who would take the severely wounded Afghans for treatment. They would arrange for the victims to be transported to the U.S. on the quasimilitary flights and sent to hospitals around the country. Then they would use the men to further their fundraising activities.

The committee also hired people to go to Pakistan to "advise" the mujahaddin militarily. One such person was retired army Brigadier Ted Mataksis. Mataksis was a well-meaning gentleman who spent weeks at a time living in Dean's Hotel while advising the Afghans on how to fight the Soviet Union. Mataksis visited Pakistan between trips to Central America to advise the anticommunist Contras and Salvadorans, and trips to Thailand to advise the Cambodian rebels as well. He once brought some Afghan commanders a secret flashlight to flash signals to each other from mountain to mountain. They were always polite to "General Ted" and gave him green tea.

Another committee representative was David Isby, an American with an acquired British accent. Isby was the author of *Jane's Book*, which analyzed Soviet weaponry. Since this weaponry was being used by the Soviet army, Isby could not resist being a regular visitor to Peshawar. He even made a few of the celebrated "foreigners' tours" the NIFA mujahaddin provided for picked visitors. The muj would take them a few miles across the border, let them take pictures, fire a few weapons, and go home. Isby wrote articles for *Soldier of Fortune* magazine on his experience fighting the Red Army with the fierce Afghan mujahaddin. They gave him copious quantities of green tea.

Andy Eiva's primary activity was to do battle with John McMahon, deputy director of the CIA. Eiva had learned of McMahon's resistance to providing the mujahaddin with any type of effective weaponry, and although Eiva was unable to create much interest in the mass media, he kept McMahon's feet to the fire in official Washington.[4]

True believers in the New Right, however, had serious problems with Eiva; he had been arrested and deported from Pakistan as a *persona non grata*. As a Pakistani intelligence official's dossier on Eiva revealed, Eiva had gone to Pakistan to help establish a clandestine radio station inside Afghanistan using small portable transmitters. The location of one of these was bombed the day after Eiva left the area, and the Pakistanis thought he had set them up. In further support of their theory, they had a file which claimed that Eiva was an East German. In fact, the Soviets were bombing the entire country of Afghanistan and Eiva was most probably the victim of circumstances. But because he had been born in Lithuania and raised in Germany, he was unable to shake the suspicions of the Pakistanis and of various of his detractors in Washington.[5]

The strangest of the volunteer humanitarians was a man named Lech Zondek. Zondek showed up in Peshawar determined to train the mujahaddin in hand-to-hand combat. On one occasion, he took a group of young Afghans to an open field to demonstrate how to disarm an attacker, handed one of them a knife, and instructed him to attack him. The man did as he was told and promptly sliced a gash in Zondek's arm that required numerous stitches. A week later, Zondek went to Kunar Province in the high mountains with the mujahaddin. He was never seen again. Several stories of his disappearance circulated in Peshawar, the most plausible of which said he had gotten into an argument with a muj and was pushed over a mountainside. Two years later, the stories took on a weird twist. The Polish labor organization Solidarity published Zondek's photograph with attached story claiming he had gone to Afghanistan to fight the Soviets "as a representative of Solidarity." They claimed him as a martyr to the anti-Soviet cause.

Other stories of humanitarian help touch on the ludicrous. More than one well-meaning individual showed up in Peshawar in order to distribute Bibles to the Afghans. The aid organization Serve was almost run out of town for proselytizing in Islam.

Every few months would see a down-and-out soldier of fortune arrive who wanted to go to war. One East German, who had escaped from prison and brought his hatred of the Soviets and his military training with him, actually led Afghans into battle in the Kandahar area.

The conglomeration of aid workers, Bible toters, soldiers of fortune, ex-hippies, and do-gooders earned the Western community in Peshawar the nickname of "The Three M's—Mercenaries, Missionaries, and Misfits."

But somehow, out of it all, aid was provided to the millions of refugees, although not very efficiently. Still, several hospitals were started and rations of food, fuel, and clothing were distributed. Many serious and dedicated people helped as well as they could with such projects as handicraft work which provided the Afghans an opportunity to earn some money.

The first two American groups were Freedom Medicine and the Mercy Fund. Freedom Medicine, started by a Reno, Nevada, firefighter, Bob Brenner, and his wife, trained Afghans as paramedics. Anne Hurd's Mercy Fund provided prenatal care for women in the refugee camps. Both grew as the years went by and expanded to take in other projects.

All of the aid groups, unfortunately, adopted the Afghan traits of distrusting each other and aligning themselves with a particular Afghan political party.

In 1983, Dr. Robert Simon of the UCLA Medical Center decided to do something about the suffering of the Afghans. Traveling to Afghanistan, he set up a medical clinic inside Kunar Province with private resources. Wishing to provide emergency medical care for the mujahaddin and villagers, he contacted Afghan Doctor Abdullah Osman who helped him build the initial clinic—in a cave.

Returning to the States, Simon was directed to Hasan Nouri, an Afghan ex-pat engineer in Southern California. Nouri and Simon then had lunch with Charles Fawcett in Los Angeles, and the International Medical Corps (IMC) was formed. Next, Nouri and Simon went to Washington and met with Walt Raymond of the NSC staff and Ambassador Helman at the State Department. As a result, $1 million was allocated to the IMC to establish clinics inside Afghanistan, with the proviso that no American citizen be allowed to travel in the war-torn country.

In the early period of IMC work, this proviso was violated, which led to the tragic death of IMC representative Charles Thorton, also a reporter for the *Arizona Republic*, who was killed when his convoy was attacked by helicopter gunships.

IMC grew to be one of the larger groups providing humanitarian assistance to refugees and mujahaddin alike. Their biggest program entailed training Afghans to work as paramedics in the far reaches of the remote country. Nouri and some others eventually separated from IMC, complaining that the organization had grown into a large bureaucracy that no longer provided simple help to people in desperate need—"to help the Afghans help themselves."

In another relief effort, the International Rescue Committee (IRC) established operations in Peshawar and placed a former priest as its director. Around 1986, IRC became the favorite of the USAID personnel in Islamabad and Washington, so much so that USAID used IRC to distribute its funding, i.e., American tax dollars, to the other groups. IRC, established as a Christian missionary organization working in Africa, even screened applicants for grants for the U.S. government. When I asked Larry Crandall, a veteran of U.S. government activities in Vietnam and the director of USAID for Afghanistan, why the U.S. government turned this responsibility over to a religious-based aid organization, he explained that USAID had neither the time nor the manpower to do it alone. USAID, incidentally, was the largest staffed section of the U.S. Embassy in Pakistan, and had the largest U.S. office in Peshawar. Crandall did not explain how his people occupied their time.

After my first trip to Afghanistan, my greatest wish was to return. In April 1984, CBS News hired me to go to Saudi Arabia to cover the oil tanker war between Iran and Iraq. Returning to New York six weeks later, I discovered that NBC News had become interested in Afghanistan. Following my appearance on the "Today" show, NBC hired me to return to Afghanistan. We arrived in Peshawar in late May.

Messengers Confusing the Message

Journalism will kill you, but it will keep you alive while you're at it.

—HORACE GREELEY, 1811–1872

The foreign editor at NBC News, Jerry Lamprecht, wanted me to go to Peshawar with Henry Champ in June 1984. In addition to working up a story, I was to do the camera work. When I explained that my sole camera experience was with the old film system of local television in the 1970s, they arranged for a professional cameraman in London to give me a few quick lessons, and assured me all would go well. In London, too, I met Champ. He was a big, affable man, and we immediately took to each other—important, we both knew, before heading into potential danger.

As soon as I arrived in Peshawar, I called Abdul Haq. He said he was heading inside, leaving immediately for the Kabul area. Since there was no time to arrange for us to accompany him, he suggested I call a few Afghans to keep me occupied until he returned in about two weeks.

The next morning, an NBC News producer, Joe DeCola, arrived. Neither Henry nor I had been told about him. DeCola, wearing brightly colored beach shorts, met us in the lobby of the hotel, unmoved by the disdainful stares of the Muslims. DeCola, it appeared, had been to the area once before with correspondent Betsy Aaron. After learning that Henry and I were headed into Afghanistan, he had elbowed his way into the project; he had spoken with Afghan "experts" in New York and "knew" just whom to contact and how to do the story.

Henry and I called New York to find out what was going on. We were told to "adjust and live with the situation"—rather difficult, given Joe's arrogance and habit of peppering his remarks with allusions to the "ragheads" and "crazy Muslims." Not a winning personality.

The following night, the three of us went to a mujahaddin office in Peshawar in a complex filled with tents housing young Afghan men. We were escorted to a large, well-furnished sitting room, far more luxurious than anything the Khalis party could boast, and introduced to Colonel Rahim Wardak and Dr. Sharooq Gran of NIFA. Wardak, a huge man with silver hair, was wearing a camouflage military uniform and a dark beret, worn at an angle. Both spoke excellent English with a slight British accent.

Wardak had been an officer in the king's army before the communist revolution in Kabul. At the time of Taraki's coup, he had been in New Delhi and had not returned to Kabul. Later, in London, he joined Pir Gailani in forming the Mahaz-i-Milli Islami Afghanistan—MAHAZ (National Islamic Front of Afghanistan - NIFA). Gailani appointed Wardak supreme military commander; the NIFA party was the only mujahaddin group to give its men military rankings. By my second meeting, Colonel Wardak had become Major General Wardak, later promoted to a full general. One of Gailani's sons told me that whenever Wardak's classmates in the regime's army were promoted, he followed suit.

Over the years I would have a mixed relationship with Wardak. He was a self-promoting braggart, a publicity hound, who was rarely involved in truly significant military operations. None of the hard-fighting mujahaddin groups had any respect for his military ability. Yet for many years he was a favorite of the CIA, which put a great deal of money and material at his disposal.[1] Because of the close relationship that developed between myself and Abdul Haq, Wardak was slightly distrustful of me. To begin with, Wardak hated Abdul's brother, Din Mohammad, whom he considered a fanatic. But, principally, Wardak was jealous of Abdul Haq's military prowess and of his extensive intelligence network in Kabul. But we got along well enough. Wardak was always open and frank with me, and spoke with complete candor about his relationships with the Pakistanis and Americans. When he came under media attack in 1989, I came to his defense. By his own admission, he had personally profited from the war, but he could have and did not seek refuge in England or in the United States.

At this first meeting, Wardak was more than eager to arrange a trip for NBC News. We agreed to leave in three or four days for Paktia Province to witness a planned attack on a Soviet garrison.

Prior to his departure, Abdul Haq had arranged for me to meet Masood Khalili of the Jamiat mujahaddin. Khalili was the son of a renowned Afghan poet and was the primary information/public relations man for Jamiat and its famed commander, Ahmed Shah Masood. He had a sharp sense of humor, spoke a beautiful poetic Engish, and was one of the few Afghans who understood the workings and importance of the Western media.

During our first meeting at his home, he demonstrated, again, the respect the various mujahaddin parties held for the Khalis organization and Abdul Haq. He greeted me by saying, "Abdul Haq is a great commander and a very good man. He is from a different party, but if Commander Abdul Haq asks something of me, I will do it."

The morning after our meeting with Colonel Wardak, Khalili came to see me. "We have three boys who have just returned from the north. They saw the Soviets using chemical gas; in fact, they were badly burned by it. I will take you to them, if you are interested." I grabbed my camera and went with Khalili to a small house in the Faqirabad area of Peshawar.

The three men in their late teens or early twenties recounted how helicopters had sprayed a yellow cloud-like substance over the Panjsher valley. The men described it as similar to light snow, only yellow, clinging to the branches of trees and bushes. The men had festering, blistering burns on their arms and faces. I videotaped their story and their wounds. There had been rumors that the Soviets were using chemicals; these were the first alleged eye-witnesses.

Back at the hotel, Joe DeCola exploded over the quality of the photography which, if not the quality of a trained professional, was not bad. Henry liked the pictures and wanted to go ahead and do a story based on them.

DeCola telephoned Lamprecht in New York; he wanted me fired. After two days of telephoning back and forth, Lamprecht decided that because DeCola was an NBC employee, he was in, which meant I was out.

Steve Olson, a freelance cameraman, was hired to replace me. Later, Rahim Wardak told me that DeCola had brought Olson to meet him the day before I met with the alleged chemical gas victims. It was also the day before DeCola had seen my camera work. DeCola later used my tape of the gas victims.

Upon hearing the story, Khalili said he could arrange for me to go on one of Commander Masood's operations. Although I now had no camera, I called the competition.

Peter Larkin was the foreign editor for CBS News who had hired me earlier to travel to Saudi Arabia. In those days of free-flowing cash at network television, Larkin was a master at "hiding in ambush" journalism—to plant a reporter in some troubled spot to wait for something significant to occur.

I called Larkin, told him what had happened, and was he interested in checking out Ahmed Shah Masood. He said yes, he would send me a cameraman immediately.

A few days later, British cameraman David Green arrived. He was a tough, rugged veteran of combat photography around the world. Khalili arranged for us to leave in two days.

That night Larkin changed his mind. "Send Green to Afghanistan; you go to Bahrain. The Iran-Iraq War might spill over." I hurriedly changed plans and traveled to Bahrain where I stayed for six weeks, but after a month of no war activity, Larkin pulled me out. I returned to New York and wrote my after-action report.

But I had to get back to Afghanistan. Since Larkin was preoccupied with Central America, I went to the only remaining competition—ABC News.

I spoke with Robert Murphy, executive producer of the ABC "World News Tonight," showed him tapes from my first trip, and explained my NBC debacle and Peter Larkin's secret army. Murphy was immediately eager to get ABC onto the Afghan story. Would I take a correspondent with me? I certainly would, as long as I was not stuck with a Joe DeCola. Murphy assured me that I would be in charge. He chose Don Kladstrup, recently from CBS, to accompany me. Murphy arranged for ABC to give me a large bundle of cash for expenses, and I was off to London, where Kladstrup would meet me. It was as simple as that; the meeting with Murphy had lasted a half hour.

Don Kladstrup was a great fellow. Tall, lanky, slightly awkward, and soft-spoken, he was somewhat anxious, being married with three children, about going to war against the Soviets with a bunch of villagers, but I was able to reassure him. We took Steve Masty with us to Pakistan. Steve, a columnist for the *Washington Times*, was a good friend. He would keep in communication with ABC New York while Don and I were "inside," as well as gather first-hand material for his columns.

Abdul Haq, back in Peshawar after a successful campaign in and out of the city of Kabul, told us of an ongoing attack on convoys on the road from Kabul to Jalalabad. He would send us along with Maulvi Jalaladdin, a subcommander operating in the area of the Kabul gorge east of the city. We were on.

We took a van from Peshawar and headed southwest towards the border crossing point at Teri Mangal. An hour out of Peshawar, the road began to scale a large mountain overlooking the Pakistani town of Kohat. The drive down was the usual nightmare.

When we reached the bottom, we were promptly arrested by

Customs police, who had instantly identified us as foreigners. We were taken to army headquarters in Kohat where we explained to a colonel that we were in the country legally and showed him our visas; he was unimpressed. After a long wait, a well-dressed, intelligent-looking man came into the office—a major from Pakistan's ISI. I showed him a copy of a letter from General Acktar, head of the ISI, praising my documentary, "Beyond the Khyber Pass," and asked the ISI agent to call the general. After some hesitation, he let us go.

The delay forced us to spend the night in Thal, the last town before the tribal areas. Nontribesmen are not permitted to cross at night.

Teri Mangal, on the border, was straight out of Hollywood. Nesting in a bowl of mountains on three sides, the small town bustled with activity. Thousands of horses and mules were jostling and stomping, ready to be rented by mujahaddin groups to transport supplies into Afghanistan. Piles of ammunition, weapons, and supplies were being loaded onto horses and mules. And a makeshift bazaar street, with shops in tents, was doing a thriving business, while several *chai khanas* (tea shops) saturated the air with aromas of kebobs, stews, and tea. Sitting on the floor, we filled up with mutton kebob, rice, and *nan*, and spent the night on the upper floor of what passed for a hotel—a large open room covered with linoleum. The floor was wall-to-wall Afghans, snoring, snorting, scratching, sleeping. Don proclaimed he would fall asleep by counting all the five-star hotels he had ever stayed in.

We were awakened at 3:00 A.M. by Jalaladdin: "*Arakat*, we must cross the border and the Jaji before the sun rises." We got the gist through our translator, assigned us by Abdul Haq, who spoke about a dozen words of English and did the rest through sign language and faith.

Our group was composed of fifteen mujahaddin and about a dozen horses loaded with materials. The trail from Teri Mangal went straight up and over the range of mountains that formed the border. Crossing over to the Afghan side, we immediately saw signs of war. The shells of two burned-out tanks had been pushed to the side of the road, and about a mile further down, a group of buildings—government outposts—was reduced to rubble. In the predawn light, the small abandoned villages looked like eerie ghost towns, the dwellings destroyed by bombs.

Every few miles we spotted long stakes driven into the ground, with colored flags or brightly colored scarves attached to the tops. They appeared in clusters, sometimes three or four, occasionally twenty or more. Jalaladdin explained that they marked the burial sites of the mujahaddin killed in battle. Walking across the Jaji valley, we saw hundreds of them.

Abandoned plots of farmland were lying fallow alongside a river which meandered down the valley. The only people we encountered were mujahaddin headed back to Pakistan, or moving down the valley, armed and grimly determined.

As we reached the north side of the valley, the sun rose over the mountains on the east. Snow-covered and glittering with majesty, these mountains were meant to stand watch over a peaceful valley, not over a cauldron of destruction and death.

The houses, or at least what was left of them, came straight out of ancient history books. Tall towers rose above the adobe walls surrounding the homes, each dotted with small holes to allow for rifles. They had been used over the centuries to defend against ground attacks, but today they were completely vulnerable to Soviet jet aircraft and helicopters; these dropped their explosives inside the walls, killing all within.

We crossed another range of mountains, this one higher still, and descended into a valley, the home of the Mangal, the Pushtoons. In the beginning, all Afghans had looked similar to me; each with his *shalwar kameez*, blanket, sandals, and either *chitrali* cap or turban. But over time, I began to notice subtle differences in appearance and in variations of dress. The styles changed from tribe to tribe and area to area. The Nooristanis in the high reaches of Kunar and Badakhshan wore wrapped leggings; the wilder tribes from Zabol to Kandahar had pantaloons with large wide cuffs; and the Kabulis somehow gave off an urbanized appearance.

The villages dotting the Mangal plain were also deserted, with the exception of the mujahaddin who used the ruined houses as resting places. Several *chai khanas* were located along the river flowing through the valley, run by entrepreneurs catering to the needs of warriors on the move. The *chai khanas* served several functions. They were a place of rest after hours on the mountain trails; restaurants that also provided fodder for pack animals; and centers for the exchange of information and gossip of the war— truck stops for pedestrians. They regularly came under bombing attacks. After being hit, most either set up shop down the trail or dug into the mountainsides and operated from makeshift caves.

We traveled for three days past Jagdalek and on to Tor Gar (Black Mountain) on the south side of the Kabul-Jalalabad highway, spending the nights in *chai khanas*. Reaching what appeared to be two small adobe huts, Jalaladdin announced we had arrived at his main encampment. A cursory look showed only three mujahaddin and the two tiny buildings. But closer inspection revealed open tents and adobe buildings hidden in clumps of trees or dug into the hillside. Over the next few days, we would spot almost two hundred fighting men, practically invisible, over a three or four square mile area.

Most of these men were from the general region, from farming families. The mujahaddin commands tended to draw their personnel from the immediate area in which they fought. The men knew the terrain, down to the last rock and tree. They had grown up here; this was their backyard, their playground. The Afghans could blend into the scenery; they were a part of nature. Like mountain people everywhere, they could see like eagles and hear like deer.

And like all people who spend their evenings and nights around campfires, they loved to tell stories and gossip. Two foreigners, the first these people had ever seen, were food for many future tales. We were also a continual source of their good-natured ribbing. We didn't know how to squat and eat; we only sat cross-legged and, always good for a guffaw, we had to stand to relieve ourselves. Moreover—terribly funny—we couldn't walk up a mountain for ten straight hours and be ready to play soccer.

Nevertheless, these kind people genuinely welcomed us and

peppered us with questions about America, a land of which they had not the least conception. Although they thought we were crazy—pleasantly crazy, but crazy—they were grateful that we had come all the way from America to join them on their *Jihad*. An objective media, freedom of the press, and the public's right to know were not concepts for general discussion around mujahaddin campfires. All they knew was that the Soviets were killing their country, and we had come to be with them—and they were thankful. And the next time we came, they would very much appreciate it if we could bring some anti-aircraft missiles with us. Simple people, but not stupid.

Jalaladdin's top sergeant was a big, barrel-chested man named Khana. Along with a smiling face and a heart full of laughter, he had the strength of an ox. When we left for the location where they attacked convoys, Khana carried two heavy recoilless rifles and turrets, one on each shoulder—a donkey could only carry one.

We walked about five miles to positions on top of a cliff, which plunged straight down for a thousand feet. Below us the highway ran along the Kabul river like a black ribbon, an occasional truck moving slowly along its length. About half a kilometer to our right (east), a military outpost sat on a wide bend in the highway. We could see soldiers and jeeps. Don and I positioned ourselves and the camera in a small pocket of the cliff, about ten feet down from the summit. The pocket or depression, where the two of us were barly able to squeeze, had a small rocky ledge that jutted out about three feet—just room enough to position the camera to shoot straight down.

We waited for over two hours. The mujahaddin were scattered up and down the cliff and in various places on top. They had RPGs, recoilless rifles, Kalashnikovs, and two dashika heavy machine guns. Finally, a group of four or five tanks began slowly grinding up the road towards Kabul. Khana decided they made a good target. He signaled his men to wait until the tanks were immediately below us and then to open fire. One muj came to our position, grabbed both of my legs under his arms, and dangled me over the ledge while I held the camera. I was in mid-air, praying he was as strong as he looked. As the RPG hit the lead tank, the camera was rolling.

In seconds, the outpost opened fire with mortars. Metallic explosions boomed around us as rockets whistled through the air above. The old saying went through my brain, "If you hear it, it didn't hit you." It was not very comforting. Abdul Haq, like most experienced soldiers, had learned to tell exactly where a missile was going by sound alone. On this day, they were so close, you could feel the air ripple as they flew past, exploding behind us.

Then the tanks began to fire onto the cliff face, a frightening and deafening experience. Things were happening so fast, I could only take pictures; I had no time to stop and think. There wasn't much I could do about it anyway, hanging over the ledge. After about ten minutes, the battle subsided—not stopped, just slowed down. I was pulled up to the ledge and I collapsed into the pocket with Don. He was busy scribbling notes on the action. Neither of us showed fear—time for that later. If, that is, there was to be a later.

The tanks, after emptying their ammunition, raced back to the outpost. One of them had been hit and was burning, but still moving. Dusk settled in and the outpost stopped firing. We scurried to the top of the cliff and began to run back. Once over the ridge line, we stopped and the mujahaddin began to regroup and count—count each other. We had started with fifty-five men. Fifty-three came back. Several had small shrapnel wounds, but shook them off. It was over. The men formed lines and began their evening prayers, and prayers for the two men who would not return. After that, we began the five-mile trek in the dark to the base camp.

The emotional shock of battle can only be realized in the aftermath. At the time, you are too tense and too busy. Fear, exhilaration, anger, anxiety, and a flow of adrenaline combine in a nearly orgasmic feeling. This had not been a major battle, but still, my first. The emotional explosions would never decrease in intensity, not with time nor place. Nobody hates war more than those who have been there. Yet, it has a perverse appeal, shared by everyone with whom I've spoken who has been there too.

*   *   *

After reaching the camp, we had a meal of cooked turnips. The warmth of the food was wonderful. For six days, we lived on turnips and *nan*. The mujahaddin had not received their winter supplies, and turnips were what they had. We would spend twenty-one days on this trip and eat turnips for the entire three weeks. I lost twenty-two pounds.

The battle was typical of what was happening all over Afghanistan. "Hit them and runaway back, hit them and runaway back," is how Abdul Haq described their tactics. "The next morning, when the helicopters come to look for us, we are gone."

The next morning, as predicted, the sky behind us was a-buzz with helicopters, and I got good pictures. With the mujahaddin and us scattered over a broad area, and under the natural cover of trees, rocks, and small huts camouflaged to blend in with the terrain, the choppers flew by without spotting anybody or anything.

Every day, all day, we could hear bombing in every direction. Jets would streak across the sky while helicopters droned overhead and the mountains reverberated with the echoes of faraway bombs. You could not escape the war anywhere inside Afghanistan.

One day Khana told us we must go to a village that had just been attacked by Soviet helicopters and ground troops. It was about ten miles away, but we must see what had happened.

Arriving in the area near the provincial line between Kabul and Nangarhar provinces, we could smell what happened before it came into view. As we approached, we saw houses blackened on the inside from the explosion of tossed grenades. Then, in an open field, we discovered the cause of the stench. The corpses of over two hundred camels, several cows, and even some family dogs were lying scattered around the field. They had all been shot with machine guns. The few remaining men had been cut down with the animals. The women and children had grabbed a few belongings as the helicopters began firing rockets into the village and had fled to the nearby mountains. Ground soldiers had moved in after them.

The mujahaddin rummaged through the smoldering ruins with machine guns. One, surveying the scene while I was taking pictures, wondered aloud in broken English, "Why, why, why camels they kill?" The answer was obvious. The camels were trucks for the mujahaddin; the Soviets had attacked a mujahaddin convoy in retaliation. The odor of death lingers and permeates your skin and clothing. It stains permanently; it cannot be washed out of your memory.

We stayed in Jalaladdin's camp for two weeks, filming the mujahaddin way of life, the aircraft, and the attack on the tanks. The day we started back, it snowed.

I thought I knew about snow, until that day in Kabul Province when the snow was pushed horizontally by the wind like white bullets. It piled up over a foot in less than three hours, and it was only just beginning. Our pace slowed to a step-by-step crawl. Don and I were each given horses, but more often than not, we found it easier to plod ahead through the blizzard on foot. Walking also helped to keep us warm.

After eight hours, with the snow up to our knees, we reached a *chai khana*. There were over 150 people inside the small, but warm, room of the tea house—women, children, babies, and old people, refugees from what we had dubbed the camel village three days before. Packing everything they could on a few horses, they had begun the trek to Pakistan, stoic and serious. The women were not veiled, and the few men with them had more important, and tragic, matters on their minds. Nobody interfered when I began, politely, to take shots. One of the most poignant scenes in the subsequent ABC stories was of these children, barefoot, walking in the snowy blizzard. Another was of an old woman, struggling through waist-deep snow, clinging to a live chicken wrapped in her arms, her sole piece of property.

The trail had turned slick and slippery from the passing of refugees and pack animals. When we reached the edge of the Jaji valley, we knew we were near Pakistan. It was night, and a *chai khana* was just about a mile ahead, across the river. Don and I were both riding on our horses at this point. The muj, freezing anyway, were crossing the river, which was covered with chunks of ice. Most were only wearing sandals. Midway across the river, my horse stumbled and threw me headfirst through the ice and into the raging river. As I jumped up, my clothes froze instantly. I had to run to avoid freezing to death. Tired and desperate, I ran all the way through the snow to the *chai khana*. Muj were wrapping blankets around me as I stripped and sat next to the fire. You learned to appreciate the basics of life in Afghanistan, such as food, warmth, survival, and your fellow human beings.

It was not over yet. Leaving the *chai khana* two hours later, we started to cross the Jaji around midnight. Throughout, rocket shells exploded around us. A Soviet fort was four miles down the valley. At night, they fired at random, knowing the mujahaddin were crossing the valley. Before daybreak, we descended the last mountain into Teri Mangal. We gorged ourselves on the first meat, the first anything except turnips, in three weeks. In exhausted relief, we knew we had great videotape of a dangerous and treacherous war. We had pictures of a remote country, and of its tragedy largely ignored—the war in Afghanistan.

CHAPTER 14

Half Kipling's India, Half Bogart's Casablanca

Unhappy the land that is in need of heroes.

—BERTOLT BRECHT, 1898–1956

Upon our return to Peshawar in mid-December 1984, we filled in the gaps in our pieces in order to give ABC an adequate, and accurate, story. We visited hospitals treating the war wounded, looked over refugees camps, and took pictures in the makeshift Afghan bazaars that were beginning to spring up on the streets in Peshawar.

One was unusually interesting. Refugees had brought old box cameras from Afghanistan. The cameras, about three feet long and two feet high, had a black hood on the back and a small lens in front, reminiscent of those used in the West in the mid-1800s. The mujahaddin would sit, strained and serious, for the photographs, and then present them to their party offices in the event they were killed. Each party published magazines with photos, or names, of those who had become *shaheed*—martyrs. Afghans poured over these magazines, pointing to this or that cousin or friend who had been killed in combat.

We also interviewed Professor Burhanuddin Majrooh, one of

the few Afghan scholars to stay in Peshawar. Most of the Kabul intelligentsia had been killed immediately following the communist revolution, and those who escaped had sought refuge in Europe or the United States. But Majrooh felt the atrocities of the regime must be documented for history's sake and stayed. He put out a monthly bulletin on mujahaddin operations and politics and collected statements from witnesses and victims of arrest, torture, and execution by the regime. He was determined the Afghan holocaust would not go unrecorded.

Majrooh was not a fundamentalist Muslim. This earned him the disdain of Gulbaddin Hekmatyar and the more radical of the mujahaddin. But other parties fed him information and contributed to his war records. A reliable source of information, he always shared it with foreign visitors and journalists to help them separate fact from fiction.

Majrooh was a regular guest at the receptions given by John Dixon, director of the newly established American Center of USIS (United States Information Service); John assisted Majrooh to obtain USIS grants for his monthly information reports. Whenever a new journalist or aid worker came to Peshawar, John would have a reception and display Majrooh. It was also the only place in town where Majrooh could partake of British liquid imports other than tea. He was an endearing old curmudgeon, who loved his country. And knew it.

Majrooh's greatest concern was that the mujahaddin would win the war before they were ready. He was afraid that, should they ever come to power, the fanatics led by Gulbaddin would be worse than the communists. And this in 1984, when no one thought the Resistance had a prayer. Majrooh was also the first person to warn me privately about the activities of the American CIA. Over and over, he would say he was convinced the CIA did not want a sensible, stable mujahaddin government in Kabul. "Why are they letting the Pakistanis give so much money and weapons to Gulbaddin?" he would ask. "Gulbaddin has no following in Afghanistan that he doesn't purchase. I remember that in his early days at Kabul University he was very close to the Khalqis"—the communist faction.

Majrooh thought that the CIA wanted to keep Afghanistan unstable for several reasons. First, an Islamic regime in Kabul, trying to spread north into the Central Asian republics, might destabilize the Soviet Union. And second, a chaotic Afghanistan would give Pakistan greater control over the north and help it to deal with its archenemy, India, to the south. With fanatics in control of Iran, Pakistan was becoming the linchpin of the region for American security. At the same time, Majrooh believed the KGB and KhAD were using Gulbaddin to disrupt the mujahaddin. Majrooh saw no contradiction in the KGB and the CIA supporting the same person for different reasons. History may prove Majrooh to have been a remarkably accurate political forecaster.

During this time, the Soviets pulled no punches in trying to prevent the Afghan story from receiving major worldwide attention. While Don and I were in Pakistan in the fall of 1984, the Soviet ambassador to Pakistan made a public statement warning all journalists to stay away. Vitaly Smirnov's exact words, "I warn you, and through you all of your journalist colleagues: Stop trying to penetrate Afghanistan with the so-called mujahaddin. From now on, the bandits and the so-called journalists—French, American, British, and others—accompanying them will be killed. And our units in Afghanistan will help the Afghan forces to do it."

The Americans did their bit to discourage U.S. journalists as well, although for reasons not totally political. When Americans did show up, the USIS officers in Islamabad and Peshawar and the U.S. Consul in Peshawar would do whatever they could do to warn them of the dangers—it was a nasty and brutal war. The U.S. officials also warned American journalists that they should have no illusions: the State Department would be unable to help should they be captured by the Afghan or Soviet armies. Over the course of the next eight years, four Western journalists were captured and eight killed in battle.

The Pakistani government seemed to be working at cross-purposes with itself in regards to Western journalists. Its Information Ministry in foreign embassies would encourage journalists to go to Pakistan and cover the Afghan War, but once there, the ISI would frequently go to great lengths to prevent the mujahaddin from taking them inside. Journalists would contact the mujahaddin, only to sit in their hotel rooms for weeks waiting for a response. Many of them would accuse the muj of incompetence, when, in fact, it was ISI pressure that prevented the Afghans from assisting. But since the Afghans resented ISI attempts to control them, those journalists who persisted usually made it into Afghanistan.

But no matter what, the ISI persisted in tapping telephones, telexes, and fax machines. Frequently, while a journalist was reporting to his or her office, the lines would go dead. I once asked President General Zia about this and he replied candidly that they were not trying to censor the story, but to keep track of what was being reported. It would have been cheaper to buy newspapers or watch television.

By the end of 1984, the news being reported in Europe and the United States was fairly consistent. The first major American newspaper stories were put together by William Branigan of the *Washington Post*. He traveled to the Panjsher valley to be with Masood, the commander of the region, in late 1983 and wrote a three-part series on his experience. He spoke of the intense destruction by Soviet bombing and marveled that the mujahaddin, given the odds, could continue to function; and he wrote about Afghan ingenuity in the face of adversity, describing a *chai khana* he had visited, built inside the hull of a downed MI-8 helicopter.

Four British journalists did considerable reporting during the early days of the war as well: Peter Jouvenal, a freelancer, who also sold videotapes to European and American outlets; John Gunston, a freelance still-photographer and former member of the British army; Arnaud Van Linden, a writer for the *London Observer* who later joined the British SkyChannel TV; and John Fullerton, described previously, who left in 1983 to work in Hong Kong. Many of the most daring and startling pictures of the war were taken by Gunston.

Jouvenal and Gunston were aficionados of war in general; they both wrote articles for *Soldier of Fortune* under pseudonyms.

The author discusses the war in Afghanistan with President Ronald Reagan, Washington, D.C., 1984.

The author, left, Dana Rohrabacher, center, and CIA Director William Casey, right, discuss problems encountered by the Afghan mujahaddin, Washington, D.C., 1985.

(LEFT:) Commander Abdul Haq and author on horseback near Jalrez, a suburb of Kabul, Afghanistan.

(BELOW:) MAHAZ Commander Major General Rahim Wardak and author prior to mujahaddin attack on Soviet post in Kunar Province.

(BELOW:) A group of tired mujahaddin return to their mountain camp following battle near Jalalabad.

Author, left, with Haji Din Mohammad, directing attack on regime outpost in Nangahar Province with walkie-talkie.

Commander Abdul Haq and author, first and second from right, take tea break with other commanders of Khalis's party, in mountains around Kabul.

(RIGHT:) Mujahaddin communications improved with CIA-supplied scrambler radios in late 1987.

Heavy artillery captured by the mujahaddin from the Soviets was frequently repaired and used in battles against their original owners.

The Afghan national sport, buzkashi, is a rough and tumble combination of polo and football, using a calf carcass. The sport has honed their fighting skills for centuries.

Mujahaddin Commanders Qari Baba, left, and Jalaluddin Haqani, right, discuss formation of Commander's Council with media in Peshawar, 1989.

Commanders (from left to right) Haqani, Sayed Jaglan, Mussa, Amin Wardak, Anwari, and Achtar Mammad at formation of Commander's Council.

The first Commander's Council nationwide meeting in Badakshan Province, Afghanistan, hosted by Jalaluddin Haqani and Abdul Haq, center.

Abdul Haq and Jalaluddin Haqani discuss strategy at first nationwide meeting of Commander's Council. Primary objective was to bring Ahmed Shah Masood into full participation.

The author with muj infantry soldier following battle in snow-covered Paghman, 1988. Hats and belts were war booty captured from Soviets.

(TOP:) Author inspecting his van which was destroyed by bomb at funeral of Khan Abdul "Gaffar" Khan, in Jalalabad, Afghanistan, January 1989.

(RIGHT:) Author pleasantly shocked to discover twisted van would still function after being bombed at funeral in Jalalabad.

(BELOW:) Mujahaddin supply depot in Teri Mangal, Pakistan, destroyed by Soviet bombing raid across the border.

Author enters Afghanistan on mule with mujahaddin supply convoy.

(LEFT:) Author as guest of villager in Logar Province being warmed by indoor wood fire.

(BELOW:) Haji Din Mohammad addresses mujahaddin who have just successfully captured Barikot, first garrison town to be liberated from Soviet control.

Author with jubilant Khandahar mujahaddin who have captured major Soviet garrison in Zabol, Afghanistan.

One of many thousands of mujahaddin battlesite graves which are scattered across the country.

A thirteen-year-old boy, already experienced in war, is part of the generation that holds hope for the future of Afghanistan.

Jouvenal started his own news service, offering material for print and television outlets worldwide. He was the only Western reporter to spend as much, or more, time as I with the mujahaddin inside Afghanistan. We were always civil to each other, but underneath ran an intense competition.

Jouvenal once accused me, through a muckraking reporter, of "having the ISI follow [him] around Peshawar." Since I had no such influence—nor intent, for that matter—I called the ranking ISI official in Peshawar and asked what was going on. He told me that Peter had brought parts of a downed helicopter out of Afghanistan and sold them to Americans. Inasmuch as he was doing this in Pakistan, the officials wanted to know more and, yes, they had been following him. He scoffed at the idea that I had had something to do with it.

A number of people came to Peshawar disguised as journalists. Some were Third World groupies, who had no connection whatsoever with any of the media. Others were trying to establish reputations as freelancers. And still others were seeking fame and fortune however possible.

One such quasi-journalist was Jeff Harmon from New York, Los Angeles, and London, or so he said. In fairness to Jeff, he described himself as a "film maker," not a journalist; he was accompanied by Alex Lindsay, his cameraman. Jeff was quite secretive about his actions, which was not strange in itself; no sensible journalist would discuss exactly what he was doing or where he was going for security reasons. It was assumed that KGB and KhAD agents in Peshawar were tracking Western journalists.

Jeff and Alex made a couple of trips inside with the NIFA group. Upon their return they wrote and performed side-splitting songs about life with the mujahaddin. But they were also intelligent men determined to film a documentary on the mujahaddin.

After each trip, Jeff would sell film shots to American and British television. Alex's filming was first-rate; he took pictures of jet air attacks and mujahaddin ground operations that rank as some of the best ever.

In due course, Jeff's documentary was released in the United States through PBS and in England through BBC television. And it was one of the most inaccurate, twisted, and outright false pieces of antimujahaddin, anti-Muslim propaganda ever. Among other distortions, Jeff's film showed a man, wrapped in chains, being beaten by the muj. He claimed the man was a prisoner from the Afghan army. NIFA officials, at a news conference after the documentary was released, produced the man and introduced him as one of their own. Jeff, the man testified, had bought the chain and they had hammed it up, false beating and all. He was not, and had never been, in the army or a prisoner of the muj.

The documentary also portrayed the muj as extensive users of hashish. While many Afghans do use hashish, a custom among many cultures, NIFA officials said that, in these instances, the men were smoking *naswaar*, a tobacco product, and that the so-called hashish pipes were, in fact, *hookahs*.

Finally, Jeff had depicted a revered tribal leader as a fanatic cleric who beheaded prisoners of war. This could be discredited off-hand by observing that beheading is not condoned by Afghan Muslims.

Jeff never returned to Peshawar. In the opinion of most Peshawarites who saw the documentary, Alex Lindsay's superb photography had been sadly abused in this travesty of a documentary.

A new diversion was instituted in Peshawar in 1984. At that time, the largest ex-pat community was the Swiss, who worked at the ICRC hospital. Black market alcohol was difficult to obtain. Other than at the occasional Dixon receptions, the only drink available was an awful concoction known as Muree beer. You could, if you were a non-Muslim foreigner, purchase this brew for consumption in your hotel room. The Swiss, however, found a remedy; they held a weekly party in the backyard of the ICRC director's house which they called the "Bamboo Bar."

Each Tuesday, they would obtain a few bottles of scotch, gin, and vodka, which they would sell for a nominal price to Western guests. Tuesday nights soon became the center of Western social activity. The "Bamboo Bar" was crowded with aid and medical workers, journalists, spies, and war groupies. Journalists returning from "inside" had a ready-made audience for their war stories. They discussed, and frequently argued vociferously, on the ability, or lack thereof, of one group of muj versus another. Aid workers exchanged the latest information on their programs, grants of money, and Afghan politics, while old hands, anyone who had been in Peshawar for over a month, would strut and expound to newcomers, most of whom were enthralled or terrified by the tales of war—often tall indeed. It was fun, as well as being a useful gathering for the exchange of information.

The Pakistani authorities turned a blind eye to the illegal public consumption of alcohol at the "Bamboo Bar." They far preferred knowing where all the Westerners were, even if imbibing, than to have them wandering about. The weekly event lasted until 1988, when a young woman was stabbed with a heroin-filled hypodermic needle by a drunken German. When she died, the "Bamboo Bar" was closed. It was the "Bamboo Bar" that inspired my flippant description of Peshawar—"Half Kipling's India and half Bogart's Casablanca."

Of the many competent, professional journalists who came to Peshawar to do stories on the Afghan War, I was fortunate to be able to travel inside with several of them, among them Don Kladstrup.

In mid-December of 1984, Don wanted to complete a piece he had been working on by interviewing Abdul Haq. We were planning a series of stories for ABC to coincide with the anniversary of the Soviet invasion—Christmas week—and Abdul was no longer a story; he was an on-going legend. He was essential to our project.

Before talking with Abdul Haq, we spoke with several men under his command to get their "feel" of the man who led them. Without exception they spoke with pride, both of their commander and of their operations. The Kabul Front, which had been started by Abdul with a crew of four men, had blossomed into a major threat to the puppet Afghan regime. Their many exploits attested to the claim.

When Kabul radio and television targeted Abdul Haq and the Kabul Front mujahaddin for attack, Abdul Haq reacted in kind. He even aimed at the Soviet army. With the assistance of Savik Shuster, a Lithuanian refugee, fake copies of the Soviet army newspaper *Red Star* and false Red Army posters were printed. The newspapers were distributed among troops in the garrisons in and around Kabul, and the posters pasted on walls throughout the city. Both encouraged defection and defiance of orders. That, and similar misinformation campaigns, inflamed the ill-feeling between the Khalq and Parcham factions of the Kabul communists, who continually blamed each other for any mishap.

The Kabul Front had grown to include tactical fighting units that completely surrounded the city. One of their ongoing operations was cutting off electric power to the city. In late December of the previous year, Abdul Haq had put out word that power to the city would be cut to commemorate the fourth anniversary of the Soviet invasion. The threat was taken so seriously that Babrak Karmal was forced to state publicly that the mujahaddin were not capable of disrupting the city's electricity and promised that the city would not be plunged into darkness. Karmal then, quietly offered a bribe, 27 million Afghanis, to Abdul Haq if he would please leave the electricity alone. Abdul Haq refused.

On a dark December night, Abdul Haq and his men hit the power station at Mahipar and knocked out the pylons that brought electricity to the city from the Sarobi and Nagalu hydroelectric power stations. Only the diesel station at Hud Khel, the largest which was inside the city, remained intact. The government hastened to fortify the station.

On the night of December 25, Abdul Haq led a small group of eight men into the city, their target—the Hud Khel power station. After slipping into the city with heavy weapons, they arrived at a safe house, the home of a brigadier in the regime's army, a longtime covert supporter of the mujahaddin. Well concealed in the man's house, they avoided discovery when a government team searched the neighborhood.

On the second night, the group left the house to conduct their operation. Crossing the river that ran through the city, the men held their weapons and ammunition high to keep them dry, and nearly froze in the icy water. Wet and cold, the men moved through the city streets to the diesel station, where they set up recoilless rifles, RPGs, and automatic rifles. One muj, sent ahead to survey the area, reported that there were tanks and nearly four hundred men at the power station. The attack, he said, would not be possible. Abdul Haq's reply was characteristic: they had promised the people they would turn off the lights of Kabul; therefore, they would turn off the lights of Kabul—even if they were killed in the doing. About 8:00 P.M., they attacked. Just as their ammunition ran out, the station caught fire and a series of explosions rocked the neighborhood. The soldiers fired back with heavy weapons as the eight muj began to retreat.

Soaking wet and freezing, the men walked through the darkened streets of Kabul. Two of the wounded men had to be carried. Suddenly a voice shouted, "Who are you?" Abdul Haq looked around and saw three hundred guns pointed at his men from the roofs of the buildings on either side, silhouetted by the fiery orange glow that burned through the night from the blazing electric facility. He and his men had no ammunition. The only possible way out was bluff and bravado. He shouted back, "We are mujahaddin. If one gun is fired, we will destroy you, like that power station behind us." He then yelled to his men that at the first suggestion of a shot, they were to obliterate them with rockets. The soldiers froze, terrified, as Abdul Haq and his men walked down the street and escaped into the darkness.

News of the raid spread to every resident of Kabul within days. The legend of Abdul Haq had earned another chapter.

The Kabul Front continued to keep the regime busy repairing power facilities. Besides destroying pylons and transformers, they attacked the power generation facilities at the huge Sarobi dam. A group of men, led by Abdul's subcommander for the Sarobi area, Agha Jan, infiltrated the dam area by climbing straight down the steep cliffs and retaining sections of the dam. For several nights they slithered up and down the dangerous cliffs and past well-guarded posts to clear the minefields that covered the area.

Carrying only explosives and timers, with no food or other supplies, the men hid during the day and moved at night. After another difficult and dangerous climb to the gates of the dam, they planted their explosives. With a roar, the blast blew apart a major section of the dam, knocking it out of commission. The mujahaddin version of the *Guns of Navarone* cost the Soviet millions in partial repairs and in inestimable loss of prestige.

The ABC interview with Abdul Haq took place in the planning room of his Peshawar headquarters. Maps of the city of Kabul lined the walls, and a large sand table showed where he planned his attacks and defenses of the areas he controlled around the city.

Don spoke with him for nearly an hour. After reviewing the history of the Resistance, Don asked, "What do you need? What help do you want from the United States?"

Abdul Haq, aware he was talking directly to an American audience, looked at the camera and said, "I am not going to ask for anything. This is my fight, my struggle. This is my problem. It is my country under attack. I am fighting to free *my* country; I am not fighting for someone else, or for their reasons. If they really want to help, then stop helping my enemy. Stop helping the Soviets: stop buying gas from them; stop giving them computers, which they use in their war against us; stop giving them food, which they send to their army in Afghanistan. If you were not helping them, they could not occupy Russia, much less Afghanistan."

Don's final question was, "Most people say you cannot possibly win. Do you think you can win?"

"We will win—or we will die. There are no other choices." The twinkle in Abdul's eye as much as said that he had no intention of dying—a message this time for the rulers in Kabul.

A few days before Christmas, Don and I arrived in New York, where we were slated to do several stories during Christmas week and to do a probable shot on "Nightline."

The producers and editors at ABC's "World News Tonight" were effusive about the "beautiful pictures" from Afghanistan, with special congratulations from Bob Murphy. I trusted Joe DeCola and Jerry Lamprecht were listening.

Most network news stories were running two minutes or less, but we ran our stories for four minutes on three nights running—major coverage for a network evening news show. Don went home to Paris, justifiably proud of a job well done. I began making plans to return for a visit with my soul.

CHAPTER 15

Lord Save Us from Our Friends

A man-of-war is the best ambassador.

—OLIVER CROMWELL, 1599–1658

By the end of 1984, world opinion had swung strongly in support of the Resistance movement of the Afghan people. A resolution demanding Soviet withdrawal from Afghanistan passed the UN General Assembly four times by an overwhelming vote. Thus it became increasingly important for the mujahaddin to show that they were a political as well as a military force.

Envoys from several countries had repeatedly invited Abdul Haq to visit their capitals and talk with their leaders. In January 1985, with the Kabul Front in good shape and heavy snow hampering military operations on both sides, he decided to accept the most imperative invitations.

Abdul Haq's first stop was London, where he met with officials of the Foreign Office. Afterward, he repaired to Number 10 Downing Street at the invitation of British Prime Minister Margaret Thatcher, who greeted him personally. From that time forward, Thatcher became an ardent spokeswoman on behalf of the mujahaddin. Over a year later, British news accounts credited that meeting as the deciding factor when the British government supplied Blowpipe anti-aircraft missiles to the mujahaddin.

The meeting could also be credited with having spurred increasing contacts between British intelligence and the Kabul
Front mujahaddin. But this had its downside—the American
intelligence community became immediately skeptical of anyone that was well liked by their British "cousins." Political
niceties aside, the CIA and SIS were not mutual admiration
societies. This was especially true during the Afghan War. As they
had during World War II, the British considered the Asian subcontinent their domain. The Americans, for their part, thought
the Brits were "meddling in our operation," as one high-ranking
spook (self-description of most agents) assigned to the U.S. Embassy in Islamabad told me.

Abdul Haq's next stop was Paris, where the French fawned all
over him. He was a guest of honor at the French Senate, after
which its president held a joint news conference with him in a
room packed with reporters eager to hear the Afghan story.

During Abdul's visit, the mayor of Antony, a suburb of Paris,
declared his city a "Sister City of Paghman," the suburb of Kabul
where Abdul had established his base of operation. During the
elaborate traditional ceremony, he presented Abdul Haq with an
ornate certificate, in both French and Farsi, proclaiming the bond
between the two cities. The framed certificate was hung proudly
on the wall of Abdul's Peshawar office until it could be properly
placed in Paghman.

The French, always looking for opportunities to expand their
arms market, were somewhat dismayed that the mujahaddin
were using only Soviet weaponry or clones thereof. The French
nevertheless committed themselves to assisting in whatever way
possible—a commitment they honored over the years.

From Paris, Abdul Haq flew to Washington, D.C., where he
stayed at my apartment, hoping to steal a few days rest. But
peace and quiet were not to be. Once the Afghan expatriate
community discovered he was in the States, he was deluged with
invitations to speak and to be hailed by his avid supporters. But
official Washington also had its eye on him.

When I drove Abdul to his various appointments and meetings, I was always introduced as "a journalist covering the war in

Afghanistan." Yet government officials never hesitated to discuss questions, however sensitive, with one of the leading Afghan commanders in my presence, occasionally in my home.

Cliff Moore, a bright young navy lieutenant from the DIA (Defense Intelligence Agency), was one of the few who asked questions of Abdul Haq in order to learn about Afghan politics and military strategies rather than to pontificate about the situation himself. Moore also thought to bring other DIA officers from all service branches to ask Abdul Haq about the tactics and weaponry of the Afghan puppet regime and the Soviets.

On one occasion, Moore inquired if Najib's recent promotion to major general and his elevation to ministerial rank as head of the Afghan secret police amounted to a significant power boost. Abdul replied that, according to his network in the city, "if Najib is not the real power in Kabul, he soon will be." This intrigued Moore. While it concurred with his own reading, he had found no support for the theory in any other agency of the U.S. government. Within months, Babrak Karmal was exiled to the Soviet Union and replaced by Najib with complete control.

Abdul Haq was his own best intelligence officer. He listened more than he spoke. When Elie Krakowski, an aide to Assistant Secretary of Defense Richard Perle, outlined the arguments on Afghan policy going on among the State Department, the Defense Department, and the CIA, he paid close attention. Perle, who breezed in and out of his office, made it clear that he had no time to meet with Abdul. But Perle's boss, Undersecretary Fred Ikle, the number two man at the Pentagon, had plenty of time. Ikle cut right through to the core issues and discussed the clandestine support given to the mujahaddin: Was it getting through? Was it enough? Was it any good? What did he need?

Later, Abdul met with the top brass of the army's Staff Intelligence Office, headed by Lt. General William Odom, who would shortly be promoted to director of the National Security Agency. These people wanted Abdul Haq to inform them in two main areas: the strategy and tactics he used against the Soviet army; and everything he knew about Soviet military operations that their satellites could not tell them.

The military experts at the Pentagon were unquestionably impressed by Abdul Haq. General Odom and his chief of staff told me that Abdul had a natural instinct for military matters and that his analytical ability was unsurpassed. Unlike their civilian counterparts, they agreed with Abdul Haq's assessment of the Soviet military machine—"They're not so great; there's just a lot of them." The military in the Pentagon were grateful for the first-hand information—and a bit envious of this commander who led battles almost daily against the Red Army.

In the meantime, Krakowski had arranged a meeting between Abdul and a man named Yossef Bodansky, a visiting scholar with John Hopkins University and a consultant to Richard Perle. The meeting amounted to a pitch by Bodansky to sell Israeli weapons to the mujahaddin. (Bodansky, the alleged authority on the Soviet military, asked no questions of the expert on the subject.) Abdul Haq said he was not aware of any religious preference of weapons, but he had no money for such purchases. "That can be arranged," Bodansky assured him. Despite several attempts by Bodansky to meet again, Abdul successfully avoided him. It was a curious episode.

After meeting at the State Department with Richard Murphy, Robert Peck, and Charles Dunbar, Abdul Haq was left wondering why the State Department was so interested in protecting the Soviets. Why, for example, were they placing their hopes on the UN negotiations on Afghanistan that were taking place in Geneva. Diplomats did not want clear-cut solutions to problems, he observed. "That would leave them with no job."

The Geneva negotiations, in any case, were ludicrous. They were ostensibly between the Afghan regime and Pakistan. The mujahaddin were not represented. Nor were the Soviets or the Americans. Yet the Afghan delegation was staying at the Soviet Embassy in Geneva, and the Pakistani delegation conferred regularly with U.S. officials. This charade went on for over three-and-a-half years.

In his varous meetings in Washington, Abdul Haq always asked why the U.S. directed the vast majority of its support to Gulbaddin Hekmatyar, given Gulbaddin's virulent anti-Americanism.

The answers boiled down to the statement that Gulbaddin had the most effective fighting force. Blank stares greeted Abdul's recital of facts: Gulbaddin had no significant fighting force inside Afghanistan; Gulbaddin had never taken part in a major confrontation with either the Soviet or regime forces; Gulbaddin had not a single commander of any renown in his outfit. But these people knew what they knew, which meant what they read and what they were told in their intelligence briefings. True, a first-hand witness of the caliber of Abdul Haq could shake them—but only temporarily. Highly classified readings and briefings always won out. After all, Abdul Haq, commander of the Kabul Front, had not been cleared for TOP SECRET—EYES ONLY.

One day, I received a phone call from the White House. Walter Raymond of the National Security Council wanted to meet with Abdul Haq the next morning. As we walked through the gates and were ushered into the Executive Office Building adjacent to the White House, I was visibly impressed. The commander of Kabul was not. "Who is this man?" he asked.

Raymond had been with the CIA for over twenty years. One of his tasks at the NSC was to keep track of events in Afghanistan. To this meeting he brought two people, Zalmay Khalilzad, an Afghan-American, and a young woman, a Pakistani-American. They grilled Abdul on the military and political situation in Afghanistan for an hour, during which, according to Khalilzad, Abdul provided them with more useful information than the total of all their previous readings and briefings. Raymond asked us to come back the next day to meet with someone of even higher rank.

The following morning, we were told to report to the Southwest Gate of the White House itself. We were cleared by security to enter the West Wing and as we walked across the front lawn of the White House, Abdul noted, "It's not very big. The palaces in Kabul are bigger."

The walls of the West Wing were decorated with large photographs of the president—scenes of him hard on the campaign trail, meeting with various world leaders, and leaving the hospital after the attempted assassination. The requisite bowl of jelly beans sat on a small colonial-style table. The atmosphere was quiet, but somewhat tense.

Walt Raymond greeted us at the door and escorted us to the office of Robert McFarlane, the president's National Security Advisor. McFarlane rose from his desk and walked us over to a corner sitting area where we were served coffee.

"Bud" McFarlane wasted no time in asking specific questions about the military and political situation in and around the city of Kabul. But I kept wondering how come I, a journalist, was allowed to sit in on the meeting.

The conversation came around to Gulbaddin; McFarlane was the only Washington official we had come across who questioned Pakistani and CIA support of him. Abdul Haq then asked, point-blank, if he, McFarlane (i.e., the president) believed the mujahaddin could win the war. "Do you?" McFarlane shot back.

"I'm not stupid," Abdul replied. "I'm not risking my life and, more important, the lives of my mujahaddin for nothing. Yes, we can win, but you must push the Soviets politically."

"We do, at every level of contact we have with them."

"You can't just talk to them," Abdul Haq insisted. "You must push them."

McFarlane asked who in the regime was the most troublesome to the Resistance. Abdul named a number of people, from Najib on down.

"What are you doing about them?"

"We attack whenever and however we can," Abdul said. "What should we do—shoot them on the streets?"

"You mean, urban terrorism?"

"Terrorism is what the Soviets are doing to me, to my country. If I start shooting these people in Kabul, which I can, they will shoot our leaders in Peshawar. Is that what you want me to do?"

The following scene has run through my mind a thousand times. McFarlane looked at Abdul Haq intently, and nodding his head up and down, said, "You have to do what you can do."

I will never know whether this amounted to a White House wink-and-nod. To my knowledge, it was never acted upon.

Gulbaddin, on the other hand, ordered the execution of several mujahaddin commanders, some on the streets of Peshawar.

As we left, McFarlane asked if there was anything he could do for Abdul during the remainder of his stay in Washington. I told him I was taking Abdul to a dinner that night to hear President Reagan speak, but thank you, no, everything was fine.

That night, in front of two thousand people and a battery of television cameras, Ronald Reagan paused in the middle of his speech to the Conservative Political Action Committee, and said, "We are honored to have with us tonight one of the brave commanders who leads the Afghan Freedom Fighters—Abdul Haq." Following a standing ovation for Abdul, the president said, "Abdul Haq—we are with you."

Two months later outside of Kabul, I interviewed Abdul Haq on camera. He was in the midst of a major assault on Soviet positions, being bombarded mercilessly by jet and helicopter aircraft, helpless to protect himself or to retaliate.

"President Reagan said he was with you," I reminded him.

"Yes, but where is he now?" Abdul roared back, as Sukoi 25 jet bombers screeched overhead. The entire sequence, from Reagan to Kabul, was used in a subsequent CBS Evening News story.

Before leaving Washington, Abdul Haq was asked by the Saudi ambassador to Washington, Prince Bandar ibn Sultan, to meet with him at his embassy.

The Saudi Embassy is a renovated bank building half a block down from the Kennedy Center for the Performing Arts. Walking into the embassy is like walking into Saudi Arabia, plush carpets, polished marble floors, Bedouin art and all. I have always marveled at the way Saudis walk. They seem to glide, as if on silent roller skates. That day, the embassy had several employees gliding up and down the hallways.

Prince Bandar's regal bearing combined assurance, authority, and ease. He was a gracious man with sparkling black eyes that absorbed everything. He greeted Abdul Haq as a brother. As we were ushered into his opulent private office, he offered Arabic cardamom coffee, and then politely, but pointedly, did what no one else had done—he had me escorted out of the office while he conversed with Abdul Haq about the Islamic *Jihad* of Afghanistan.

Afterwards, Abdul told me that he had been surprised to learn the Prince, and the entire royal family were not members of the strict Wahabi sect of Islam. He said he had complained to the Prince that Saudi Wahabis were coming to join the Afghan *Jihad* and were proselytizing Wahabism. The Prince had responded that their actions were beyond the control of the King and the government. Abdul said without further elaboration of other topics discussed that the meeting had gone well.

That afternoon, I answered a knock on my front door. A tall dark man in an immaculate suit handed me an envelope and requested that it be given to Abdul Haq. Abdul later called the prince and thanked him. The envelope held a stack, several inches high, of $100 bills. Abdul said he would give it to his party.

As he left the United States, Abdul told me to come to Pakistan as soon as I could. He was planning to continue his operations in the city of Kabul. This time he would send me to the city. I would be the first television reporter to go there since the war began.

CHAPTER 16

Spies, Lies, and Videotapes

Treason doth never prosper: what's the reason? For if it prosper, none dare call it treason.

—SIR JOHN HARRINGTON, 1561–1612

In January 1985, at a party given by a friend in his home on Capitol Hill, a man approached me and said, "Kurt, I'm so glad you're OK. We worried because we learned the Soviets knew of your whereabouts in Afghanistan." I turned and saw a balding man with horn-rimmed glasses and a mustache. He was standing with a short, reddish-blonde woman. I had never seen either of them before.

Reaching into his coat pocket, the man withdrew a small leather case, flashed an identity card, and said, "I'm Jay Pollard, with the Naval Intelligence Service." He introduced me to his girlfriend, Anne Henderson. I was intrigued that an intelligence service was interested in my travels. After blurting out his tidbit of information, he became secretive. "We can't talk here with all these people, but let's get together soon." We made plans to have dinner the following day.

It never occurred to me that this meeting was probably not accidental. Over the next year it was disclosed that Jay Pollard was a double agent, working on the side for the state of Israel. He would join that growing list of Americans in the 1980s that were convicted of espionage and put in jail for life.

Over dinner, Jay was bubbling at the opportunity to discuss Afghanistan with someone who had been there. Unlike the other intelligence officers I had met who probed for news, Jay burst out with his own information—on Soviet troop deployment and from ELINT (electronic intelligence) sources. He and Anne Henderson appeared to be genuinely interested in the plight of the Afghans. Occasionally, Jay would stop himself, look around the room, and then whisper, very cloak-and-daggerish. But a few minutes later, he would once again be pouring out information from classified sources on Afghanistan. Since he claimed he had documents pertaining to my personal safety, we set a date for another dinner in a couple of days.

We drove to a restaurant. As I was parking my car, Jay reached into his pocket and handed me a sheaf of papers. Each was marked with stamps indicating they were classified. Glancing through them, I saw they were sitreps (situation reports) on military activity in Afghanistan. The documents gave dates and locations of regime and Soviet military movements, and of ongoing sweep operations. Other papers referred to life in the city of Kabul—reports from the bazaars, political gossip, whatever. They were quite similar to the sitreps issued by the American press officers in New Delhi, Islamabad, and Peshawar each week. There was no question that I was interested, and for the exact reason Jay had suggested—my safety when I was inside Afghanistan.

Our relationship grew into a friendship of sorts as we met for dinner or cocktails. Jay purported to be an ardent supporter of the Reagan administration, and Anne Henderson worked for the National Rifle Association. They both frequented events sponsored by conservative organizations in Washington, and we would occasionally go together to receptions and other such events.

In the spring of 1985, Anne and Jay told me privately that they were going to be married. Jay said he had an uncle who had offered to pay for a lavish wedding at the Ritz Hotel and a honeymoon in Europe. Anne Henderson began sporting a beautiful, and obviously expensive, diamond and sapphire ring.

One night I received a telephone call from Jay. He told me he and Anne were in Paris and that they were going to be married the next day—so much for the wedding at the Ritz. Since I was preparing to leave for Afghanistan, could I stop in Paris on the way? Two nights later, I was in London and called Jay's room at the Hilton Hotel in Paris. A man answered the phone. When I asked for Jay, he countered: Who was I? Where was I? What did I want? When I asked who he was, he said that Jay had left Paris, he didn't know where he'd gone, and hung up. Months later, when I queried Jay about the man, Jay said it had been his uncle. According to Wolf Blitzer's book, *Territory of Lies*, written two years later, the man must have been Israeli intelligence officer Raphael "Rafi" Eitan, the top controller of the Pollard case. Eitan, the former deputy chief of operations for the Mossad who was involved in the Adolph Eichmann affair, now headed a small, highly covert, intelligence section of the Israeli Defense Ministry called "Lakam." Passed over for promotion as head of the Mossad, he was described as having a "score to settle with Mossad."

At the time, I had contracted with Sam Roberts, the new foreign editor for CBS News, to cover the Afghan War, and I told him that a man in Washington was providing me with classified information on Afghanistan that would help in my travels across occupied Afghanistan. Roberts cautioned me: in a situation such as Peshawar and in a war such as Afghanistan's, many people would jump at the chance to implicate me as an intelligence agent. He reminded me that good reporters frequently learned more about such intricate situations than intelligence officers. This could cause problems. His final warning was not to fall for the bait.

On my return to Washington in the late summer of 1985, I realized I had not heard from Jay Pollard and Anne Henderson for some time, so I called Jay at his home and asked what he'd been up to. Jay said nervously that he would get back to me and hung up. About twenty minutes later, there was a knock at my back door. The only way to that door was from the alley, enclosed behind a high wall. It was Jay. He said he didn't want to be seen on the street, and that Anne, now Anne Pollard, would show up later. He then produced a bunch of highly classified documents and asked if I thought Pakistan would want to buy them. I laughed—I couldn't believe he was serious—and said the Pakistanis provided me with information, not the other way around. In retrospect, alarm bells ought to have gone off loud and clear. Jay left that evening the same way he had arrived— over the wall and down the alley—without further explanation.

A few days later, Jay called and asked me to meet him at a café on Connecticut Avenue. Upon my arrival, Jay told me he had interesting information on the Soviet army in Afghanistan. We left in his car and drove to the Naval Intelligence Service complex in Southwest Washington. He showed his identity card to the security guard and took the elevator while I waited in the lobby. Ten minutes later he signed out and we went to his car in the parking lot. As he started up, he reached into an inside pocket of his overcoat and handed me a hefty packet of papers. They were all marked TOP SECRET and were purported to be Soviet military plans for the Asian subcontinent. It was like reading a spy novel, except that these were official U.S. government documents. As we drove, Jay laughed about how easily he had sneaked the material past the lax security at NIS headquarters. And would the Pakistanis be interested in buying the material? That night I read the documents in detail. They were mind-boggling. I gave the papers back to Jay the next day—they were too hot to handle. Jay's only comment was to say I was missing an opportunity to make a lot of money.

Jay was constantly scheming to make money. He would come up with one idea after the other for brokering arms deals. One day, he told me the Argentines were manufacturing an antitank missile called "Cobra," similar to the one the Taiwanese were making, and thought we should find a way to sell it to the mujahaddin. At his request, I accompanied him on a visit to the office of the Argentine defense attaché on Connecticut Avenue. Here we met with a colonel, who affirmed that his people would like very much to sell the weapon to the mujahaddin. Jay said he would find a third party to pay for them.

We then went to an office of a South African Embassy commercial attaché section near 19th and M streets. The man in charge knew Jay on a first name basis. Jay explained the Argentine antitank missile and asked how funding could be obtained. The man asked Jay if his employers knew what he was doing, and Jay assured him, "All the way up to Gates." The officer then told Jay he would get back to him. I was never informed of any follow-up. When I asked Jay who "Gates" was, Jay said, "He's the guy at the CIA in charge of this type of stuff."

On November 19, 1985, I returned to Washington from another trip inside Afghanistan. I had been in my apartment barely five minutes when the doorbell rang. Two FBI agents wanted to speak with me. When I let them in, they asked if I knew Jonathan Pollard. I said yes. I assumed he was the subject of a background check for a promotion he was expecting at the NIS. I was dead wrong. Jay, just moments before, had been arrested at the Israeli Embassy and would be charged with espionage. They said they would want to speak with me again, and asked, "What are you going to do?" meaning, "What are your travel plans?" I told them I was going to call CBS and report the arrest. The agents, somewhat taken aback, left.

I called Rita Braver, the CBS Justice Department correspondent, and told her the whole story. For the next several days, I would work with her and producer Charles Wolfson on the Pollard spy story, which by now was a lead story throughout the country.

My second FBI interview took place in the office of my attorney, Robert Barnett. The FBI told us that Jay had confessed to selling classified documents, and had implicated me by stating that I was part of his spying operation and had bought classified documents from him. The case was going to the grand jury and they wanted to subpoena me to testify. They implied that I would also be investigated. As the case progressed, the naval interrogators became convinced that Jay was using me as a red herring to throw them off the trail of the Israeli agent who had, in fact, bought the secrets. In his book, Wolf Blitzer, then of the *Jerusalem Post* and later with CNN, stated: Jay "then admitted that the person to whom he had been selling the documents for more than a year was not Kurt Lohbeck, the American friend he had earlier named. He acknowledged that he had falsely identified Lohbeck so as to throw the agents off the real trail."

As the facts emerged, we discovered that the highly classified documents Jay was charged with selling to Israeli Intelligence agents related to the Mideast, Iraq, Syria, and Israel, not the lowly sitreps he had shown me. After he pleaded guilty at his sentencing hearing, Jay's attorneys filed a document alleging that I was working for a very highly placed person at the White House; i.e., Robert McFarlane. McFarlane, who was subsequently hit by the Iran-Contra affair, was getting a foretaste of disinformation and misinformation.

Following his guilty plea to espionage, Jay was sentenced to life in prison. Most news reports attributed the harsh sentence to a still classified memo sent by Defense Secretary Caspar Weinberger to the federal district judge, stating that the information Pollard had sold to the Israelis made this the most damaging of any peacetime espionage case. An acquaintance who worked for an intelligence agency showed me what was purportedly the Weinberger letter. The documents, even those marked TOP SECRET, which Jay had given me, paled in comparison to these secrets.

Several years later, Joseph DeGenova, the U.S. attorney who prosecuted both the Pollards, said the investigation conducted by the FBI for his office completely exonerated me of any wrongdoing. FBI and NIS investigators discovered that Pollard's "confession" was preplanned to allow the Israelis, who had no diplomatic immunity, to escape the country. The plan worked; they got away.

During the sensational media coverage of the Pollard affair, Jay and Anne claimed they were dedicated Zionists, whose only sin had been their attempt to defend Israel. Yet in all my dealings with Jay, I cannot recall his ever mentioning Israel or Zionism. I was not even aware that Anne Henderson Pollard was Jewish until her arrest. Jay's reasons for selling government secrets to Israel, in my somewhat informed opinion, was not a deep personal commitment to Israel, but a personal commitment to his wife and to his pocketbook.

Jay wanted to wine, dine, and travel first class and to bedeck Anne with jewelry. He never concealed that he was an intelligence analyst. In fact, he boasted about it, proudly displaying a courier card that allowed him to avoid customs and immigration checks at ports of entry, calling it his "get out of jail free card."

I had already learned how loose were the lips, from the top down, of official Washington. Jay's problems began when a professional, who happened to be an Israeli, offered money to keep them flapping.

When Jay lied about me to the FBI, I was, of course, upset. What he did was a crime, and crimes deserve punishment, but it has always bothered me to think of Jay Pollard locked in the cages of the federal penitentiary for the remainder of his life.

As the Pollard story was unfolding, but before the arrest, I left for Afghanistan to take Abdul Haq up on his offer to include me in his next operation against Kabul and document it for CBS News.

On my arrival in Peshawar in May 1985, I found that several European journalists were preparing to cover the mujahaddin spring offensive. John Gunston had already gone inside, and Arnaud van Linden was preparing to go. Abdul Haq asked if it was OK for a Norwegian journalist to accompany me. I said of course. It would be good to have company and Norway had no publications competing with CBS.

I was introduced to the Norwegian, a tall blonde named Paul. We left Peshawar with one of Abdul Haq's lieutenants, Zabet Walid, and a large group, over twenty-five, mujahaddin. Abdul Haq was taking another route to the Kabul area and would meet us inside.

It took us six arduous days to reach the outskirts of Afghan's capital. My first view of Kabul was at night from Paghman. Kabul was beautiful, the mountains surrounding the city like the sides of a bowl. My imagination roamed over the historic battles of a disparate group of armies—British, Greek, Mongol, Persian. But the dream was soon split by the sounds of battle from the current war, the sky streaked with rocket trails going to and from the city. Occasional explosions would light up different areas in and around Kabul. Zabet Walid explained that different operations were taking place in all parts of the city and its suburbs. His purpose was to maintain the action. This would not be a quick firefight in the remote mountains, but part of ongoing assaults on the Soviet and regime armies right at the heart of their operation.

CHAPTER 17

Street Gangs and Armies

Insurrection—by means of guerrilla bands—is the true method of warfare for all nations desirous of emancipating themselves from a foreign yoke. . . . It is invincible, indestructible.

—GIUSEPPE MAZZINI, 1805–1872

The day before the operation in Kabul was scheduled to begin marked the first day of the holy month of *Ramazan*, a month of Muslim fast—no intake of food or water from sunrise to sunset. Being June, this was a long portion of each day. Although exempt from fasting by the Holy Koran while participating in *Jihad*, most of the men in Abdul Haq's command, though not fanatic, were serious; they adhered to the fast.

Zabet Walid planned to attack a post in the Darulaman section of Kabul. In the early evening, three teams of four men each moved into place with recoilless rifles (RRs) and RPGs. Two single-barrel rocket launchers would be placed a couple of hundred yards from the post, while assault teams moved in to the walls surrounding it. The attack would begin at 11:00 P.M. Two of the assault teams were in place by 9:30. I was with Walid in a bombed-out abandoned house about two hundred yards from the main gate of the post. Just before ten o'clock, we saw a truck

138

approach the post. One muj with an RR thought a soldier in the truck had spotted him. He fired a round into the truck. With that shot, the battle exploded around us.

The post security guards had been on alert; they were manned and ready. Heavy machine gun and small arms fire erupted between the guard towers on the post and the two assault teams in position. Walid immediately ordered the men in our position to fire their rockets to cover the men in the open field.

After two rounds were fired from our house, we were spotted, and artillery began pounding the walls around us. By now the third team was in place, shooting the RPGs and RRs. Then silence. The entire outburst had lasted fifteen minutes. It seemed like hours. Now we had to get out.

With Walid in charge, we left the house in single file, about five yards apart, and crossed the open field. The night was lit by a half-moon, but it was bright and to our right. To our left, the lights of the city gave off a subdued glow. We could dimly make out shadows of movement behind us coming from the post. Walid was unconcerned, which I hoped meant that the shadows were members of our assault team returning.

After about fifteen minutes, I realized we were headed toward the city—the street lights were only about three hundred yards ahead. I asked Walid where we were going. "They will expect us to run to the mountains," he smiled. "We will go into the city. They won't think of that." I couldn't argue with him. Who would ever voluntarily go from the frying pan into the fire?

Occasionally we could hear, and feel, bullets whizzing past our heads. The tracer fire was eerie. Red trails appeared to meander aimlessly, as if in slow motion. From certain angles it was impossible to tell in which direction the bullets were heading. The mixture of machine gun fire with occasional rocket blasts made a confused background of sound. Suddenly, the sky lit up in instant daylight. A flare. Directly overhead. The flare had been fired from the post we had just attacked. We froze. We huddled in whatever shadow was available from the low scrub brush in the field. The flare hung over us for about five minutes as it descended slowly on its kite-like parachute. In its glare, the machine gun fire increased and I understood why the direction of the tracer fire was so confusing. The machine guns, two hundred or so yards apart, were spraying their rounds waist high, like a house fan oscillating from side to side. The guns were creating a fence of live ammunition around the city.

When the flare fizzled, Walid ordered us to move on, but to crawl, or crouch, and let the bullets pierce the air over our heads. We managed to squiggle between two of the machine gun emplacements and reach a paved road, with street lights and curbs. We had arrived inside the city of Kabul.

We ran down the street for about two blocks to some buildings that looked like warehouses. Behind one of them we stopped and rested, waiting for the others to join us. The respite was welcome; adrenaline had been pumping for over three hours. With eighteen men we began to move again, cautiously, three men a few blocks ahead of us and three behind at the same distance, our front and rear guards.

Shortly we reached a residential district. At each street corner we peered around buildings and, if safe, scampered across one at a time. Twice we saw small groups of militia patrolling the streets and we'd hide in the shadows until they passed and then scurry across.

I yearned to shoot a videotape of the streets, in particular the militia patrols, but it was too dark. I couldn't even get an image in the viewfinder. Walid was nervous when I unwrapped the camera. He wanted to keep moving. Earlier in the evening, I had gotten some great footage of the city from the safe house where we met the assault teams. I knew they were the first television pictures of Kabul taken with the mujahaddin, but, like any journalist, I wanted more.

We continued moving through the city like cat burglars until we reached a large house with a wall around it. It was Walid's father's house. Several of the men stayed outside while eight of us entered. We were led to the guest room located on the top floor and two old men brought rice and chicken—the first real meal we had eaten in almost a week. I fell into a deep sleep, exhausted and unable to grasp where I was. It was 1:30 in the morning.

Walid shook me to groggy awareness—4:00 A.M. We must leave quickly, Walid told me. "There is a patrol coming." I was instantly awake. We ran down the stairs and out a hole in the back wall.

The moon had gone and it was very dark as we raced through several streets until we reached an open area where Walid stopped abruptly. "We must be careful of mines," he warned. We tiptoed through the open field between Kabul and the foothills nearly three miles ahead of us. We were headed south, out of the city, when we turned to the northwest towards Paghman. After walking a mile or so, we came to a small orchard, which gave us a little cover. A small stone wall about three feet high ran along one side.

The dawn was beginning to cast a grayish light as we settled down to spend the day. Walid sent two men to get water from a nearby canal for tea to go with the fruit and biscuits he had brought from the house, and the muj built a small fire in a recess of the wall to boil the water.

As we were drinking our tea, the men seemed tense. Walid explained that the three men in our rear guard, only ten minutes behind us when we left the house, had not arrived.

A short time later, an old man came to the orchard from the city and reported what had happened. Soldiers had arrived almost on our footsteps and captured the men moments after they left the house. Walid and the men accepted the news stoically, but they hurt. Their assignment had been to protect me. Was a two-and-a-half minute television story worth the lives of three young men? The old man said the three had made a disturbance to give us time to get away. I cried inside—a tragic waste—for me. Nothing could justify their sacrifice.

The sun began to rise and I looked around. We were right in the middle of the two highways leading south from the city. Military trucks and occasional tanks were moving in both directions. A half kilometer to the east, a large post was serving as a road checkpoint, stopping all traffic. I laid my camera on a rock, aimed at the post, and watched through the extender on the lens as the soldiers checked each vehicle. The Soviet Fourth Army Headquarters at Darulaman was less than a mile away. Walid crawled up to the rock, pulled me back into the trees, and pointed to the sky. Two helicopters had left the Soviet base and were circling a large convoy that was leaving the main gate. On one circle, they flew directly over our orchard, less than a hundred feet overhead. I took pictures of them while Walid nervously calculated whether the sun was reflecting off my lens into the pilots' faces.

We slept sporadically during the day. At one point, large convoys came towards us from the city on the roads to either side of us and foot soldiers walked between tanks, less than three hundred yards on both our flanks. Had some Soviet officer decided he wanted a fresh apricot, we would have been finished.

That evening, we moved. In two hours, we reached Arghandeh. During the day, Arghandeh belonged to the regime soldiers and police. At night, it was a mujahaddin camp.

We slept in a mosque. In the middle of the night, I heard a loud argument, partially in English. In the dim light of a single lantern, I saw John Gunston arguing with Walid. Where had he come from?

Gunston was trying to convince Walid to take him back to Paghman and send someone else with me to Tezin. Walid took me aside and, when he asked for my advice, I told him that he should follow whatever instructions Abdul Haq had given. Walid told Gunston that he would proceed to Tezin. John was furious. He had come to Arghandeh from the mountains outside Paghman when he got word that Walid had arrived, but his guide had refused to go into Paghman itself without a more senior commander, such as Walid.

Early the next morning, we prepared to leave. John was packing his horse when the first jet screamed over our heads with such force that we could feel the heavy vibrations. A bomb exploded near us, and I grabbed my camera. Jet attacks are usually over in seconds, but this time they made repeated runs on the village. I saw a little boy, with terror in his eyes, watch the planes howling above. John and I both got close pictures of the bombing of the village. The shots became a dramatic part of the CBS story of my trip to Kabul.

By midmorning we had left Arghandeh. Relations between John and me were strained. He vented his frustrations by complaining incessantly to Walid and anyone else within earshot.

Paul, on Walid's instructions, had rejoined us in Arghandeh right after the bombing. By nightfall we had reached the picturesque village of Lalandar, where we stayed in the local Khalis commander's house. By the middle of the night, I realized I was sick—I had a fever and couldn't hold down any food. It was a hell of a place to get ill.

By morning, I felt miserable. This was the same village where we had been attacked by helicopters and ground troops only a week before. And reports spoke of troop activity near Mosai, our next destination. We waited until dusk before moving out. Upon reaching the road to Mosai, we could see headlights from numerous vehicles. Walid went to a nearby house to ask for refuge, but the owner refused to let us enter. He was afraid of retaliation—Soviet troops had searched his house three times the previous week. He did, however, offer us food and fodder for our animals.

We waited on the flat plain just north of Mosai until past midnight, when we were sure there was no activity on the road, and reached the town before dawn. The local commander, a cousin of Walid, was happy to have foreign guests and set out a big meal for us. But to me, even the sight of food was nauseating. Luckily, nature saved me. Suddenly, the house began to sway, the walls vibrated, and our tea cups bounced on the floor. It was a powerful earthquake, but it was over quickly. The muj laughed it off—earthquakes were common in these mountains. My lack of appetite had gone unnoticed, and Paul and I went to sleep. The next morning, Paul told me of the aftershock; I had slept right through it.

In the morning, Walid decided to go to the *marqaz* (military base camp) in the mountains east of Mosai and see if they knew where we could meet Abdul Haq. With daylight, we could see the effects of the war on the town. Many sections had been utterly destroyed by the bombing, and the outskirts were dotted with numerous shells and the wreckage of tanks and other vehicles. The cemeteries had been recently enlarged, grimly decorated by countless mujahaddin flags. The trip up the winding trails of the mountains was torturous. By the time we reached the camp in late afternoon, my condition had deteriorated—hot and cold spells, a high fever.

Although it was a warm evening, I was freezing. Wrapped in a blanket, I tried to sleep by hugging the cooking fire. But within moments I heard a familiar voice. Arnaud van Linden had arrived from Tezin, en route to meet us in the Paghman area. We left in the morning.

The trip across the Chakaray flatland was hot and miserable, with neither food nor water. With every village across the large, flat valley showing signs of heavy bombing, we were constantly on the alert for aircraft. The Soviets were wrecking the country.

Moving in single file along a well-trodden trail, I could do nothing but droop on my horse as the fever continued unabated. But I was startled into full awareness when I heard John, Paul, and Arnaud having a loud argument with one of the muj ahead of me. Then, suddenly, the muj raised his Kalashnikov and appeared to be pointing it at them.

When I reached them, the three foreigners said we had to talk—about Zabet Walid. They had decided—I never discovered the instigator of this bright idea—that Walid was an incompetent commander. They claimed that the young muj had tried to steal their canteens, recently filled at a well, and blamed Walid for his lack of control over the men. Abdul Haq must be informed. Somehow—in my dazed state nothing was too clear—matters were patched over.

Finally, we reached Tezin and were welcomed by Ismarak, the commander for Tezin, like members of the family. After taking one look at me, Ismarak put me on a *charpoi* (bed made of woven jute rope with wooden frame) and ordered soup. Abdul Haq was not there; he had left, and Ismarak didn't know where to, perhaps Hisarak. Abdul Haq never discussed his movements.

The next morning we set out for Hisarak, a journey that took us over the most rugged mountains I'd ever seen. It was twelve full hours before we reached the Khalis *marqaz* in the mountains overlooking Hisarak.

But Abdul Haq was there. He enveloped me in a bear hug, shook hands with John, greeted the others, and, expressionless, inquired why Arnaud was back and where had we met John. I told him I was sick.

The setting sun signaled the time for prayer and breaking the fast. Abdul Haq had the cook make fresh sheep liver kabobs for me, but, thanking him, I said I couldn't eat a thing. He ordered me to eat all of them, so I did. You don't argue with the commander of Kabul. As usual, he was right; I felt better.

Later in the evening, he told the man involved in the altercation to come to his tent. After asking the muj what had happened, he made the man apologize to John, Paul, and Arnaud. Then Abdul explained what the man had said: "He had been marching all day without water. When the time for breaking fast approached, he asked you in Pushtu if he could have a small drink from your canteen. When you didn't understand, he pointed to the canteen with his rifle. He wasn't stealing anything; he just wanted a drink. I ordered him to apologize because you are our guests and we cannot argue with a guest." Arnaud felt terrible, but John became defensive. "All journalists complain," Abdul Haq said, ending the matter. "You are no exception. I am sorry I cannot give you automobiles, but we don't have them in these mountains."

Afghans tend to be generous to a fault. They have nothing, but share everything, and guests are treated like royalty. Many of us do not deserve it. Strange, but most problems I have witnessed between Westerners and Afghans have boiled down to a misunderstanding of the Afghans' attempts to help. This was one more of the thousands of lessons I would learn about these people.

CHAPTER 18

Wars and Rumors of Wars

The conventional army loses if it does not win. The guerrilla army wins if it does not lose.

—HENRY KISSINGER, B. 1923

We spent several days in Abdul Haq's base camp in Hisarak. The setting was magical.

As Abdul Haq moved through the areas surrounding Kabul, he would be besieged: subcommanders awaiting instructions or in desperate need of weapons and ammunition; village elders coming to pay their respects; widows asking for relief; eager young men begging to enlist; villagers needing food or money. Abdul Haq had become a great chief who had to attend to every need of his people. No request was too small; no plight too mundane; no one too humble for his attention. The country was in chaos, and the people needed someone in whom they could put their faith—their hope for survival.

Old men would approach Abdul Haq pleading for an assignment to carry contraband or messages into the city. They needed to feel useful, valuable, part of their nation's struggle. Empty patriotic rhetoric was not enough; Abdul always made sure that each left with his or her dignity and pride renewed. It was not an easy responsibility with his limited resources.

146

This role of the major commanders in the war-torn country was never appreciated by the diplomats or covert operatives from the West. They viewed the war in strategic terms, in terms of the latest political pronouncement. They never saw, and therefore never understood, the relationship among the commanders— Abdul Haq, Ahmed Shah Masood, Ismael Khan, Jalaluddin Haqani, Mullah Malang, Amin Wardak, and others—or among the commanders and their people.

To begin with, the term commander was misleading. These men were *khans* in the true tribal meaning of the word. They were chiefs of culture, superior to their status as "war chiefs." The population that remained in the devastated country and their refugee brothers and sisters in Pakistan gave willing allegiance and devotion to these few men.

Steeped in American or European tradition, the diplomats saw only the military role played by the Abdul Haqs of Afghanistan. They dealt almost exclusively with the political leadership—the party leaders. They would frequently "order or tell" a party leader to have this or that commander do this or that. The political leaders of each of the seven parties relied on their military commanders to enhance the standing and reputation of their respective parties. Although the overwhelming majority of the military commanders was affiliated with a particular political party leader, this was primarily because weapons and money were distributed through the party system, not because each commander had an undying loyalty to any particular party leader. The party leaders would dutifully nod their heads, knowing full well that if orders were to be issued, it would be the other way around.

Throughout history, the Afghans had repeatedly turned back their would-be conquerors, and out of each successful resistance, leaders arose who led the mujahaddin into battle and the people to survival. It was happening in the 1980s, as it had happened over the centuries.

Abdul Haq was required to move his encampment every few days for security. The regime would spare no effort to capture or kill him if it could ever find him. At each camp, a stream of old men and a few women would appear carrying messages from inside Kabul. The communications from his network would be written in code on cloth and sewn into the hem of clothing or the lining of blankets. When the elderly messengers were patted down by militiamen at checkpoints, there was no paper to give them away. The envoys would then return with instructions from Abdul Haq to his operatives in the city.

By 1985, Abdul Haq had penetrated every arm of the regime's government. Often, he would have copies of papers destined for Najib before Najib ever saw them. The same was true in the Defense, Interior, and other ministries. Most of the documents related either to Soviet and Afghan army operations or to political disputes within the regime.

On one occasion, Abdul's network distributed pro-mujahaddin leaflets throughout the city. More galling yet, a leaflet was placed on every desk in the Defense Ministry. The minister was so enraged that he picked three trusted officers to investigate the matter—the very three who had personally distributed the leaflets. Gleefully, they identified several hard-line communists as the offenders. The suspects were severely punished.

After spending six weeks inside Afghanistan, I took my videotape to CBS in London for editing. Tom Fenton, CBS's chief European correspondent, narrated the story, which was produced by Peter Bluff, a true professional and a pleasure to work for. He transformed a month's worth of disparate videotape into a flowing story that accurately depicted the events.

At CBS, I worked with Peter, Al Ortiz, Steve Glauber, Doug Sefton, Susan Zirinsky, Harry Radliff, and others. Each was a first-class professional who, unfortunately, received little credit outside the industry. The correspondents, known inside the industry as "lips," are hired to be shown off on camera and, as a result, receive all the kudos.

After the Kabul story aired on CBS, my reputation became

solidly established as "the Afghan reporter." I was asked to write stories for newspapers and to appear on television on the news analysis shows.

In 1981, prior to being selected to replace the legendary Walter Cronkite, Dan Rather made a trip into Afghanistan with the mujahaddin. His series of stories was hard-hitting, powerful, and according to many people at CBS, gave Rather the edge over Roger Mudd to become anchor of the CBS Evening News. In subsequent years, CBS "adopted" Afghanistan. Dan wanted regular coverage of the story, and what the anchorman and managing editor of the Evening News wanted, he got.

Shortly after returning to Washington in the summer of 1985, I went to a banquet featuring a speech by Jonas Savimbi, the leader of UNITA, the Angolan rebel organization. Vice President George Bush was also speaking. A couple of hours before the banquet, I placed reserved signs on four seats; each table had eight settings. As I did so, two men with radio plugs in their ears, obviously security people, reserved two seats next to mine. When we returned for the banquet, we took our seats. A few minutes later, William Casey approached the table and sat down at his reserved seat—the one next to mine.

The next two hours were engrossing. I introduced myself to the director of the CIA, and he nodded and mumbled that he knew who I was. Soon we were discussing the war in Afghanistan, and he quizzed me about the country, the people, and the mujahaddin. This was more than a mere dinner conversation; Casey pulled a notebook from his pocket and began to write extensive notes; I was happy to oblige.

At one point, Casey asked me what the Afghans thought of the Pakistanis. I replied that they had mixed reactions. They were grateful to Pakistan and President Zia ul-Haq for the refuge they were providing the Afghans, but they were somewhat resentful that the Pakistani military, through the ISI, was telling them how to run their war. More important, they abjured the Pakistani buildup of Gulbaddin Hekmatyar into such a powerful force. But didn't Gulbaddin, in fact, have the strongest fighting force? I smiled, "Surely your sources of information refute that." It then hit me that his probings were not so much for pure information as to elicit a fresh opinion, any opinion, other than what his people were giving him.

Casey went on to say that during his several visits to Pakistan, he had visited mujahaddin training camps and met with Zia and General Acktar. "I have great respect for Acktar," he told me. "He is a real patriot, and he knows these people. Our aims—what we are trying to accomplish there—are very close."

Casey asked if I thought the mujahaddin could win the war, and I said that I was convinced that the Soviets would be compelled to leave.

"Why would they do that?"

"Because they are losing face throughout the Third World, exactly where they want to make headway, particularly with the Islamic countries."

"Yes," he mused, "they are going to lose this one."

Casey asked if the mujahaddin were getting enough weapons. Like all journalists in Pakistan, I said I had heard rumors of Pakistani officials siphoning off supplies intended for the mujahaddin, although the weapons would be of little use because they were of a much lower class than the Pakistanis'. But the rumors persisted.

"What's the biggest problem for the mujahaddin?" Casey asked. (At this point, Dana Rohrbacker, then a speechwriter for President Reagan, came up and joined the conversation.) I answered Casey's question: "Aircraft. They are at the complete mercy of jet and helicopter attacks. They say they need Stinger missiles." Casey was dubious, though; if such weapons were provided, wouldn't they likely be given or sold to Iran? The Afghans, I countered, had no great love for the Ayatollah Khomeini; they were interested in their own war. Besides, Iran was Shii'a Muslim, Afghanistan was Sunni, and there was great animosity between them.

Switching the subject, I brought up the Orlikon issue. I told Casey that although money had been appropriated by Congress to purchase forty Swiss-made Orlikon anti-aircraft cannons, after talking with commanders from every mujahaddin group, I had discovered that only six cannons had been delivered to the mujahaddin. Moreover, several people I knew, avid supporters of the contras in Nicaragua, were delighted because the contras had recently acquired heavy anti-aircraft cannons. I asked Casey point-blank if the Orlikon cannon had been redirected to the contras. He answered, candidly, "You'll have to check with Gates at the office on that."

With that, he got up and went to chat with the vice president and Jonas Savimbi. Casey's wife, Sofia, seated next to her husband, joked that her husband had barely touched his dinner. When he returned, Casey said he wanted a further discussion with me about Afghanistan and left.

The name Gates at the CIA still meant nothing to me. The next day, I called the Agency and asked for "Mr. Gates." I was transferred to a secretary who said Mr. Gates was tied up and took my name and number. I called two or three more times that week, but never got through.

Some months later, Stinger anti-aircraft missiles reached select groups of mujahaddin, including Abdul Haq. Soon, the mujahaddin were bringing down an average of one jet or helicopter a day. The cost to the Soviets of continuing their occupation of Afghanistan rose dramatically. The Stingers unquestionably caused the turning point in the war.

In 1987, Dana Rohrbacker, still working at the White House, told several journalists that according to Bill Casey my conversation had tipped the scales in his mind in favor of providing the Stinger missiles.

The Orlikon story, however, would not go away. I was now spending most of my time in Afghanistan, where, among other things, I met and talked with mujahaddin from every party. They had all heard of the Orlikon, a long-barreled cannon designed for aircraft, particularly helicopters. I videotaped one in operation near Barikot, in Kunar Province, and used it in a CBS story. I was told of five others—two in the Jalalabad area, two in Paktia, and one in the north. But where were the other thirty-four?

I went to Sam Roberts, CBS foreign editor. If they had been sent to the contras, I told him, let's find them. Sam's interest was piqued and he agreed to send me to Nicaragua to look for the Orlikons. This was September 1985, over a year before the Iran-Contra story broke.

I arrived in Tegucigalpa, Honduras, headquarters of the contras much as Peshawar was to the mujahaddin. I had been given a name of a Honduran, the widow of an American and a friend of Fred and Dixie Zumwalt, employees of USAID in Pakistan. I called, explained how I had come on her name, and was invited to join her and a few others who were coming over that evening.

At dinner, I said that I was in Honduras to connect with the contras and study their methods of warfare in order to compare them with the Afghan mujahaddin. She asked one of her guests, a top-ranking colonel in the Honduras army, if he could help, and he smiled and said he knew someone who might. I was told to wait at my hotel the next day until I was contacted.

The contact came early, eight o'clock in the morning, a young Nicaraguan with the unlikely name of "Frank" who took me to a contra office. In due course, I was introduced to a "Colonel Gomez," who had been a member of Anastasio Somoza's air force and was now a top field commander for the contras. I discussed my forays into Afghanistan and brought the conversation around to the problems the mujahaddin had with aircraft. Colonel Gomez explained that only recently, the Sandinistas had acquired Hind 24 and Hind 25 helicopters from the Soviets. Gomez then volunteered that the contras had a few anti-aircraft cannon. The problem, he said, was that they were too heavy to transport through the jungle. When I told him that the mujahaddin had lugged an anti-aircraft cannon to the top of a 15,000 foot mountain, he asked what kind it was, and I said, "Orlikon." "That's what we have," he smiled, "but they are too awkward to move around." When I suggested I would like to see them in action, he said we could leave the next morning for Nicaragua.

The next morning at the airport I met Colonel Gomez, two

young men, and an elderly Brit named Colin Mitchell, who said he had been to Peshawar several times and was now "investigating" the contras for friends in London. He did not elaborate.

We got into a small twin-engine plane piloted by Colonel Gomez. We flew across the border and over the jungle to a small dirt airstrip hidden along the banks of a river. Under the jungle cover near the airstrip was a dug-in contra base camp under the command of a young man, a Nicaraguan, with the *non de guerre* of Commander Ben Franklin. Most of the men in the camp, about seventy-five, were armed with American M-16 automatic rifles.

After a light lunch, Commander Franklin gave me a tour of the camp. I took video pictures of the camp and his men, and Colonel Franklin said he would try to take me to see the Orlikons in a day or two. Along the line I asked Colonel Gomez how they obtained them and he said they had been presented by private donors from the United States.

Gomez wanted to fly back to Tegucigalpa that afternoon, but no problem, I could come back in a couple of days. After recrossing the border, Gomez landed at a small military encampment to deliver messages from headquarters in the city, and off we went again.

We climbed to about eight thousand feet. Suddenly we heard a loud crack. It felt as though a huge rock had hit the tail of the aircraft. The plane lurched into a spinning dive and headed straight down, spinning like a top. One man, who had not connected his seatbelt, was flying around the cabin, Colonel Gomez was yelling, and someone else was screaming his "Hail Marys." I looked into the pilot's compartment and saw him straining, veins popping, as he pushed his foot on the rudder with his every ounce of strength. Mitch and I looked at each other; we knew the plane was crashing, we couldn't survive. When we were less than one hundred feet from the ground, Gomez managed to stop the spinning and yank the wheel back, pulling the nose up just as the plane hit ground. By some miracle, it slammed into the ground on its wheels. We staggered out wondering why we were alive. A crack stretched right across the tail, through the aircraft.

When Gomez put his hand on it, the tail fell off. We never discovered if we had been hit by Sandinista fire or if metal fatigue had simply torn away the tail of the "donated" aircraft. At that moment, there was not an atheist among us.

We got a ride back to the city. Gomez came to the hotel every morning to say he was waiting for word to take me back to Commander Franklin. While I lingered, I met as many of the contra officials in Honduras as I could find. They were interesting, but they lacked the total dedication of the mujahaddin, as if the Nicaraguans were relying on Americans to make decisions for them. The contras appeared to me to be conducting more of a surrogate operation, something the mujahaddin would never permit.

The second trip with Commander Franklin did not materialize. Perhaps someone got wind of my true mission. I would have to keep digging to get the whole story.

I returned to New York, where Sam Roberts immediately dispatched me back to Afghanistan. The Orlikon story would have to wait. We wondered if diverting Afghan weapons to the contras was such a big deal, anyhow. A year later, we found our answer when the White House itself was shaken by the Iran-Contra mess.

CHAPTER 19

Into the Jaws of the Enemy

The next war criminals will come from the chemical and electronics industries.

—ALFRED KRUPP, GERMAN ARMS MANUFACTURER,
1907–1967

By the fall of 1985, support for the Afghan Resistance was growing strong in the United States and across Europe. Media interest was also increasing. In the maneuvering before the upcoming October summit meeting with Mikhail Gorbachev, President Reagan had stated several times that an end to the Soviet invasion of Afghanistan was key to improved relations between the superpowers. The Soviets' only response was to step up their military operations against Afghanistan in the summer and fall of that year.

During those days, I was spending most of my time with the mujahaddin. Every day, if our own position was not being attacked—at times we would come under attack from up to a dozen HIND 25 helicopter gunships at a time—we could hear the heavy metallic thuds and roars of bombing in the next valley or over the next ridge. Not a day passed that we did not hear the screams of MiG 29s and SU 25 jet aircraft tearing up the valleys to the mountaintops. The distinctive rasping of a rocket exploding from a helicopter became a dread sound among villagers and mujahaddin alike. The copters were like huge deadly bumblebees from which it was impossible to escape.

In early November I was in Paktia Province with mujahaddin under the command of Jalaluddin Haqani. The muj had been laying siege to a division headquarters of the Soviets at Asham Khel. Every morning they would launch rocket and small arms attacks from the mountains surrounding the large military base, fire their weapons for about forty-five minutes, and then move to a different part of the mountains. Like clockwork, the jets from Kabul would arrive half an hour later to bomb and strafe the positions the muj had just left. It made for great videotaping; the all-important "bang-bang" needed for network news stories was a daily event. Unfortunately, the feeling of mujahaddin invincibility was contagious.

One morning I was sitting on a mountainside drinking tea with several muj in front of a couple of adobe huts used by the muj for storing equipment. A jet thundered through the valley below us, its loud report causing a jolt in the air that could be felt. Looking skyward, I saw what appeared to be a round silver basketball hurtling directly towards us—a bomb headed straight into our teacups.

One man pushed me hard to the ground and threw himself on top of me as the silver basketball slammed into the trees about ten feet up the slope from us. I can still hear the sound as it broke through branches before exploding. Instantly, the ground around us burst into flames. The cold crisp mountain air was quickly converted into an inferno, the flames spreading like spilled liquid. I realized that was exactly what it was—napalm.

I ran past the burning door of the hut and grabbed my camera while a muj beat my back. Excited at the prospect of taking pictures of napalm, I hadn't realized my clothes were on fire. As he smothered the flames on my back, he noticed that his own clothes were burning. After wrapping ourselves in blankets I began taping the hellish scene.

The gel of napalm had made a circle about twenty yards in diameter causing flames to leap all around us. Trees and bushes were burning, and the wooden door frames of the two huts crackled until fifty or so men appeared to beat out the fires. In one area the jelly-like substance had, for some reason, not ignited. I found an empty can and took about a quart of it and sealed it tightly. My videotape was the first real proof that the Soviets were using napalm in Afghanistan, a fact they had vehemently denied in several different world forums.

After the chaos had subsided, I realized I had received a horrible burn on my backside, located where I could never show off my war wound. Sitting was impossible, standing was painful, and lying down was not much better.

As always in the aftermath of such an attack, the men began to joke about it. Humor is the best remedy for fear. Seeing that I did not fully understand their jokes, they pointed to the second hut. I walked painfully over to the burned-out door and looked inside. It was crammed to the ceiling with over a thousand claymore antitank mines. The napalm bomb had landed two yards above the roof of the hut. Had the napalm set off the mines, none of us would have lived. I understood why the mujahaddin were always saying "Allah Akbar." It had to be more than good luck.

That afternoon I began the journey back to Peshawar with a great story on tape. When Vietnam provided a picture for the American television audience depicting the ravages of napalm, it engendered an effective horror of it in Southeast Asia. The reaction would be the same for the Soviet use of it in Afghanistan.

I reached Peshawar early the next morning after a painful trip, spending most of the time lying in the back of a pickup truck. Once in Peshawar, Abdul Haq insisted on seeing my battle wound. He was the only person I would allow to see it. He was genuinely concerned, even if he couldn't refrain from joshing me a little.

After trying for almost three hours to place a telephone call to New York, I finally reached Sam Roberts and told him what we had on videotape. He told me to take the next plane to London. I said I hadn't slept for three days and I was hurting. What about I sleep for a full day and then look into flight schedules? He said take the next possible flight.

I called the airport and discovered the only flight for the next twenty-four hours was a PIA flight to Moscow, with a six-hour layover in the Soviet capital before connecting to London. I called Sam back and said, "Of course I can't take this tape to Moscow, so I'll have to get to London the day after." Sam said take the flight via Moscow.

When the plane reached Afghan airspace, a jet fighter with a big red star on the tail appeared to escort the PIA 747. Then the long trip north across the Soviet Union. I have never felt more paranoid in my life. My briefcase contained videotapes of a Soviet atrocity, and I was flying nearly six hundred miles per hour towards Moscow. It was discomfiting.

Sheremetievo Airport in Moscow was a huge marble building with uniformed men and women everywhere. The large hall was dimly lit. After I had wandered around, holding onto my briefcase with a white-knuckled grip, for about an hour, a man in a leather jacket came up to me and asked in a thick accent if I was English. I said, no. He offered to buy me a beer. He must be KGB; I was being arrested. I followed him tamely into the restaurant where he ordered two beers.

They tasted like liquid cardboard. All the uniformed people in the airport, he said, were there because Gorbachev was leaving in a few hours for the summit meeting with Ronald Reagan in Geneva. I suddenly understood why Sam was so anxious for me to leave immediately for London, and what a genius he was. If I reached London with the napalm story during the summit it would be one powerful story. If I had trouble getting the tape through the USSR that would be equally powerful, if not quite so comfortable. Such decisions were why people like Sam had such jobs.

Upon my arrival in London, the people at CBS were excited about the story, as were the producers in Geneva where the CBS Evening News had moved for the summit. Doug Sefton produced the story with me; Steve Kroft narrated it.

November 17, 1985, was the opening day of the first summit between Gorbachev and Reagan. CBS's lead story showed them greeting each other. The second story was of Nancy Reagan and

Raisa Gorbachev meeting for the first time. The third story was my videotape. The opening pictures showed a jet ripping low through the sky and the spitting flames on the ground as Steve Kroft narrated, "The Russian jets came in low. When the dust had settled Kurt Lohbeck, on assignment for CBS News, had finally proven what the Soviets have long denied—they are using napalm in Afghanistan!"

CHAPTER 20

We Deceive
Ourselves

*A politician will do anything to keep his job—even become a
patriot.*

—WILLIAM RANDOLPH HEARST, 1863–1951

In the winter of 1986 battle lines were being drawn inside Washington over the war in Afghanistan. Unlike the policy debates over Central America or Africa, Congress, crossing party lines, was eager to supply the Afghans while the State Department dragged its feet.

A joint Senate-House task force on Afghanistan was formed which included Democratic Senators Chris Dodd, Bill Bradley, Paul Tsongas; and Republican Senators Gordon Humphrey, Orrin Hatch, Al D'Amato, and Steve Symms. The House Afghanophiles were led by Democrat Charlie Wilson and Republican Bill McCullom. Nearly every measure requiring congressional support for the Afghan Resistance passed both Houses of Congress overwhelmingly.

Those who hesitated to provide overt military support to the mujahaddin were, more often than not, officials of the State Department, but there were also a few figures from private policy foundations such as Selig Harrison of the Carnegie Foundation and Raymond Gartoff of Brookings Institute. These busily wrote op-ed pieces warning of the dire consequences involved in helping the Afghans to free themselves from the Soviets. The Soviet army, they argued, could not be defeated, and, anyway, the Afghans, a backward people, would only benefit by having the Soviets drag them into the twentieth century. But this opposition fell on sterile ground; this time, the media was not interested.

The only opposition to the Agency giving any aid at all to the Afghans came from the State Department. Professional diplomats such as Robert Peck, Richard Murphy, Gerald Helman, and Charles Dunbar were horrified at the prospect of any direct confrontation with the Soviets, and they said so. Another set of opponents within the labyrinth of Foggy Bottom were the Indian lovers, those who had served in New Delhi, or come up through the ranks under John Kenneth Galbraith, Chester Bowles, or Daniel Patrick Moynihan, each of whom had fallen for Hindu mysticism and/or Ghandiism while serving as ambassadors. India, with its morass of human misery, was the only non-Soviet bloc nation openly to support the invasion of Afghanistan. For Prime Minister Rajiv Ghandi it was not only a question of marching to Moscow's drumbeat, but of opposing any position taken by Pakistan. If Pakistan aided the mujahaddin, India was against them.

The CIA ignored these voices in the State Department, although its own were hardly full-throated. Bill Casey took his orders directly from the president. He didn't need any consensus from diplomats and he wasn't about to ask for one.

For American conservative political groups, on the other hand, Afghanistan was a cause célèbre. This was a fight against the Red Army itself, not a mere surrogate battle such as those taking place in Nicaragua or Angola. Ronald Reagan himself had declared that the mujahaddin were the "moral equivalent of our own Founding Fathers."

Surprisingly, most liberal and even pacifist groups also supported the Afghan Resistance. For some it was a way of legitimizing their opposition to the Nicaraguan contras by showing that they did not, in general, support Soviet imperialism. They could safely continue to criticize Reaganism generally by lamenting this Soviet "blunder" in particular.

Whatever the struggles going on inside Washington, one fact emerged: in the 1980s, no major publication editorialized against aiding the Afghan mujahaddin.

Abdul Haq and other political strategists among the mujahaddin lamented this fact. The CIA loved it. Abdul reasoned that if even a small segment of the media or press was to oppose support, it would be debated in the Western world. If it were debated openly—not just in the inner councils of government—then real and effective assistance might emerge from America and Europe. As it was, the faceless dissenters in the State Department were able to keep the level of aid low.

The CIA, for its part, was jubilant: with no domestic debate on Afghanistan it was free to conduct its part of the war unobserved and unquestioned. For William Casey and the team he had assembled to assist the war, the situation was ideal.

This freedom for the CIA was particularly welcome because the National Security Council and the CIA were constantly battling during the Reagan presidency over covert actions.[1] Early in his administration the president issued a National Security directive that required an annual review of all "CAs," or covert actions. Its purpose was to articulate what a particular covert action was attempting to achieve and to ensure that it was doing so. The CIA was, naturally, not pleased with this annual review requirement. The agents were accustomed to being given a directive and then proceeding with a free hand.

In regards to Afghanistan the debates between the CIA, NSC, State, and Defense Department was frequently heated.[2] Many of the White House NSC staff thought John McMahon, deputy director of the CIA, resisted any covert program that directly confronted the Soviets. Most in the CIA policy sections were content to "bloody the Soviet's nose," unable to envision the possibility that the Soviets could actually be made to retreat from Afghanistan. In this, the CIA had strong supporters at the State Department. The National Security Advisor, on the other hand, took the position that our covert programs ought to have a definite goal, that it was not sufficient simply to ship a lot of weapons to the mujahaddin. This argument was held by all of Reagan's NSAs—Judge William Clark, Robert "Bud" McFarlane, and Admiral John Poindexter.

The CIA, in short, resented interference from any other agency, including the White House. William Casey was torn. A true believer that Soviet advances should be rolled back worldwide—that the Brezhnev Doctrine should be challenged— he was also now heading the Central Intelligence Agency and felt he must defend his people. To the frustration of the Reaganites at the White House, he would waver this way and that.

Another serious point of contention in the internal government debates on Afghanistan was the role of the Pakistanis. From the beginning, the CIA had relied on the Pakistani ISI to determine who was who among the mujahaddin and how to fight the battles.[3] Due to the close relationship between Casey and General Acktar, the CIA willingly accepted the role of advisor and of supplier of materiel and intelligence. The CIA station chief in Islamabad rarely planned military operations or vetoed ISI political mischief in its dealings with the mujahaddin.

The CIA personnel in Pakistan, moreoever, were notoriously unlearned in the culture and political intricacies of the Afghans. While many of them enjoyed Afghan culture and deeply respected the people with whom they dealt, few understood the history of the mujahaddin or the country.[4] One high-ranking member of the NSC staff explained it to me; he said they had no understanding of "the otherness of others."

But these policy arguments stopped short of the ISI-inspired buildup of Gulbaddin and Ahmed Shah Masood at the expense of the other Afghans who had much broader-based constituencies. One CIA official in Pakistan told me he backed Gulbaddin because "fanatics fight better." Masood was picked because, as Ed McWilliams, U.S. envoy to the mujahaddin, stated, "We feel it is right to support minorities in Afghanistan and elsewhere in the world." These policies would lead to deep distress for the mujahaddin—and for the Afghan people.

* * *

The CIA is a large bureaucracy with thousands of employees and a variety of missions. Not all of them involve cloak-and-dagger activities, guns, or wars. One of the most active sections of the Agency deals with propaganda. It disseminates misinformation, disinformation, and frequently, where able, puts a "spin" on the news.

The propaganda activities of the Agency in Afghanistan were not limited to influencing information coming into the United States. The agents also needed to influence the people of Afghanistan and Pakistan. In this regard, they were in their element.

Living in a mostly illiterate society, the Afghan people rely on rumor and word-of-mouth for their information. The busiest bazaar in Peshawar is named "the Storyteller's Bazaar." Here Pakistanis and Afghans crowd into the teashops and kabob parlors to feed as well on the latest news or gossip. No people thrive on gossip more than the Afghans. No organization can dream up and spread rumor better than the CIA. The two were made for each other. When the rumor mills of the KGB and the Afghan communist government were added to the mix, very strange stories indeed circulated in the war-torn country.

In the early years of the war news coverage was scarce. The few reporters venturing to Peshawar relied heavily on the U.S. and British embassies for information. In response, the American Embassy in Islamabad issued weekly situation reports (sitreps) on the Afghan War. These same sitreps were also given to Western reporters stationed in New Delhi. The reporters receiving the sitreps were told that, in return, all information must be credited to "Western diplomatic observers." The information, of course, came directly from the CIA or CIA sources. Until late 1986 when it was closed, the U.S. Embassy in Kabul was still staffed by three or four people, all connected with the Agency, who provided information of activities in Kabul and the surrounding areas. Other CIA sources provided war information from elsewhere in the country.

The sitreps rarely gave negative reports on the mujahaddin and only reported Soviet military successes if the ensuing atrocities had more impact. The sitreps, plus the fact that very few Western reporters traveled into Afghanistan, allowed the CIA and the State Department to control the flow and tone of news about the war. And this, in its turn, helped the CIA to keep a leash on various mujahaddin groups. Those who cooperated closely were promoted for their prowess and battle strength. Those who went their own way were disparaged or, worse, ignored.

The U.S. government also did its best to keep control of the reporting by influencing whom reporters could talk to or which Afghan groups they could contact for information or travel into Afghanistan. The British Embassy did the same with its reporters. I would often receive both American and British sitreps and I discovered that frequently they were word-for-word identical. In one case the British weekly report referred to the "Afghan Defense Ministry." In retyping the report some British clerk forgot to change the American spelling of "defense" to the British "defence."

Control of the news caused serious problems within the Afghan Resistance, most particularly the hype and sheer falsehoods distributed about Gulbaddin Hekmatyar. For years, the information officers, embassy officials, and consular officials reported that Gulbaddin's party was the "best organized and strongest fighting force in Afghanistan." This was not true and it was never true. It was true that whenever the mujahaddin of any party achieved a battlefield or political victory, Gulbaddin's office took the credit.

On more than one occasion when I was with a group of mujahaddin during a significant military operation, it would be several days before I could get back to Peshawar. Upon my arrival, I would discover that Gulbaddin and the American information offices had already put out stories crediting him with the successful battles I had just finished videotaping. When I pointed out that Gulbaddin's people had been nowhere near the activity, the officials would shrug and lay it to the difficulties of getting accurate information in a primitive situation.

Gulbaddin's office took full advantage of the situation and opened an operation called the Afghan News Agency (ANA), which churned out reams of fairy tales presented as battlefield reports. Frequently, news agencies cited reports by the ANA as if it were an independent and objective agency.

Far and away the most blatant U.S. government attempt to influence the news from Afghanistan was the Afghan Media Resource Center. In 1985, Walt Raymond of the NSC staff at the White House went to Senator Gordon Humphrey with an idea. Raymond explained that the scarcity of reports on the Afghan War was due to the danger involved in gathering the news. Raymond asked Humphrey to sponsor a bill to fund training for Afghans in the use of video cameras. These Afghans could then cover the war, and the organization, created by the legislation, would distribute the videotape around the world. Gordon Humphrey was happy to help, and the bill quickly passed.

Although several Afghan support organizations and a few professional video companies gave proposals to the USIA, the program went to Boston University and its controversial dean, Joachim Maitre. Maitre, an East German air force pilot who defected in the 1950s, was a strident anticommunist and had worked his way up to become dean of Boston University's School of Journalism. Maitre had made a propaganda film supporting the Nicaraguan contras, thanks to funding by LTC Oliver North of the NSC staff at the White House.[5] And now, this Afghan program had been created by Walt Raymond, whose office was down the hallway from North's.

AMRC had mixed results in the first couple of years. Since it was all but impossible to find any Afghan who could be an objective and accurate journalist, students for the project were provided by the mujahaddin parties, of which nearly 90 percent were from Gulbaddin's Hezb-i-Islami or Rabbani's Jamiat-i-Islami. Maitre's operation would then distribute or sell the video around the world. Much of it was dispensed in the United States, even though the law specifically prohibits the USIA from doing so. Even the three American television networks purchased some of the tape. On the "West 57th Street" story, we pointed out that CBS News had broadcast some of their scenes, although the producers responsible claimed they had not been aware that the tape was a USIA product.

After about two years, the USIA was instructed to turn the program over to qualified Afghans to operate as an Afghan news agency. Boston University was phased out of the project, and a member of Gulbaddin's Hezb-i-Islami, Haji Daud Khan, was hired as manager.

Walt Raymond and Gordon Humphrey readily admitted that the project was designed to put an anti-Soviet and pro-mujahaddin spin on the war. Neither of them quite grasped that a free press and media only have credibility if they are independent of the government. If their motive of airing the horror of the Afghan War was admirable, their method was open to question.

This program and other CIA propaganda projects opened a valid debate among Western journalists. Citizens of free countries have a need, indeed a right, to know what is happening in the world. In a situation such as Afghanistan, where the physical danger of covering the story prevents such coverage, how does the story get out?

Since this type of "spin control" by the government was known, it was not a significant problem for major media outlets. Not so well known was the fact that Western intelligence agencies hired foreign journalists, or that intelligence operatives themselves posed as journalists. U.S. law prohibits our intelligence agencies from hiring U.S. citizens who are journalists or covertly posing as such. By hiring foreign journalists, the letter of the law is kept but the spirit is circumvented.

In Afghanistan, it became known by mujahaddin commanders that several British and French journalists were also employed by the CIA and European intelligence agencies.[6] A typical, but tragic case was that of Dominique Vergos.

Vergos, a Frenchman, arrived in Peshawar in 1985 from Paris with a reputation as a fashion photographer. Dominique announced, to anybody who would listen, that he was going to cover the war for various French magazines, and he made several extended trips into Afghanistan with the mujahaddin.

In Peshawar, Dominique demonstrated considerable knowledge of the mujahaddin—their internal squabbles, commanders, battle strategies, and so on. Yet, he never showed any of his published photographs. Most freelance shooters carry their scrapbooks with them. Dominique's British wife, who worked for Afghan Aid, also displayed a deep understanding of the mujahaddin military.

In January 1989 Dominique was killed in the frontyard of his home in Peshawar. He had been shot in the head with an AK-47 automatic rifle. Before police arrived at the scene, a Britisher, widely assumed by the community to be working for SIS, cleaned up the scene of the crime. An American from the consulate, who arrived on the scene, told me Dominique's home had all the equipment and trappings of an intelligence cell. A Pakistani household employee, charged with the killing, was later released for lack of evidence.

Shortly after his death, Dominique's daughter from a previous marriage arrived in Peshawar. Natalie Vergos wanted to familiarize herself with Afghanistan and the situation that led to her father's murder. At her request, she accompanied me on a short trip to Afghanistan. As bombs were exploding around us, she said she knew her father must have relished this sort of situation and added that he had worked for "the Americans" for a long time and was proud of being an intelligence agent.

In a border city like Peshawar, the situation was frequently confusing. Numerous freelance journalists and some aid workers had a fantasy of becoming—or of being—"spooks." They liked to give the impression that they led a double life. And yet, the city did, in fact, have an abundance of people who worked covertly for the various governments—American, British, French, German, Saudi, Libyan, Iraqi, Pakistani, Afghan, and Soviet.

In the 1980s, Afghanistan was strategically important to a number of countries. It was the only spot where the Soviet army was actively engaged in combat. It was a testing ground for the weapons systems of the East and the West. And it was a battleground within Islam between the fundamentalists promoting Pan-Islam, and the more nationalistic Muslims. In aggregate, these currents created an atmosphere of distrust among the foreign residents.

CHAPTER 21

Extremely Intolerant

Fanaticism consists in redoubling your effort when you have forgotten your aim.

—GEORGE SANTAYANA, 1863–1952

A Muslim must accept and abide by five tenets:

1. Believe that there is but one God (Allah) and that Mohammed was the Messenger of God (Prophet).
2. Pray five times daily facing the holy city of Mecca.
3. Keep the dawn-to-dusk fast each day during the month of Ramazan (Ramadan).
4. Give *zakat* (alms) to those in need to the equivalent of 10 to 25 percent of his/her income or material worth.
5. Perform *Haj* (pilgrimage to Mecca) at least once in a lifetime if physically and financially able.

The practice of these five items is what constitutes a Muslim, no more, no less. Most Muslims argue that there can be no division in Islam, such as "fundamentalist" or "moderate." Acceptance of the five tenets makes each individual a fundamentalist, and moderation is the very basis of Islam, according to the teachings of the prophet Mohammed.

The word Islam means "Peace." When a Muslim greets another he says, "Asalam alai-kum" (Peace be unto you).

All this notwithstanding, Western observers and participants in the Afghan imbroglio insisted on labeling the various Afghan groups as "moderates" or "fundamentalists." This was probably because their own Christian culture has split into sects, which range from Catholics on the one side to Jim Jones fanatics on the other, with just about everything else in between.

Yet it would be proper to label the three parties headed by Gulbaddin Hekmatyar, Abdul Rasul Sayyaf, and Burhanuddin Rabbani as "fanatic." All three, particularly Gulbaddin and Sayyaf, are strong advocates of the internationalist movement called "Pan-Islam."

Pan-Islam calls for uniting Islam into a world without borders. Antinationalistic, it teaches that the Holy Koran is the only set of laws required for all Muslims. The Pan-Islamic movement is promoted, frequently with violence, by the Ikhwan, known in the West as the "Muslim Brotherhood."

Founded in the *madrassas* (Islamic schools) of Cairo, Egypt, during the reign of King Farouk in the 1940s, the Ikhwan has opposed and/or fought against all monarchies and secular governments in the Islamic world. In Afghanistan, as in most Arab countries, the aims of the Ikhwan are frequently in conflict with the tribal traditions of the populace. The Ikhwan has nevertheless increased its strength in recent decades primarily because of the twin bogeymen—Soviet communism and Western secularism.[1]

The Soviet Union was based upon atheism, an anathema to Islam. Moreover, its appetite for expansion, evinced since its early days in power, was seen as a threat to the neighboring Islamic countries.

Western culture is also viewed as a threat because it is, in essence, secularistic and materialistic, twin evils, according to Islamic belief. Muslims are not enemies of practicing Christians or Jews. Any adherent of "the Book," whether the Koran, Bible, or Torah, is considered to be a believer in the one God. And all are children of Abraham. But Muslim fanatics believe that the so-called Judeo-Christian culture has been superseded by international hedonism and materialism.

The Ikhwan has been successful throughout the Islamic world, primarily among the poor and uneducated masses. But numerous wealthy Muslims have also supported it as a political movement since the days of Gammal Abdul Nasser in Egypt. They have viewed the Ikhwan as a means to eliminate the monarchies in several Islamic countries and thus to enhance their own economic status.

The Ikhwan has become a potent political force in recent years in Pakistan, Jordan, Algeria, Egypt, and Saudi Arabia. In 1990, its adherents captured the national legislature in Algeria, and through the Jamaat Islami party in Pakistan, they ousted Prime Minister Benazir Bhutto and replaced her with a government more in tune with their extremist goals.

The movement had little influence in prewar Afghanistan, since tribal hierarchies wielded strong control over the sparsely populated country. But following the Soviet invasion in 1979 millions of refugees were herded into camps in Pakistan and Iran, torn from their tribal roots. Subjected to the rhetoric of war—the Soviet invasion of Afghanistan was depicted as an atheist attack upon all Islam—the refugees became susceptible to recruitment by the fanatic advocates of Pan-Islam.

In Pakistan, moreover, the seven political parties of the Afghan mujahaddin had large control over the distribution of supplies to the refugees, and since a large proportion of this largesse was given to Gulbaddin's Hezb-i-Islami to hand out, his following multiplied.[2]

Support for Afghan members of the Ikhwan came from a number of sources throughout the Islamic world. The followers of Sheik Bin Baz, the blind and elderly leader of the Wahabi sect of Muslims in Saudi Arabia, contributed large sums of money. Saddam Hussein and Muammar Khadafi also supported the more fanatic factions of the Afghan mujahaddin.[3] But the largest backing of Gulbaddin came from the CIA. Huge amounts of U.S. aid also went to Ahmed Shah Masood of Rabbani's Jamiat-i-Islami. Both have been longtime advocates of Pan-Islam. Their mutual hatred had its roots in the early days of the Resistance when they began vying for power in the northern provinces of Afghanistan.

U.S. support of these factions can be attributed to the influence of the late President Zia ul-Haq of Pakistan and his Intelligence chief, General Acktar. Zia was a fervent believer in Pan-Islam and wanted to create a federation of non-Arab Islamic states. He told me in an interview in 1987 that Pakistan, Afghanistan, Iran, and Turkey were natural allies and should be united under the "brotherhood of Islam." Zia, moreover, convinced American policymakers that such unity would be effective against Soviet expansionism.

In 1990 and 1991 Zia's successor in Pakistan, General Aslam Beg, refused to condemn Iraq's Saddam Hussein following the invasion of Kuwait. He had no hesitation in denouncing the U.S.-led war against Iraq, which was a "victory" by Saddam over the "Zionist-controlled American forces." Although Saudi pressure forced Pakistan to send a token contingent of troops to Operation Desert Shield, Pakistan stated they were sent to Saudi Arabia only to protect the holy shrines in Mecca and Medina.

Gulbaddin Hekmatyar also denounced the American operation against Saddam Hussein. In stark contrast, the parties of Younas Khalis, Gailani, and Mojadidi sent a battalion of mujahaddin to join Desert Storm troops and were commended for it.

In short, the overwhelming majority of Afghans, indeed Muslims in general, do not support the fanaticism of the Ikhwan, or the Pan-Islamic movement. The Afghan Resistance was motivated by a nationalistic determination to protect its homeland from a foreign invader and an alien ideology.

Yet the strife and chaos of war allowed the more fanatic factions to gain a foothold in Afghanistan. The strange cooperation between Islamic extremists and Western intelligence agencies was never openly questioned until after the Soviet withdrawal in 1989. At that time Representative Anthony Beilenson, chairman of the House Permanent Select Committee on Intelligence, called for an end to all assistance to the mujahaddin because of our support of the extremists.

In a letter to the *New York Times* (May 23, 1989) Beilenson described American policy in Afghanistan since 1980: "Some of the largest and best equipped factions [of the Resistance] are made up of Islamic fundamentalists whose goals for a new Afghanistan are in stark contrast with our own. We may have been willing to ignore the ideology of the rebels while they were fighting the Soviets, but now that they are fighting only their own countrymen and are trying to form a new post-occupation government as well, we face an entirely different situation that demands a cutoff of our military aid."

Representing the nonfanatic factions, Abdul Haq answered Beilenson in a letter to the *Times* (June 9, 1989). "If the advice of Mr. Beilenson is taken seriously, it would suggest that: (1) The United States was not supporting the people of Afghanistan for their freedom, but using these people to kill their enemy. (2) The two superpowers may be playing a game with small countries, trading one country for another. (3) The United States does not care about human lives, only pieces on their world game board.

"We respect the American people as much as anybody else. Yes, there are a few fanatics among us, yet the majority of us are against them as much as anybody else. . . . The struggle of our nation is for the establishment of a system that assures human rights, social justice, and peace. This system does not threaten any nation. Mr. Beilenson's view of the future of Afghanistan is in stark contrast to ours."

For their part, the moderate factions of the mujahaddin seemed to do little during the war to head off the growing influence of Gulbaddin and his Hezb-i-Islami; for example, they included him as a full partner in their councils and alliances. But it is generally believed that this was primarily motivated by fear. Since Gulbaddin had a habit of ordering the assassination of his opponents, the mujahaddin leaders thought they could best— and most safely—control him by outvoting him in their meetings.

Gulbaddin carried his intimidation of the moderate factions to other parts of the world. When Mojadidi and Gailani visited the United States, their meetings with exiled Afghans were disrupted by shouting fanatics. In one instance, when Dr. Mohammed Yousef, a former Afghan prime minister, came to Los Angeles to address the Free Afghan Alliance in 1986, several dozen Hezbi supporters created such a din that he was forced to cancel his speech.[4]

Although the Islam fanatics gained political strength in the refugee camps and with foreign supporters, their power inside of Afghanistan was negligible. Every significant military operation against the Soviets was conducted almost entirely by other groups. In October of 1986 one particular operation caused more damage to the Soviet occupation army than any yet.

CHAPTER 22

Goliath Begins to Fall

War's a brain-spattering, windpipe-splitting art.

—LORD BYRON, 1788–1824

The summer of 1986 saw the heaviest fighting of the war in all parts of the country—with the exception of the Panjsher valley, where Commander Ahmed Shah Masood had negotiated a truce between the Soviets and his forces, in what threatened to become a habit, having done so on several previous occasions.[1]

Although Masood claimed he had forced the Soviets into these pacts, the agreements were obviously beneficial to the Soviets. In exchange for keeping the communist forces out of the Panjsher, Masood agreed not to attack supply convoys traversing the single highway from the Soviet border into Kabul. This, of course, gave the Soviet commanders a secure land route to the capital and allowed them to concentrate their resources against the mujahaddin supply routes.

Military commanders of the other parties were livid. If Masood had instead helped them to coordinate their attacks on the Soviets and to keep up the pressure nationwide, they could have crippled their common enemy.

Masood avoided a direct confrontation with the other commanders by the simple expedient of never venturing outside the

Panjsher valley. Believing that his motives for isolation were patriotic, his Tajik people and journalists in general extolled his courage.

This strategy also helped enhance his international reputation as the "Lion of the Panjsher" (the word *panjsher* means "five lions" in Farsi). The Panjsher valley is located only fifty miles from Kabul by road. To reach it, the mujahaddin in charge of supplies were forced to find a route over the mountains of Nooristan and through the treacherous terrain of Badakshan Province. Heavy snows completely closed the trails from November through April, and during the spring and summer months it took a month or more to complete a one-way trip from Pakistan to the Panjsher.

The few intrepid journalists who risked the trip always returned with tales of danger and derring-do. Here the terrain— the high mountain passes were snow-packed year round—was as deadly as the Soviet army. Horses and mules slipped and fell thousands of feet into mountain gorges, occasionally with their riders or handlers. More than one journalist returned only with their stories, their equipment—cameras and film—having been swallowed by the jagged landscape on the roof of the world.

But those who managed to arrive in the Panjsher were struck by the beauty of the vast valley which stretched for over one hundred miles through Kapisa and Badakhshan provinces. Hundreds of side valleys and finger ridges branched out on both sides along its entire length. The rich farmland was irrigated by ancient *kerezes* which were terraced throughout the valley as it descended down towards Kabul.

The terrain was also a guerrilla commander's dream. Regular army military posts were located in the various towns along the river which wended its way through the center of the valley. Guerrilla bands could swoop down on them and as quickly vanish up into the many side valleys, safe from counterattack by land or air.

When a journalist or other visitor finally reached one of the many camps set up by Masood's mujahaddin, he would frequently have to wait days for the elusive commander to make an appearance. When Masood did arrive, he would share tea or a light repast, talk for an hour or so, and just as mysteriously disappear.[2] Few journalists were ever granted more time by the Lion of the Panjsher. Richard MacKenzie of *Insight Magazine* was one of them, and he became a great admirer of Masood, much as I was of Abdul Haq.

Having survived the ordeal of the trip into the Panjsher, a visit with Masood was tantamount to a royal audience, which seemed to immunize him from the usual journalistic grilling about his policies or tactics. Moreover, captive audiences (literally) needed his support for the rigorous month-long trip back to Pakistan. I don't remember ever having seen a report even slightly critical of Masood, a situation that led many to believe that Masood was the overall commander of the mujahaddin.[3]

Since much of Afghanistan was snowed in during the winter months, the heaviest fighting generally occurred in the spring and summer. Mujahaddin and Soviet commanders alike supplied their outposts in the early fall sufficiently to last nearly five months.

In September 1986, reports from Abdul Haq's network within the regime's Defense Ministry revealed that the Soviets had amassed a huge supply of munitions at the 4th Division headquarters in Darulaman on the outskirts of Kabul. These munitions were to be distributed nationwide before winter set in. Unable to interdict them along the Salang pass without being forced to confront Masood's defenders directly, Abdul Haq decided to attack the huge military base in Kabul before the deadly supplies were dispersed.

It would not be easy. Over two thousand Soviet and nearly three thousand Afghan army soldiers were garrisoned at the base, the area was protected by an armored battalion, air cover was only minutes away at the Kabul airport, and minefields encircled the base in a strip over a kilometer wide.

Abdul made his plans carefully. It would have to be a small, but potent operation. He had precise information on where and how the various rockets, bombs, and other munitions were stored and he knew the exact routines of the perimeter guards and of activities inside the base, which was located alongside Kabul's Lake Qarga.

For three weeks he moved men and material into his main *markaz* (base camp) in Jalrez, twenty miles southwest of Kabul, in small groups so as not to alert the KGB or KhAD. From Jalrez, small attack groups fanned out to Paghman and Arghandeh close to the base. Their assignment was diversionary.

At dusk on October 19th, Abdul Haq and three of his men crossed the Paghman plain near Lake Qarga to within five hundred meters of the outside wall of the base near the main gate, where there was heavy traffic. The four men carried a rocket launcher and three 103mm rockets. At 9:00 P.M. they began setting up the heavy launcher just as the assault troops started to shell the western side of the base with rockets and mortars. From a small rise in the terrain, Abdul Haq could see into the base.

At 9:45, with the base guard occupied by the mortars, he fired his first rocket. It sailed one hundred feet over the bunker, his target, and landed half a kilometer beyond the base. He adjusted the sights, loaded a second rocket, and fired again. It missed, ten feet to the left of the bunker.

His third and final shell was an incendiary rocket. At exactly 10:00 P.M. he fired. The rocket slammed into the door of the bunker. Nothing happened. He had *seen* it tear through the metal door. Minutes later—an eternity—a small fire erupted behind where the door had been. Then an explosion, and the entire bunker blew apart. Smaller bursts of flame spewed out of the bunker like giant fireworks.

As Abdul Haq and his three men raced back towards Paghman, a tremendous eruption shook the ground beneath them, like a major earthquake. The entire sky over Kabul lit up with the brightness of a midday sun. A huge fireball rose a thousand feet over the city, seemingly held aloft by a gigantic mushroom cloud. The roar of the blast echoed back and forth from the mountains ringing the city. Abdul Haq and his men couldn't breathe as the oxygen was sucked out of the air around them, but they continued running with the heat from the inferno searing their backs. Minutes later a second monster blast—the entire Kabul valley seemed to vibrate once again. And another imposing fireball and mushroom cloud shot up into the sky.

Reaching the outskirts of Paghman, exhausted, they looked back at what they had wrought. The base was afire, with dozens of secondary explosions occurring every few minutes until well past daybreak.

Over the next several days word got out about the extent of the damage. Over one thousand Soviet and regime soldiers had been killed, and the hospitals and schoolrooms were filled with the wounded. Najib and two members of his cabinet had left the base only half an hour before the attack. Multimillions of rubles worth of bombs, rockets, and munitions had exploded in their faces—an entire winter's supply gone in a few short hours. Nearly every glass window in the city had been shattered. It was the largest and most destructive mujahaddin operation of the entire war.

Diplomats, journalists, and others began speculating about what had happened. One story told at the American Club in Peshawar by British war correspondents had it—on the very best authority—that the perpetrators of the inside job had thrown satchel bombs into trucks entering the base. An American diplomat, with equal certainty, told a news backgrounder that an Afghan army general, a rival of Najib, had done it from inside the base. The regime announced that a campfire at the base had gotten out of control. Not to be left out, Gulbaddin's Hezb-i-Islami magazine took credit saying that Gulbaddin himself had directed the massive operation with five hundred of his men. Unknown to them all, the operation had been videotaped.

The British Embassy was located in a section of Kabul which overlooked the base at Darulaman. Abdul Haq had asked a British agent in Peshawar to inform the people at the embassy to watch the base on the night of the 19th. They did, and Michael Reagan of the embassy staff had a video camera.

Shortly after the Qarga explosions, I was given the videotape by a British diplomat. They also sent copies of the tape to the U.S. Embassy, which in turn provided a copy to Saul Gefter of the USIA. Back in Washington I had the tape transferred to the American video system, called Steve Glauber, producer on my latest story, and asked him to hold the story—I had something on the Qarga explosions.

When Glauber took a look at what appeared to be a nuclear explosion, he was elated—the explosion was included in the CBS News. From that time on, I was point man for the Afghan story at CBS. And Abdul Haq's reputation skyrocketed like the fireballs he had caused.

The event severely shook the rulers in Kabul. Within weeks the Soviet command in Kabul was shaken up, and General Boris Gromov was given overall command of Afghanistan. Najib had three top generals arrested and personally took command of the Defense Ministry. Not only had the loss been expensive, but the Soviets were unable to supply their major commands, which allowed the mujahaddin to strike harder in the winter and spring of 1987. The damage to the morale of the regime's army, moreover, was enormous. The number of desertions in Kabul and Logar provinces increased dramatically. One mujahaddin commander, Agha Jan, reported that he had more deserters from the Afghan army than original mujahaddin in his group.

The successes of the mujahaddin during 1986 began to have a profound effect on the Soviets. During a visit to India late in the year, Mikhail Gorbachev described the Soviet adventure in Afghanistan as "a bleeding wound." The UN-sponsored proximity talks between Pakistan and the Afghan regime began to receive serious diplomatic attention.

Perhaps most important, following the attack on Qarga, the Soviet media began to devote much more attention to the war. The Soviet magazine *Orgoniok* ran a series of articles, written by Artyom Borovak, which actually described the condition of Soviet soldiers in the faraway wasteland of Afghanistan. The articles, moreover, had an antiwar tone, unheard of in previous Soviet propaganda. Artyom, son of a well-known Soviet propagandist, represented himself as an independent journalist, although the two encounters I later had with him made his self-description dubious. All that aside, by late 1986 the Soviets were unquestionably beginning to rethink their Afghanistan venture.

The Soviets had not won the hearts and minds of the people of Afghanistan. The decisions by Ronald Reagan and William Casey to up the ante and drive a hard bargain with the Soviets was working well, at least within Afghanistan. But in the end, the situation of the superpowers was being determined by the Afghans themselves. And they continued to fight, bravely and successfully.

CHAPTER 23

Money is the Root of All Evil

Force and fraud are in war the two cardinal virtues.

—THOMAS HOBBES, 1588–1679

The Afghan people had two of the most important ingredients for resistance—the motivation to liberate their country, and the manpower to do so. All Afghan children are regaled with tales from their history of repelling foreign invaders. They are proud of being a militant culture. From the day the first Soviet soldier set foot in Afghanistan, the mujahaddin Resistance had more men willing to take arms than it could use. What the muj needed and could not provide were guns and butter—weapons with which to fight the invading army and food to supply their fighters and feed the millions of refugees. A variety of U.S. government agencies stepped in to fill these needs. It was not a simple operation.

Early in the war, the American CIA and Pakistani ISI decided that Warsaw Pact weaponry would be used. The reason was twofold. First, in the early stages of the war, most of the weapons used by the mujahaddin were captured from the government which was being supplied by the Soviet Union, or from Soviet units themselves. Secondly, although the whole world knew the United States was backing the Resistance, some people in Washington didn't want American or NATO weaponry used directly against the Soviet army.

Brezhnev's people, on the other hand, didn't care what type of weapons they used to kill freedom fighters.

Although it did not figure in the decision not to use American weapons, there was another good reason. Soviet small arms—Kalashnikovs (AK47 assault rifles), dashikas (heavy machine guns), makarovs (pistols), and so on—were designed to be "peasant proof" and were used around the world by Marxist insurgency groups. An AK47, for example, breaks down into just four pieces that cannot be reassembled incorrectly. Soviet small arms work even if wet, dirty, or grimy. American-made M-14s and M-16s are not so reliable and require considerable training to clean and repair.

To supply an army the size of the mujahaddin to fight in a country the size of Texas with Soviet-style weaponry was not easy. Bill Casey's procurers began scouring the globe.[1] The first cache of Warsaw Pact weapons was found in Egypt. Israel also had a supply, some captured during the Six-Day War and others from Palestinians in Lebanon. But it was not enough. Following upon an arrangement with China instigated by former Defense Secretary Harold Brown, and using the ISI as go-between, the CIA contracted with the Chinese government to manufacture rocket launchers, AK47s, and heavy machine guns. Much of the purchasing of weapons was handled government-to-government, with the CIA dealing directly with the Chinese, Egyptian, and even Polish governments. A great deal more was thrown to the open arms market.

As word got out to the international subculture of smugglers, gun runners, and arms dealers that the CIA had a blank check to purchase Soviet-style weaponry and ammunition, a bizarre international bazaar took form. The Bank of Credit and Commerce International handled the financing, which involved hundreds of millions of American and Saudi-supplied dollars.[2] BCCI was later described by Casey's successor Robert Gates as "the bank of crooks and criminals international." Because Saudi and American funding was commingled in various "Afghan

War" accounts, accounting also entered the realm of "plausible deniability."[3]

The founder and chief executive officer of BCCI was Agha Hasan Abedi, a Pakistani banker from Karachi. In addition to Abedi, BCCI's major owners were Saudi and Emirate Arab political and banking figures. Abedi kept close ties with Pakistani President Zia and ISI director General Acktar. Any high-ranking Pakistani military officer who retired was immediately given a position with BCCI upon Acktar's request. Since Acktar handled the supply network to the Afghans, BCCI was as important a link to the CIA as his personal relationship with Bill Casey.

Casey undertook a variety of operations described as "off the books"—not accounted for in detail by the CIA's record-keeping apparatus. He referred to them as jobs undertaken in his role as advisor to the president. BCCI was used to provide similar "off the books" assistance. This was later documented in the Iran-Contra affair and in the Senate Foreign Relations Subcommittee investigation of BCCI.

Big- and small-time arms dealers all tried to get in on the act. Many did. Perhaps the biggest was Adnan Khashoggi, a Saudi arms dealer and businessman who openly fronted for the Saudi government in much of his operations. Khashoggi had a two-pronged role in supplying arms to the Afghan mujahaddin. He was involved in procuring and redistributing weapons and munitions to the mujahaddin through Pakistan's ISI logistics network. And he was a watchdog on the expenditure of Saudi funds for such hardware. In this capacity he worked as an agent for Prince Turki, director of Saudi Arabia's Intelligence Agency and nephew of King Fahd. Over the course of the war, it has been reliably reported that Prince Turki distributed over $1 billion in cash through BCCI and Pakistan's ISI to the mujahaddin.[4]

Arms dealers were contracted to supply weapons to the mujahaddin through the port of Karachi.[5] Many of them supplied the Nicaraguan contras as well. At least one contract obtained by Adnan Khashoggi called for NATO-type weapons to be sent to Honduras for the contras and Warsaw Pact weapons to

Afghanistan for the mujahaddin—paid out of a single BCCI account. This particular deal was made although the Boland Amendment prohibited lethal weapons from being sent to Nicaragua. But Khashoggi argued that the account was actually two: the Nicaraguan portion of the contract was paid by the Saudi funds in the account; and the Afghan portion was paid by the American funds.[6] Most lawyers would contend that commingled funds cannot be separated.

BCCI was also reported to have moved money to the mujahaddin through the National Bank of Oman, 29 percent of which was owned by BCCI.[7] The *Wall Street Journal* (October 23, 1991) quoted a member of President Zia ul-Haq's cabinet as saying, "It was Arab money that was pouring through BCCI. The bank which carried money from Oman to Pakistan and into Afghanistan was the National Bank of Oman." The Bank of Oman had a large branch in Peshawar.[8]

By late 1986 there were so many agencies spending and distributing so many hundreds of millions of dollars for so many countries that no agency could keep track of it all.

The Brezhnev Doctrine, promulgated after the ill-fated Prague Spring, declared that any state that had once gone socialist would never be permitted to revert to its original form of government or to any other; e.g., Eastern Europe, Cuba, North Korea, Ethiopia, Afghanistan, and so on. The Soviets could aggress—as witness the "liberation" movements around the world—but not the free world. The Reagan (Casey) Doctrine declared that no such communist de facto conquests should or would go unchallenged. It insisted on combatting and rolling back the communist acquisitions and thrusts wherever they occurred; e.g., Nicaragua, El Salvador, Angola, Mozambique, Afghanistan. It was a worldwide struggle.

In a conversation with me in 1985, Bill Casey compared countering communist revolutions to a football game. Separating policy in Nicaragua from Afghanistan, he maintained, would be like putting two running backs on the same football team in different uniforms and on separate playing fields. He was the coach of one team on one large playing field. When he offered me the analogy, I told him of a speech I had attended in 1960 at which Congressman Walter Judd gave a similar description in talking about an alleged rift between Mao Tse-Tung and Nikita Khrushchev. Judd said, "When the right halfback runs off in one direction and the left halfback goes in another, you don't say, 'They got their signals crossed.' Those *were* the signals."

This helps explain the international nature and intricacies of the financial operation. Arms dealers such as Khashoggi were used in most of the CIA and Saudi Intelligence operations as a normal way of doing business. Khashoggi, using BCCI to transfer funds and contracts, was also important in the Iran-Contra arms deals in 1986. Lieutenant Colonel Oliver North of the NSC staff used him to provide weapons to Iran and the contras.[9] It was all part of a single worldwide policy. Khashoggi had a single American client, the CIA.

In 1985, Eden Pastora, the picturesque Commandante Zero of the Nicaraguan contras, compared wars with Abdul Haq. Both had attended a banquet in Washington in March honoring freedom fighters around the world. I translated from the Spanish. Pastora said he first became aware the CIA was cutting him off from its supply network when Khashoggi's representatives stopped socializing over drinks with him in Costa Rica. Pastora's "crime" was that he was insufficiently subservient to CIA liaison officers. As the single most successful commander to fight against Anastasio Somoza, he felt that he could conduct his own operations without CIA control, that he knew his own country better than the newly arrived Americans—rank insubordination.

In short, passage of the Boland Amendment which prohibited the CIA from providing lethal support to the contras had no seeming effect. The CIA simply asked the Saudis to pick up the tab. They did for a time, allegedly through the BCCI accounts.

Widely circulated rumors claimed that huge amounts of weaponry—from 30 to 50 percent, according to members of the Senate Foreign Relations Committee—slated for the mujahaddin did not reach Pakistan. One administration official was

. quoted in the *New York Times* (March 27, 1987) as saying, "It is true that there still isn't enough accountability. There is still a need for better monitoring."

The stories prompted Representative William Gray, chairman of the House Budget Committee, to request a Government Accounting Office investigation. Gray said, "If funds have indeed been diverted . . . we want to be informed of the amounts involved and the eventual recipients." The result of the audit, given to Congressman Gray and the committee, is still highly classified.

Once the weapons were manufactured, purchased, and shipped to Pakistan, it was up to the ISI to get them to the Afghan commanders.

Unlike Angola and Nicaragua, where the CIA dealt personally with UNITA and the contras,[10] the CIA, for the most part, kept its distance from the mujahaddin until 1985. U.S. money, weapons, and military expertise, and even CIA's satellite reconnaissance and Soviet military communications intercepts, were funneled through the Pakistani ISI.[11] Rumors soon arose that a percentage of weapons and money was being siphoned off by Pakistani generals.

In Pakistan, General Acktar's deputy, General Mohammed Yousaf, was in charge of the day-to-day activities of ISI. Several dozen of Yousaf's ISI personnel were trained by the CIA in guerrilla and urban warfare. They in turn ran training camps for the Afghans. Yousaf and his top commanders planned attacks, battles, and specific operations for the mujahaddin, relying on information supplied by the CIA. Frequently, ISI officers would accompany the mujahaddin on these operations.[12]

In 1985–86, the American escalation of supplies coincided with the escalation of hostilities by the Soviets in an attempt to end the war. While many in the State Department were giving up hope for the mujahaddin, and elements in the CIA were reluctant to improve the quality of support, several congressional friends of Afghanistan (Charles Wilson, Gordon Humphrey, Orrin Hatch, Bill Bradley) began to push for stronger military aid for the Resistance. This pressure, along with Bill Casey's approval, led to the signing of National Security Directive 166 by the president, which raised the level of assistance significantly. "Bud" McFarlane changed the discussion within the Intelligence community from the Carter doctrine of "harassing" the Soviets to one of actually defeating the Soviet military.

Whether from China, the Middle East, Eastern Europe (including Czechoslovakia), or CIA weapons plants in the U.S., all materials were shipped by boat to the port of Karachi, or by cargo plane to Pakistani air force bases. From there they were trucked by Pakistani NLC (National Logistics Cell) trucks to various arms depots, from which Afghan commanders would pick up their allotments. Occasionally large shipments would be trucked directly to Afghan depots in Landi Khotal, Miram Shah, Teri Mangal, Quetta, and other locations right on the Afghan border.

The tons of munitions were treated cavalierly by Pakistanis and Afghans alike, haphazardly stacked up in crudely crafted bunkers, which caused several accidents. One occurred at a Jamiat depot near Chitral during the winter of 1987. Rooms full of rockets and thousands of boxes of bullets were to be transported by mule caravans to Commander Masood. The compound also housed several Soviet prisoners of the Jamiat. One night the Soviet prisoners revolted, and the mujahaddin surrounded the prison building. Several of the Soviet soldiers climbed to the roof of the building with a couple of rifles and an RPG (rocket-propelled grenade) they had gotten hold of, as two Pakistani ISI officers arrived to take charge.

There were conflicting reports as to who fired first, the Paks, the muj, or the Soviet POWs. It became irrelevant when after several shots, the entire compound exploded, killing the Soviets, two Pakistanis, and several Jamiat mujahaddin.

The most significant explosion brought down the government of Pakistani Prime Minister Mohammad Khan Junejo.

On April 12, 1988, I received a midday phone call at my home in Peshawar. It was a Pakistani newspaper reporter with whom I had covered several stories in Islamabad, where he then was. In a tense voice trembling with fear, he shouted, "The bombs, Mr. Kurt, the bombs are raining down upon us this very moment as we speak. It must be an attack from India." I tried to calm him down and find out what he was talking about. It was impossible. He was screaming that bombs were going off all around him in Pakistan's capital city.

I hung up the phone and called the U.S. Embassy and was told by Ed Abington of the political section that, indeed, there were repeated explosions in the twin cities of Rawalpindi and Islamabad. Although no one at the embassy knew what was happening, they were discounting an attack from India. A phone call to the Pakistani Information Ministry suggested that a coup was in progress against President General Zia ul-Haq, "but this of course cannot be confirmed." I jumped in my jeep and headed for Islamabad.

Two hours later as I approached the capital city I found that all roads had been closed by military roadblocks, but I was able to convince them I was a foreigner, maybe even of the official variety, and was allowed to pass. A large black cloud hovered over the area between the congested urban area of Rawalpindi and the more serene government complex of Islamabad. In the distance, I could hear occasional explosions. Pakistani civilian citizens were scurrying about in no particular direction, with women crying and everyone scared witless.

I saw one military roadblock with jeeps and tanks and several high-ranking officers. Arriving at the command center of the roadblock I spotted Lieutenant General Imran Khan, a corps commander whom I had met previously. He recognized me and welcomed me with a grin. "You don't have to go to Afghanistan for war today," he said, and laughed. I didn't see the humor. Then he explained that there was no attack from India, no military coup—ISI's main ammunition dump had blown sky high. Thousands of rockets had exploded and rained down upon the two cities. Most of them were thrown into the air and propelled several kilometers, not by erupting, but from the force of the ammunition blasting off. Rockets by the hundreds were lying around roads, residential areas, schoolyards, and government parking lots just waiting to explode. An army officer told me that hundred of others had gone off and killed dozens of people.

General Imran took me to the site of the blazing depot as I videotaped, thinking that surely more than just "dozens" had been killed. The general speculated that the KhAD or KGB had committed sabotage. I later learned that a good friend, mujahaddin commander Mir Zaman from Kunar Province, had been instantly killed while picking up a shipment of munitions for his region.

For the next several days the blast was the only news in Pakistan. Some members of Parliament were outspokenly critical of ISI for storing such weapons, and in such quantity, in highly populated areas.

Prime Minister Mohammad Khan Junejo had been on a state visit to Korea when the incident occurred. Before rushing back to Islamabad, he communicated to his office that he was going to suspend the top-ranking military officers of the country and conduct a thorough investigation, but President Zia and General Acktar had no intention of permitting such a probe. When Junejo arrived, he was informed that Zia had dissolved Parliament and that he was no longer prime minister. New elections would perhaps be held in ninety days.

Numerous theories cropped up about the cause of the havoc. Many blamed the Soviet and Afghan governments; rival mujahaddin factions blamed each other. One little heralded report caught my attention. A team of auditors from the Inspector General's office of the U.S. Defense Department had been scheduled to arrive in Pakistan to conduct an audit of weapons going to the mujahaddin. For years, Pakistan had been rife with rumors that top military figures were skimming weapons from the mujahaddin and selling them elsewhere, including the highly secret Stinger missiles. It seemed convenient that the major ammo dump in the country would blow up just days before an American military audit. The truth will never be known. President Zia and General Acktar were killed four short months later.

CHAPTER 24

Chaos and Confusion

The weak have one weapon: the errors of those who think they are strong.

—GEORGE BIDAULT, 1899–1983

By early 1987 it was evident that there were deep divisions within the Soviet government over their predicament in Afghanistan.

In addition to occasional Soviet media reports disparaging the Afghan policy, Mikhail Gorbachev and others in the Soviet hierarchy began to speak of withdrawing from Afghanistan. But during this same time period the Soviet army again stepped up military activities throughout the country, and KGB operations spilled over the border into Pakistan.

Terrorist bombings became commonplace in Peshawar and other Pakistani border spots, during which hundreds of Pakistanis and Afghan refugees were killed. KGB and KhAD terrorist groups were responsible, according to a State Department news release, for over 235 civilian murders in Pakistan during 1987, more than all other terrorists activities in the world combined; the Afghan KhAD made the Palestinians look like amateurs. Cross-border bombings by Soviet and Afghan regime aircraft also increased.

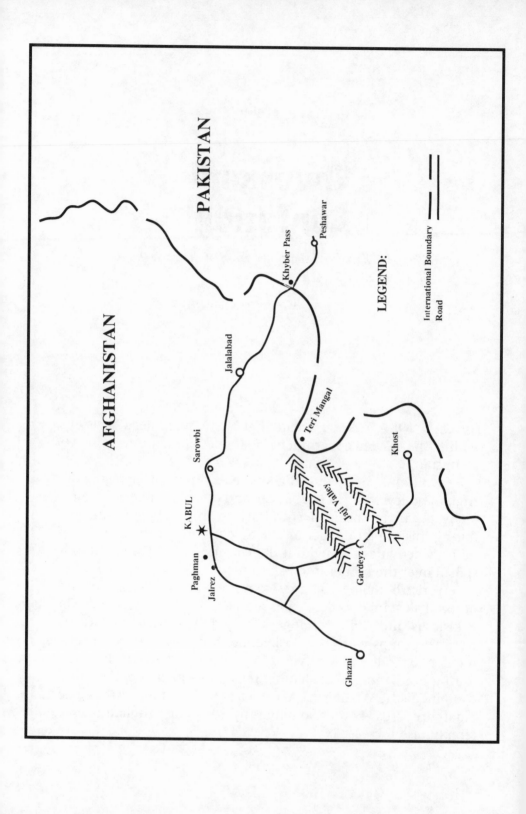

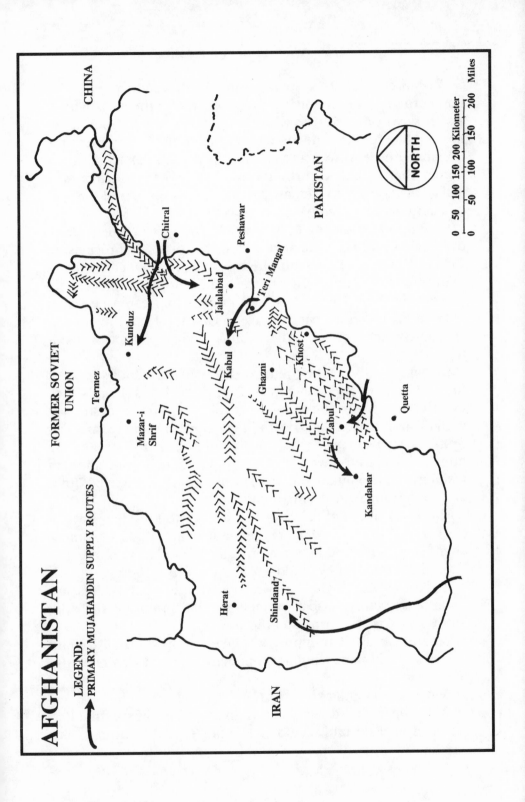

On March 23, 1987, Soviet bombers attacked the Pakistani border town of Teri Mangal, a supply center for the mujahaddin. At the downside of a pass which curled through the mountains into Paktia Province, the town was strategically important to the mujahaddin because it was at the tip of a finger twist in the border that extended further west into Afghanistan than Jalalabad. Crossing into Afghanistan at Teri Mangal saved the mujahaddin days or even weeks of travel time.

Early in the morning of March 23, three jet bombers swept over the border and unloaded dozens of bombs and rockets on the bazaar area. Over a hundred people were killed, twice as many injured. Hundred of horses, mules, and donkeys were destroyed. Shops, teahouses, and mujahaddin campsites were obliterated. It was a clear message to Pakistan from the Soviets: "If you continue to support the mujahaddin, you too will suffer."

Arriving on the scene the next day with CBS correspondent Richard Wagner and cameraman Derrick Williams, I was struck by a sharply contrasting picture. The town was utterly destroyed, with the pungent smell of death permeating the air, the carcasses of animals lying exposed to the high mountain sunshine. Yet, the mujahaddin groups were quietly going about the business of loading their supply caravans as if nothing had happened. Within days Teri Mangal was being rebuilt.

The government of Pakistan sent a letter to President Reagan asking that the United States lease several AWAC or similar aircraft so they could better protect their border. By offering to lease the aircraft, they could avoid a fight in Congress,[1] and it would allow American crews to operate the aircraft. Besides, Defense Secretary Caspar Weinberger had promised such defenses to Pakistan during an official visit in late 1986.

Senator Gordon Humphrey was given a copy of the Pakistani letter and he became a public proponent of providing air defense to Pakistan.

Two weeks later, Pakistan announced that one of its F-16 aircraft had been shot down by an Afghan jet (one of six) that had intruded on Pakistani territory. The news was confirmed with pride by the Afghan government.[2] But according to Steven Weisman of the *New York Times*, reporting from Kabul, the Afghan government said the plane had been hit and crashed inside Afghanistan near Khost.

The Pakistanis and their friends on Capitol Hill—Gordon Humphrey, Charlie Wilson, and others—began pushing to provide early warning aircraft to Pakistan. The incident of the Pakistani jet allegedly shot down by a missile while chasing Afghan aircraft out of their country was promoted as a perfect example of why such defenses were needed. Within months, the United States had provided Pakistan with Orion aircraft equipped with early warning radars. These U.S. navy aircraft were a downsized version of the AWAC.

The incident of the F-16 downing received major news coverage in Pakistan. The American jet was considered top of the line. If they were vulnerable to MIG-29 or SU-25 attack, it would seriously shake Pakistan's feeling of security vis-à-vis neighboring India, which had a stableful of such Soviet aircraft. The Pentagon and the U.S. air force should also have been concerned.

I contacted the Peshawar office of mujahaddin commander Jalaluddin Haqani, whose mujahaddin were in control of Paktia Province, including the Khost district. I asked if they could take me to see the downed Pakistani jet in the Khost district. They said they would contact Haqani and get back to me. The next morning one of Haqani's top subcommanders called to ask me to come to their office. There I was told not to quote them, but that Haqani's field headquarters in Paktia had sent a radio message stating there was no such crash site near Khost or anywhere else in the province. They had mujahaddin positioned throughout, and if a plane had been downed, they would know about it. But since the Pakistanis said the incident had occurred, Commander Haqani thought it the better part of wisdom not to deny it. Somebody had taught the Afghans the art of "plausible deniability."

My inquiries to American officials, overt and covert, drew a blank. Nobody was talking. The only news came from the public releases issued by the Pakistani government and the State Department.

I learned no more about the incident until late July 1987 when I heard that the *Los Angeles Times* had run a paragraph buried in a Sunday, July 19, story on Afghanistan. The paragraph read: "A Pakistani air force F-16 accidentally shot down a companion F-16 previously reported to have been hit by a Soviet-made missile last May in combat over Afghanistan, U.S. sources said. 'It was pilot error,' a U.S. intelligence source said of the fighter's loss. Following the incident, Administration aides quoted Pakistani counterparts as announcing that six Soviet-made Afghan aircraft had entered Pakistani airspace and that two Pakistani jets chased them back across the border. In so doing, one of the Afghan jets downed the F-16 with an air-to-air missile, Pakistani officials were quoted as saying. Administration sources said some Pentagon and State Department officials aided in the cover-up." I began to wonder if any government, anywhere, knew how to tell the truth.

The Afghan government knew, of course, that they had not shot down the Pakistani F-16. But when they were given credit, they decided to up the propaganda ante. The next week, in May, they announced that an Afghan civilian airliner had been shot down by an American Stinger missile killing thirty-six civilians, mostly children. The so-called civilian airliner was "on a regularly scheduled route from Kabul to Khost," never mind that there were no such things as civilian flights to Khost, or anywhere else in Afghanistan outside of Kabul. Khost, a border town, was at the time under a total siege by the mujahaddin. Two Antonov 26 military transport planes had been shot down by the mujahaddin in the spring of 1987.

On May 7, the Afghan government took three dozen foreign reporters to Khost. The military planes transporting the journalists spewed antimissile flares as they spiralled down to the airport in a maneuver to avoid ground missiles. The journalists were then taken to the alleged crash site of the "civilian airliner."[3] The Afghan communist officials could not explain why the civilian airliner was painted in military camouflage and outfitted for military transport. Despite this farce, the regime received worldwide sympathy for the innocent children.

These propaganda wars were going on at a time when the political divisiveness in Moscow and Kabul was coming to a head. On April 30, the director of the KGB, Viktor Chebrikov, visited Afghanistan. He took a tour of border posts—the KGB was in charge of border security—which had recently been under attack by the mujahaddin, and announced that the Soviets would never abandon their Afghan brothers. That same week Gorbachev said they would withdraw as soon as possible.

In Kabul the political turmoil was out in the open. In the first week of May, former Afghan President Babrak Karmal, ousted in 1986 and replaced by Najib, was arrested and, according to the Chinese government, incarcerated in the Pul-i-charki jail.[4] They cited their own diplomats in Kabul as the source of the reports. Several days later the Kabul government announced that Babrak had traveled to Moscow for "medical treatment."

Abdul Haq issued a "situation report" on the political situation in Kabul, gleaned from runners in his network in the city who smuggled information out to him. It stated that a power struggle was taking place between the Parchamis and the Khalqi factions of the Afghan communists, and Babrak had been removed so as to give absolute control of the Parcham faction to Najib. While Najib's clique within the Parcham faction was controlling the regime, Abdul Haq reported, General Mohammad Gulabzoi, a top Khalqi, had gained greater power in the ruling council and several top Khalqis were released from prison. Moreover, Babrak's brother Baryalai remained in the ruling Parcham council. Abdul Haq's network reported that the primary reason for KGB chief Chebrikov's visit to Afghanistan was to straighten out the feuding Afghan communist factions.

In the spring of 1987 Najib began to promote his new program of "National Reconciliation." In a grandiose gesture, he offered to share power with any dissident who would lay down his arms and join his government. In short order, the regime began to issue names of mujahaddin commanders who had accepted the offer. None was real. At this point, a new ministry of National Reconciliation was created and it was announced that "powerful nonparty figures such as Ismat Musleem and Abdul Rashid Dostam have joined the government." The two men were leaders of mercenary militias, paid by the regime for years to fight the mujahaddin.

All this was timed to coincide with renewed interest in the United Nations-sponsored negotiations. Originally convened by Secretary General Javier Perez de Cuellar in 1980, the talks were meaningless until March 1987 when the Soviets, through their Afghan puppets, suddenly proposed a withdrawal of troops—a full withdrawal, 115,000 at that time—within eighteen months. The Soviet side and the Americans, through the Pakistanis, had already agreed to end outside interference once the Soviet withdrawal actually started. But there was one big obstacle to a diplomatic settlement—the makeup of the Afghan government after the Soviets withdrew.[5]

The mujahaddin would never consent to allowing the present regime to continue to rule the country. They had fought the war; they wanted to win the victory.

Another issue that concerned the mujahaddin was the favoritism shown to Gulbaddin at the expense of the real fighting forces. In this they had a champion, Pakistani Foreign Minister Sahabzada Yaqub Khan. He was the lead negotiator for the Pakistan/American side of the proximity talks. The tall, ramrod-straight retired general was highly respected throughout the diplomatic world. He had been a full participant in Zia's coup d'état against Zulfikar Ali Bhutto and was now the sole opponent within Zia's inner circle of the policy favoring Gulbaddin Hekmatyar. Yaqub privately wished for a more modern and secular Pakistan, and he was appalled at the influence of the mullahs and the militant Jammat Islami over policy making in Pakistan.

But while Yaqub Khan was Zia's point man in international relations, he was out of the loop in the area of supply and support to the mujahaddin. So he used his influence in the UN talks to push for a settlement which would assure a broad-based government for a postcommunist Afghanistan.

Yaqub Khan's key deputy on the Afghan issue was Najmuddin Sheik, who was director of the American desk in the Foreign

Ministry. Najmuddin attended nearly all of the Geneva negotiations.

In March of 1987, Yaqub Khan instructed Najmuddin to accept in principle the proposal from the communists regarding a timetable for Soviet troop withdrawal, but to hold out strongly for a broad-based government to replace Najib's regime—not, that is, to include it.[6]

In a background briefing in Islamabad, Najmuddin stated that Kabul would have to become more "flexible in sharing power with non-Communists before national reconciliation [could be] taken seriously." The Pakistanis, he went on, would not push the mujahaddin or the Afghan refugees to accept the present communist government.

At the same time as the Pakistani diplomats were insisting that the mujahaddin take part in any future government, they were careful not to confront the Soviets directly. Yaqub Khan stated publicly, and Najmuddin privately, that at the Geneva talks, Pakistan was attempting to allow for a Soviet troop withdrawal leaving the puppet regime in place. (The mujahaddin, of course, interpreted "broad-based" as meaning inclusion of the various mujahaddin groups only.) "We are quite clear that there has to be an honorable peace," stated Najmuddin. "A superpower is not going to be humiliated in Afghanistan," he continued. "Afghanistan in the future should also not become the kind of a base that in any way threatens Soviet security."

In early 1987 the Pakistanis were optimistic that a settlement could be reached over Afghanistan. But, as mentioned, they were receiving conflicting signals from the Soviets. Yuri Vorontzov, deputy foreign minister to Edvaurd Shevardnadze and a frequent diplomatic visitor to Islamabad, conveyed Gorbachev's wish to get out of Afghanistan without appearing to have been defeated. It was the Soviet's turn to seek what Richard Nixon and Henry Kissinger called "peace with honor" in Vietnam. But while the Kremlin political leadership was looking for a way out, the military and the KGB, e.g., Chebrikov, were hell-bent on military victory.

To this end, increased numbers of *spetznaz* troops were deployed to the country. The *spetznaz*—elite commando troops similar to the Green Berets—operated in small groups and tried to get behind the lines to disrupt mujahaddin supply routes and assault their *markazes*, or camps. For the most part they were unsuccessful, primarily because the guerrilla tactics of the mujahaddin did not call for "lines of battle." Russians dressed in the local *shalwar kameez* fooled nobody. More often than not, they fell victim to mujahaddin ambushes rather than the other way around.

Soviet bombing also increased dramatically in 1987, but by this time there wasn't much left to bomb. In one trip from the Pakistani border to the outskirts of Kabul, I traveled through dozens of villages. None was inhabited, all were destroyed. The purpose was to deprive the mujahaddin of the support offered by the villagers, and this they achieved.

By the end of May the Geneva talks which had held so much promise earlier in the year appeared to fall apart over the issue of a postcommunist broad-based government. Secretary of State George Shultz in early May stated that the United States had called upon India—the only non-Soviet bloc country to continue friendly relations with Kabul—to pressure Kabul to compromise. But he was rudely rebuffed when the Indian Foreign Ministry announced that it was "unrealistic to expect Kabul to be anything but dominated by the People's Democratic party" and that "The Soviet Union is entitled to a friendly Government at its southern border." Mujahaddin leader Younas Khalis shot back: "Afghanistan is 800 miles from the Russian border. They have already annexed the Wakhan Corridor into the Soviet Union. [If] India want[s] a friendly government on this border, that would be Pakistan." What Khalis meant, of course, was that the Russians wanted land adjacent to theirs on a continuing basis, that is, all land—everywhere.

The talks scheduled in Geneva for the last week of May were canceled. A Western diplomat in Kabul was quoted as saying,

"The light has receded farther back into the tunnel. In my opinion, the Russians would like to get out of Afghanistan, but they don't know how. And we in the West would like to cooperate and help them, but we don't know how either."

The Soviets began floating the name of former King Zahir Shah as taking some part in a settlement. Mikhail Gorbachev told the Italian communist newspaper *L'Unita* that Moscow could accept the king in a coalition government. While the parties of Gailani and Mojadeddi had always tended toward the monarchy, none of the other political leaders responded favorably. Abdul Wakil, the regime's foreign minister, said Zahir Shah would be welcome in Kabul, but that the PDPA would continue to run the country.

By this time the war was over eight years old. Many among the millions of refugees began hoping the king would assert himself and take a leadership role. They remembered the days of peace, nearly two decades before, when he had sat on the throne in Kabul. But the royal gambit, whether by the Soviets or Mahaz, was not relevant to the battlefields of Afghanistan, where the killing continued. Zahir Shah was sitting comfortably in Rome and had passed up every opportunity to join the fray. Leadership belonged to those who were leading the fight.

The peace talks, in an Orwellian way, involved only Pakistan and the puppet regime in Kabul; they excluded the real parties—the Soviets and the mujahaddin. The seven mujahaddin parties felt with justification that they ought to be participating directly in the Geneva talks. It was they, after all, who were fighting and dying in the national struggle against the Soviet invaders.

In a move to assert leadership, the mujahaddin alliance in late May announced it would hold elections among the refugees and inside Afghanistan to chose an interim government. The message to the Geneva negotiators was clear—the only acceptable solution would be an Islamic Republic of Afghanistan led by the mujahaddin. The alliance, which at the time was headed by Khalis, announced that it would elect a 270-member parliament representing every province in the country and that it would take six months to organize and hold the elections.

The regime reacted quickly: it said that it too would hold elections, in June, to choose representatives to a national reconciliation council. I was on the outskirts of Kabul in the village of Tezin when the regime was conducting these so-called elections. Over the previous two years, Tezin had been depopulated by Soviet ground and air assaults, and several mujahaddin groups used the valley as a staging area for attacks or forays into the city. On the day of the "elections," an air bombardment of the valley began shortly after sunrise and continued throughout the day.

As the attack began, we left our makeshift campsite and moved up a mountain to escape the unusually heavy bombing. Halfway up, we saw bombs raining on our campsite. Our cook who had stayed behind to prepare an evening meal was killed instantly.

Safe on the mountaintop, we waited out the air attacks. I turned my portable shortwave radio to the Radio Afghanistan English report in the early afternoon. The regime announced that the day's elections were proceeding smoothly and that voting was heavy in the Tezin valley. As the announcer read the propaganda, over a dozen 1,000-pound bombs were blowing the few remaining buildings to smithereens. Nobody was left to contest the results of the "elections."

On my return to Pakistan, I learned that Congressman Charlie Wilson was in Islamabad lobbying President Zia on behalf of what Wilson by now called "my mujahaddin."

Charlie Wilson yearned to go inside Afghanistan with the mujahaddin. He wanted to watch them fight the Soviets. He had attended the funeral of more than a hundred young men from his congressional district in Texas who had been killed in Vietnam, and now, in Afghanistan, he said, "I want the Russkies to count bodybags going back to Moscow." He asked me if I could find a commander who would take him "inside."

Abdul Haq agreed to arrange a short trip just over the border at Teri Mangal. Wilson would be taken along with Tony Campaign, who operated the Mercy Fund in Washington, D.C., and Mark

Acuff, an adept journalist with an irreverent sense of humor, both great admirers of the Afghans.

Abdul's men would drive them to Teri Mangal, across the border into Paktia Province for a few hours, and back the next day.

But the ISI got wind of the trip and sent a high-ranking delegation to Abdul Haq's office. "You are absolutely forbidden to take the American congressman into Afghanistan," a Pakistani colonel ordered. Abdul Haq talked the ISI into a deal. Abdul would take the three Americans by jeep about fifty miles down the road from Peshawar towards Teri Mangal. When they reached the tribal territory they would be stopped by another group of mujahaddin and informed that there was trouble ahead between two groups of tribesmen. A firefight was taking place and they would be unable to cross the area. Alas, it would be a great disappointment not to enter Afghanistan, but these crazy tribesmen were frequently such a problem. ISI agreed, but with a warning that nothing had better go wrong!

Decked out in full Afghan regalia—*shalwar kameez, chitrali* hat, and blanket—Charlie Wilson twisted his tall, lanky frame into the jeep. The three Americans and three Afghan escorts left my home at six o'clock in the morning headed for the adventure of war.

Twenty-five miles out of Peshawar they came to the tribal town of Dara Adam Khel. Dara has a worldwide reputation as a center for the manufacture of arms of every size, shape, and calibre. The tribesmen copy AK47s, pistols, rockets, Uzis, Colt 45s, anything. Charlie Wilson, a gun fanatic, needed a weapon before he could go to war. At a gunshop in the Dodge City of Pakistan he purchased a copy of a Soviet Makarov 9mm pistol. As is the custom in Dara, a customer must try out his purchase before the sale is final. The tall clean-shaven American made quite a picture, still remembered, when he went onto the main street of Dara and fired his newly purchased pistol into the air. Satisfied, he spiralled himself back into the jeep and headed into the tribal territory on the border with Afghanistan.

An hour later their jeep was hailed by four young Afghan

warriors on the side of the road. Much shouting and gesticulating took place. Four hours later a chagrined Charlie Wilson dragged himself into my living room, cursing the unruly tribesmen of Pakistan. Wilson immediately called the office of General Acktar, ISI director, and was patched straight through to Pakistan's number two man. Wilson recounted his experience and demanded to be taken into his beloved Afghanistan. Acktar nearly blew the deal by telling Charlie he was too valuable to the mujahaddin and to Pakistan to risk his life in Soviet-occupied Afghanistan. But after much arguing, Acktar promised to send his personal helicopter the next morning to bring Charlie for a meeting with himself and President Zia.

Charlie Wilson asked me to drive him to the American consulate where he would spend the night. On our arrival, we discovered a formal reception in progress in honor of outgoing American Ambassador Dean Hinton. Charlie, looking like the tallest muj in Pakistan with a bandalero and pistol thrown over his shoulder, sneaked up the staircase to avoid the six hundred dinner guests.

As I started to leave, a hand grabbed my arm and a voice boomed, "Let's get out of the way and you tell me what the hell's going on." It was Ambassador Hinton, one of the State Department's best diplomatic troubleshooters, who was headed for El Salvador. But first he wanted to know what had been going on with the most important member of Congress as regards the Afghan War. I told Hinton the complete story, including the ISI deal and the conversation with Acktar. He shook his head in disbelief.

That would have been a fitting end to the Wilson Goes to War in Afghanistan story. Unfortunately, it was merely the prelude.

George Crile, a producer of CBS's "60 Minutes" program, was working on an Afghan story built around Charlie Wilson and had made several trips to Pakistan to do research on the story.

I was planning to call on Crile in Islamabad when I received a report from a muj in Paktia Province that the Pakistani army was moving into Afghanistan near Teri Mangal. I didn't believe it. Pakistan might be the primary supporter of the mujahaddin, but

President Zia would never authorize an invasion of a Soviet-held country. But within hours I received several similar reports. At the office of Commander Haqani's Paktia Front I asked a friend to radio to Paktia Province in Afghanistan and ask what was going on. The report came back: about two hundred ISI troops were in the Jaji valley securing an area about ten miles inside the country.

I called Don Decesare at the foreign desk in New York and was told to investigate further. After calls to every contact I had in the ISI and the army I learned that indeed the sovereign country of Afghanistan was being invaded by a contingent of ISI troops—on behalf of CBS News!

George Crile had arranged to go into Afghanistan with Charlie Wilson and Harry Reasoner to tour a mujahaddin camp and interview Wilson inside Afghanistan. And General Acktar had been true to his word. To prepare for the CBS excursion, a couple of hundred of Acktar's soldiers, dressed in Afghan garb, went into Paktia Province to secure an area for the filming.

I telephoned Decesare and confirmed that an invasion was taking place; we—CBS—were invading Afghanistan with two hundred soldiers, I explained. Decesare went ballistic. He told me to do nothing until I heard from him; he was going to call CBS News President Howard Stringer immediately. About an hour later Decesare called back and told me to just sit tight and pray nothing happened.

The invasion lasted about three hours, and the military force, the camera crews, Crile, Wilson, and Reasoner returned to Pakistan and headed for Islamabad and a few drinks at the embassy. The trip was a featured part of a "60 Minutes" segment.

The Messengers Kill Each Other

Doctors bury their mistakes. Lawyers hang them. But journalists put theirs on the front page.

—ANONYMOUS

Throughout 1987, I made continual trips into Afghanistan. While still low in the priority of American and European news reporting, the coverage was intensifying. The increasing number of freelance journalists that poured in alarmed the Soviets and the Kabul regime, particularly since they felt they were making headway at the Geneva talks. As a result, they made a determined effort to stem the flow of news. Directorate Five of KhAD—the section of the Afghan secret police that operated outside of Afghanistan—was responsible for terrorist activities, assassinations, and covert operations. It was now assigned the task of targeting foreign journalists.

Bounty prices were placed on the heads of certain foreign journalists. The bounties would be paid—dead or alive.[1] The more intrepid of the regulars covering the war were honored with the going price for their deaths or capture: 1 million Afghanis. That was only $5,000, but for those of us on the morbid list—Peter Jouvenal, John Gunston, Richard MacKenzie, and myself—the idea of being worth a million anything was quite invigorating.

Humor aside, the threat was real. Jouvenal and I were the only ones living full-time in Peshawar and making regular trips into Afghanistan with the mujahaddin. Nearly all the other journalists who regularly covered the war lived in the U.S. or Europe in between trips to Pakistan.

One night Peter's house was hit by machine gun fire and a grenade. The local police said not to worry, it was due to a nearby tribal marriage ceremony. While marriage ceremonies in Pakistan and Afghanistan do get raucous, the bullet holes in his wall were not the result of matrimonial enthusiasm. Following the incident we both began employing armed Afghan guards at our homes and cut back greatly on our wanderings about the city.

Jouvenal was quoted in the *Christian Science Monitor* in an article by Ed Girardet, a daring reporter who made several Afghan forays, as saying, "It's a lot riskier now with the threat of spies informing on you or walking into ambushes." The "now" referred to Pakistan; inside Afghanistan was no longer the only risky area.

In August I traveled to the outskirts of Jalalabad with Commander Abdul Qadir, who operated in the areas surrounding the city. French journalist Alain Guillo accompanied me. Alain was a short, mustachioed man with sparkling eyes that revealed a great sense of humor.

We crossed the border north of Teri Mangal with a group of ten muj, including Qadir. Traveling by horseback, we rode straight up alongside a winding, rocky riverbed to the top of the mountains forming the Pakistani-Afghan border. We had left Peshawar during the hot, muggy, oppressive days of summer in the Northwest Frontier Province. Now, within hours of crossing the border, we were riding horses through snow on the peaks. These mountain trails, hundreds of which snaked along the border, followed stream banks and water runoff trails. The travel was treacherous as trails frequently wrapped around mountainsides with sheer dropoffs of many hundreds, occasionally thousands of feet at the edge of the narrow walkways. Men, horses, mules, and donkeys slipped over from time to time. Rescue and/or retrieval was impossible.

As always upon entering Afghanistan the panorama was majestically beautiful. Alain, Qadir, and I were on horseback, but our muj escort were scampering up the mountaintops like goats. These young men were born and reared in these mountains, and it seemed the higher the altitude the stronger and more agile they became. The opposite was true for most Westerners.

Arriving at one of Qadir's *markazes* near Deh Bala on the southern side of Jalalabad we saw one of the reasons the mujahaddin were able to survive in their fight with a superpower army. As we rode into a small clearing among the pine and pinon trees, nothing suggested it was a military base of operations—until fifty or so men came out to greet Qadir, their commander. Close inspection displayed caves, with small entrances, dug into the mountain, each cave housing about ten men. Others were crammed with rockets, missiles, and ammunition. Implanted in the larger trees, much like disguised eagles aeries, were antiaircraft guns. From the ground it would be extremely difficult to spot the base, from the air it would have been impossible.

Sitting around the fire inside a well-dug cave with a fire to keep us warm reminded us of paintings depicting the lifestyle of early cave-dwelling mankind. Alain and I became fast friends. He joked about the meaning of treason in France. Treason, he said, had nothing to do with government secrets or betraying the military but everything to do with an expert wine grower caught taking a flight to California.

During the first week, we joined Qadir's mujahaddin in two assaults on a Soviet/regime outpost at Achin. Returning to the camp one night Qadir announced he was going to attack the main Soviet headquarters next to the airport in Jalalabad the following day. We would leave immediately—it was near midnight—and head to the edges of the city.

We walked the remainder of the night down steep canyon walls and through narrow gorges to the floor of the Nangahar valley within ten miles of Jalalabad. This was the very spot where the Afghan tribes had laid siege to the British army which had been holed up in Jalalabad in the 1840s. In these very gorges, the British force of thousands was wiped out, with the exception of a lone survivor left to tell the story. Walking in the moonlight through the finger arroyos, arrayed like the spokes of a wheel emanating from the city, was like walking back in time. We were with a small force of about thirty men, lightly armed and ready to strike at the foreign occupier of their city.

As the early morning sun sliced through the darkness we came upon a complex of farm houses. Inside the pervasive adobe wall we saw an ancient Soviet-built truck. It had a large flatbed, used to transport produce in better days. That day it was a mujahaddin transport service. Thirty of us clambered aboard. Alain and I jumped on blindly, ignorant of our destination. The sight of this truck overflowing with armed warriors cascading along the river valley would have been comical if it had not been deadly serious. We drove within sight of the Jalalabad airport and the headquarters of the Soviet 66th Division Infantry, the men laughing and joking with each other, oblivious of danger.

Just east of the airport was a huge government-run farm. Built as a collective with Soviet assistance in the 1960s it meandered along the Kabul river for nearly twenty miles. In the center of a large tangerine orchard were some fairly modern buildings, once the administrative center for the farm. Now they housed Soviet soldiers and a field command center for their units operating in Nangahar Province.

Qadir directed his men to set up three rocket launchers they had hidden in a cache dug alongside a stream. He had received intelligence from within the Afghan army in Jalalabad that a meeting of ranking Soviet officers would take place at noon in an old movie theater. He was going to disrupt the meeting. He pointed out the theater through binoculars, a large white building with a black roof. I was able to zoom in close with my camera.

A few minutes after twelve o'clock he ordered the rockets launched. With a deafening roar the three launchers began expelling loads. Each launcher was located in an arroyo, which prevented the flash from being seen. Minutes later explosions and fires were erupting throughout the farm complex. At least two rockets slammed into the black roof and set it ablaze.

Qadir barked commands for immediate retreat. In small groups of three or four we left in several different directions. Alain and I accompanied Qadir as we headed towards the steepest, most rugged-looking mountain. Tired from lack of sleep, exhausted from our morning climb down, but alert with apprehension of a swift retaliation from the Soviets, we ran through the network of arroyos towards the mountain. The *shalwar kameez* clothing and blankets we wore blended with the ground around us. A man standing still or squatting just ten yards away was nearly invisible.

Within half an hour, ten helicopters began crisscrossing the sky above us. They came in low, sweeping back and forth, looking, looking for the mujahaddin. Each time they approached, Qadir would order, "Stop—don't move." Twice helicopters flew directly overhead not one hundred feet off the ground. Both times we escaped detection. It was another reminder of the frustration the Soviet military must feel—exactly what the British generals must have felt 150 years before.

It was well past sunset when we came to another of Qadir's *markazes*. I always felt a sense of accomplishment at reaching mountain summits—a feeling that would last until one of the muj pointed to the next mountain ahead. It would always be higher and steeper than the one just surmounted.

We had a good story. But Alain wanted to see a different part of Afghanistan and a different group of Afghans. He wanted to travel to the northern province of Faryab which was adjacent to the border with the Soviet Union. He made arrangements with the leader of a passing caravan of munitions to hitch a ride north—his Uzbek interpreter would help him contact the commanders of that region. Qadir warned Alain that the region he was entering had several renegade militia commanders who worked one week for the regime and one week against them. "These people are not Muslims, they believe in money," Qadir stated. But Alain ignored the advice and left the next morning headed north. Qadir and I left for Pakistan.

Three weeks later the regime in Kabul announced it had captured a foreign spy, a Frenchman named Alain Guillo. A militia group in Faryab Province was credited with capturing Guillo "while spying on military maneuvers of the Afghan army." It was subsequently revealed that a militia commander named Habibullah, who had worked for years as a mercenary for Najib's KhAD, had sold Alain for 200,000 Afghanis.

The regime turned the capture and trial of Guillo into a major event, and it became an immediate *cause célèbre* in Paris. He was tried, found guilty of espionage, and sentenced to death. The French government vigorously protested. But the regime was determined to use Guillo as a propaganda device. After dallying for over ten months, they told the French government that if a high-ranking member of the government went to Kabul, Guillo would be released. By complying, the French government would be giving de facto recognition to the puppet regime. French President Mitterand nevertheless complied, and a deputy prime minister arrived in Kabul and took Alain home.

Upon his release, Alain told horror stories of torture and crude prison conditions. His capture had a significant effect on the war coverage as a number of journalists decided the risk was too great and opted out of travel with the mujahaddin. The fact that Habibullah was not a mujahaddin commander made little difference.

Earlier that summer, I received a visit from a man named Lee Shapiro, who was putting together a documentary on the war and wanted to discuss the situation with me before making an extended visit to Afghanistan. Lee, personable and dedicated, had received financing for his project from CAUSA, a division of the Unification Church of the Reverend Sun Myung Moon. He had been a member of Moon's church for several years. Lee planned to spend up to six months inside with a group from Gulbaddin's Hezb-i-Islami. The briefings he had received from American officials led him to believe "the Hezbs" were the best fighting force and, besides, although Gulbaddin was the most controversial of the muj leaders, he was not well known to Western audiences.

Lee had hired James Lindelof to be his cameraman. Jim had volunteered as a worker with the International Medical Corps (IMC), made his first trip to Afghanistan in 1985, and become a passionate promoter of the Afghan cause.

Both of them were well prepared mentally and logistically to travel to the war zone. They knew the dangers, had discussed them with experienced hands, and decided to proceed. In July they left Pakistan and ventured into Afghanistan.

In early October, they were with a large group of Gulbaddin's soldiers northeast of Kabul in an area where the Hezb was in frequent conflict with forces loyal to Jamiat's Ahmed Shah Masood. On October 15, their guide and interpreter, Abdul Malik, returned to Peshawar with the news that Shapiro and Lindelof had been killed in an attack by four Soviet helicopters in the Sanglakh valley. Lindelof had been killed instantly by a rocket fired during a strafing run; Shapiro had been wounded by a second helicopter's machine gun; and most of the men had fled into the mountains. When the helicopters landed, Soviet soldiers shot and killed Shapiro and took his equipment.

Qaribar Rahman, a deputy of Gulbaddin, told U.S. officials the two had been buried near Maidan Shah about twenty-five miles from Kabul.

Another version of the tragedy circulating in Peshawar maintained that the guide Malik was actually a Tajik member of Jamiat. According to this story, the Hezb group accompanying Shapiro and Lindelof encountered a group of Masood's men. Malik, afraid of retaliation from his own party if he were caught with Gulbaddin's people, fled back to Pakistan. In the resulting armed clash between the two groups of mujahaddin, Shapiro and Lindelof had been killed.

It was impossible to confirm or deny either version. What did emerge as true was that the war had become very dangerous for foreign news reporters. Shapiro and Lindelof brought to seven the number of foreign journalists killed covering the war.

Almost two years later, in June 1989, another incident confirmed that the regime was continuing to target foreign journalists and use them for their own political and propaganda purposes.

American photo-journalist Tony O'Brien moved to Peshawar in 1988 and rented an apartment adjacent to my house. We became fast friends. Tony lived in Santa Fe, New Mexico, where I grew up, and had worked his way up from photographer for the *Albuquerque Journal* to top international photo-journalist with pictures regularly published in *Time, Newsweek,* and other major publications.

In early 1989 Abdul Haq arranged to sneak Donatella Lorch of the *New York Times* into the city. Out of it came several major stories and a feature article. It was not only a journalistic coup but an incredible feat for a woman in the strict Muslim society. Donatella's supersuccess whetted the appetite of others, among them Tony O'Brien.

Tony had traveled inside several times with Abdul Haq's forces. Although he had for some time requested to venture into Kabul, he was now determined to do so. Tony received hushed approval from Time-Life, Inc. to make the trip. After weeks of pleading with Abdul Haq, Tony convinced Abdul to help him. He appointed Jaglan Hamid, a key figure in Abdul Haq's intelligence network, to arrange the details. The extensive operation took time to put in place. In early June, Tony was smuggled into Kabul city.

Once in the city he was moved from one "safe" house to another, but several in the network balked at giving Tony a tour of the city. Tony, a tall 6'3", looked like a giant to these people. Donatella had hidden throughout her trip under a full *burqa,* a head-to-toe veil worn by many Afghan women, hardly possible for the tall, lanky American male. As it turned out, their fears for his safety were justified, but the danger came from a different quarter. One of the men Jaglan had asked to hide and move Tony had gone over to the KhAD, and he told them a foreigner was venturing into Kabul. One night, as Jaglan's men moved Tony into a home of a member of the network, the double agent gave the signal.

The house was quickly surrounded by KhAD agents and neighborhood militia. Tony was arrested along with several others. He was taken to a KhAD office and interrogated. Although he had been inside the city for three days, the KhAD had not arrested him hoping to trap as many members of Abdul Haq's network as possible. As it was, they only captured two members, since Abdul Haq kept the various cells in ignorance of each other.

The next night Abdul Haq's brother called and told me to come quickly to their office in Peshawar. There he said they had received a radio message from their headquarters in Jalrez: Tony had been caught. They informed the American consul Mike Malinowski.

Abdul Haq was furious. For the first few days I thought he would kill Jaglan Hamid. Tony was the first American to be captured. Beyond the fact that Abdul liked Tony, he was distraught both by the thought that Tony might believe he had been betrayed by people who were truly his friends, and by the penetration of his network.

It was three days before the regime announced it had captured an American, stating they would charge him with illegal entry. The diplomats were relieved that he had not been charged with spying. They credited this to two factors: he was American, unlike Guillo; and he was connected to *Time* magazine. Even communists knew whom not to upset.

Close friends of Tony in Pakistan mounted a major effort to help him. The U.S. government also moved, and in due course the regime notified the State Department they would "allow" a diplomat to go to Kabul to discuss Tony's situation.

But Abdul Haq was ahead of them all. From the first news, he had set his mind to gaining Tony's release, and the following week, his mujahaddin entered Kabul city and captured a ranking member of the PDPA Central Committee. Abdul sent me a message to give to Malinowski saying he was setting up discussions with Najib to trade his prisoner for Tony. After conferring with the embassy, Malinowski relayed a message to Abdul asking him to hold off for a while—the U.S. was sending a consular officer from New Delhi, Miss Renny Smith, to Kabul to talk to the regime. Abdul sent a second message giving the Americans until July 15 before he proceeded to do what was needed to release O'Brien.

On July 1, I accompanied Abdul to Paghman on the outskirts of Kabul. The next day the situation took a strange turn. Abu Khalid, a deputy of Yassir Arafat who ran the Palestinian Liberation Organization office in Kabul, announced that O'Brien would be released by the Kabul government in response to a personal appeal by Yassir Arafat. (Arafat, scheduled to arrive in Kabul the next week, claimed to be attempting to mediate a settlement in the war. It was never clear whom he was mediating with since the mujahaddin refused to deal with him. His only contacts were the Soviets and the regime.) On hearing this news, Abdul Haq sent a message to Najib offering the exchange of prisoners. He jumped the gun on his self-imposed date of July 15 because he heard the Americans wanted "to examine the PLO proposal."

On July 5, Abdul launched a huge attack on the Afghan army base at Lake Qarga. While accompanying a muj who was operating a Milan antitank missile, I was hit by a tank shell and severely wounded. Abdul had me driven back to Peshawar where I was sent to the States for surgery (more on which later).

On July 18, the regime notified Renny Smith that if the United States sent a diplomatic note to be delivered personally by a high-ranking American official, Tony O'Brien would be released—a move reminiscent of its ploy with the French. The exchange of cables between Kabul, New Delhi, and Washington lasted over twenty-four hours. The U.S. was not going to send a "high-ranking diplomat," but we did send a "diplomatic note" to Smith to hand personally to the regime's foreign ministry.

On July 20, Tony was released to Renny Smith at a ceremony and a mock news conference at the Foreign Ministry. The two of them took off for New Delhi.

Tony had been held captive for six weeks. Abdul Haq traded his prisoner for three of his men who had been jailed previously. The two members of his network who had been caught during the incident remained in Pul-i-Charki jail until released by Abdul Haq himself two years later.

In some instances journalists attacked each other. A frequent criticism, frequently correct, was that one or another became too close to the commander or faction he or she traveled with "inside." In other cases it was ideological or personal. These last were the motives of Mary Williams Walsh.

Mary Walsh first came to Pakistan in early 1988. Her husband, Lawrence Walsh, had traveled with the mujahaddin of Qadir a year before. Lawrence said he was writing a book on insurgent movements around the world and he wanted to include the Afghan mujahaddin. He admitted to his preconceived notion that the Afghans were wild fanatics and puppets of the warmongering Reagan/Casey doctrine to boot.

But after a considerable time spent with Qadir in Nangahar, he changed his tune. Qadir, he now opined, was an "amazing and wonderful human being," and he and his men were Muslims who took their religion seriously without being fanatic about it. "These people are motivated by their own goals and they are the most generous people I've ever met," Lawrence asserted.

Qadir liked Lawrence and gave him a mountain man's equivalent of the red carpet treatment. After Lawrence left Peshawar he wrote to Qadir, and Qadir, who had difficulty reading English, asked me to help.

Lawrence's wife Mary worked for the *Wall Street Journal*. When she first traveled to Peshawar to write a feature article on the Afghans she came to my house at her husband's behest. Qadir welcomed her as the wife of his very good friend Lawrence, and again rolled out his red carpet. He provided her with a vehicle and driver and gave her a ring and a carpet. Mary complained to Steve Masty and me that she did not understand why Qadir was showering her with gifts. "Does he think he can get into my pants?" she asked. I tried to explain the Afghan concept of hospitality to her. Qadir felt obligated to receive with all honor the wife of his good friend. Nothing more. Mary returned the gifts, with the exception of the vehicle and driver which she needed to get around.

Mary Walsh then wrote an article that astonished and confused Qadir and the other mujahaddin. Her article implied, among other things, that the mujahaddin were indeed American stooges. And she described Younas Khalis as a used clothes peddler. Khalis, the only of the seven party leaders who commanded the respect of all the others, was thoroughly perplexed. When she left Pakistan, she wrote to thank me for my hospitality and assistance during her stay in Peshawar.

Some time later, Mary traveled officially to Kabul. By this time she had been transferred to the *Wall Street Journal*'s Hong Kong bureau. One of her Kabul articles was a glowing report on a militia commander, the butcher Ismat Musleem. He was described as a Robin Hood character who drank copious quantities of brandy, and thereby an OK guy in this stodgy Muslim society. His numerous concubines and mistresses were brushed off, but there was no mention at all of the plundering, raping, and murder for which he was famous.

Needless to say, when copies of the story reached Peshawar the mujahaddin offices broke out in an uproar. Qadir was embarrassed and lost face for having, in effect, sponsored her.

Months later, I received calls from several people in the United States saying that a Mary Walsh was investigating my background for what appeared to be a coming attack on me and others covering Afghanistan in the *Wall Street Journal*. The reports continued for an entire year.

In early February 1989, Mary and Lawrence Walsh arrived in Peshawar along with hundreds of international journalists. The media frenzy was caused by the final Soviet withdrawal scheduled for February 15. It seemed as if every assignment editor wanted to cover the expected storming by the mujahaddin of the walls as the last Soviet soldier departed. All of them wanted to be in Afghanistan when it happened. Mary and Lawrence were no exception.

Qadir was occupied with his siege of Jalalabad at the time. But he was upset enough with Mary Walsh to issue orders that she not be brought to his area of control. He was helped in this by the ISI which instructed all the mujahaddin offices not to take the horde of new journalists into the country due to the heavy fighting taking place during the Soviet withdrawal. Most of the journalists had no idea of the dangers and difficulties entailed. The general journalistic response to being kept out of the killing fields was to condemn Pakistan and the mujahaddin for "trying to control the news."

I had no such problems. Having traveled and lived with the mujahaddin for nearly seven years, I could get into the country on a moment's notice. And I could keep the competition—American television networks—from going to the same places I covered.

While most of the international news corps was concentrating in Jalalabad, close to the Pakistani border, I focused on Kabul, the "heart of the country." I arranged to take CBS correspondent Anthony Mason, producer Joe Halderman, and cameraman Jonathan Partridge to the outskirts of the city and telexed Don Decesare, CBS foreign editor, that we would have exclusive coverage of the upcoming battle for Kabul. Whether this was "news management" or all's fair in love and war is a matter of interpretation.

Mary and Lawrence Walsh stayed in Peshawar for several weeks and interviewed dozens of people, not about the war or the politics of Afghanistan, but about me. One day they appeared together at my home/office to interview me.

I served them coffee and asked Mary what she was doing talking to so many people about me. In response, she handed me a typed list of about twenty questions and set a tape recorder on my desk. I turned on a tape recorder of my own. "What are you doing?" she asked testily. "If you feel you need to record this, then so do I," I said. She didn't like that at all.

Her questions concerned my closeness to the mujahaddin and to Abdul Haq in particular, my relations with an ex-girlfriend, and whether I gossiped about her, Mary. I answered each question and then asked her to leave. Happily, I kept the tape.

Late in the summer of 1989 CBS received rumors that a "slam story" was about to appear by Mary Williams Walsh—this time not about me, but about Mike Hoover who also did considerable freelance work for CBS.

On September 27, 1989, it hit—not a *Wall Street Journal* story by Mary Walsh, but a big feature story in the tabloid *New York Post* by Janet Wilson. The series sported such headlines as "DAN RATHER AIRED FAKE AFGHAN FOOTAGE" and a cutesy "THE RATHERING STORM." The articles accused Mike Hoover of faking battle scenes and news accounts in Afghanistan, including the footage shot by him during an operation called "Operation Blackout." This mujahaddin operation, led by Rahim Wardak of Mahaz, had been successful and was typical of mujahaddin raids in the area outside Kabul. The muj would blow up the electric pylons supplying power to Kabul, the regime would replace them, and the muj would take them out again. Hoover's pictures of this operation was part of a Columbia/duPont Silver Award given to CBS for its continuing Afghan coverage.

When the *New York Post* articles hit the streets, all hell broke loose inside the CBS newsroom and in the Peshawar offices of the mujahaddin.

I received the first phone call from Don Decesare followed by one from CBS Vice President Joe Peyronnin who quizzed me about Hoover's operation. The most emotional call came from Rahim Wardak. "How can they say these things?" he demanded. "Everybody knows we conducted this operation." I recorded his story in detail and faxed it to Peyronnin in New York.

The stories had dredged up several people with axes to grind. An Afghan ex-pat with British citizenry, Habib Kawyani, was quoted as stating that Hoover's battle scenes had actually been shot in Peshawar. Kawyani had complained for months that Hoover owed him money for a previous trip into Afghanistan. Another Afghan named Etemadi said Hoover directed the battle for a movie.

I found Etemadi at his brother's home, and he said the only journalist he had ever talked with was Mary Walsh. He had never heard of Janet Wilson. He swore the only thing he had said to Walsh was that a scene of refugees, supposedly shot on location, had not been. Nothing else.

Beat Kraetlli, another "source" for the story, as well as Kaw-yani and Etemadi, stated they had never met Janet Wilson, only Mary Walsh.

The most startling quotes in the article came from Joan Konner, former NBC employee and present dean of the School of Journalism at Columbia University in New York, one of the most prestigious in the United States. The school sponsored and picked the Columbia/duPont Awards. Konner was quoted as saying CBS might have to return its award for faking battle footage.

This incensed Dan Rather. Rather called her and questioned her professionalism in making such a statement without checking the story with him or CBS. He told her the award was "at this moment en route back to you" and indicated the perfect place to put it. Konner was on the spot. CBS had made a veiled threat no longer to participate in the duPont Awards. Without it, the awards would lose all meaning. But Konner's involvement in the CBS bashing had more string to play.

I gave all the information I was able to gather to the executives at CBS. While not present during Wardak's attack on the power system, I had enough evidence to prove it had taken place.

CBS announced it would make a thorough internal investigation of the charges. Peyronnin summoned me to New York. I left the next day.

In New York I found CBS had done its own research on the story. We learned from a source inside the *Wall Street Journal* that Mary Walsh had gone to her editors with the Hoover story and a personal attack upon me, using Dan Rather as a vehicle to trash CBS. The *Journal* editors had turned down the stories because they were filled with factual error, had no purpose, and appeared to be a personal vendetta. Mary Walsh was livid and appealed to the editor-in-chief of the *WSJ*, to no avail. Mary Walsh then resigned or was fired, depending upon who told the story.

Three weeks later the Hoover section of her stories appeared in the *New York Post*. Janet Wilson said she had researched her own material.

CBS announced publicly that the footage had not been faked.

Rather and I felt the Hoover stories were merely the first shoe to drop; the second was sure to fall.

It did. Another bombshell in the January/February 1990 issue of the *Columbia Journalism Review*. I was the target. This time with Mary Williams Walsh's byline. Joan Konner was the publisher.

The lengthy article was emblazoned with a large photo of me with my pet falcon on my arm, surrounded by armed mujahaddin. The thrust of the article claimed I was a conservative zealot who had duped CBS and through it the American public into blindly supporting the mujahaddin. Describing me as the eyes and ears of CBS in Afghanistan it derided my friendship with Abdul Haq, and accused me of writing flattering reports about the mujahaddin, when in reality they were factious bickerers. All in all, I was unfit to be a journalist. The article was obviously a personal vendetta against me. It served no other purpose.

CBS again announced an internal investigation. Peyronnin again summoned me to New York. I took my cassette recording of Walsh's interview and left immediately. At the CBS affiliate meeting in Los Angeles, CBS News President David Burke and Dan Rather were asked about the attacks upon me and Mike Hoover. Dan Rather said, "These guys have courage. They have frequently risked their lives to bring this story out. I admire them and have complete confidence and respect for them." David Burke questioned Mary Walsh's motive in attacking me for appearing to support the mujahaddin in my reports. Burke stated, "Who should he be supporting? The Soviet invaders?"

A month later, the leftist publication *The Progressive* reprinted much of Mary Walsh's *CJR* piece with an added story attacking the executives of the *Wall Street Journal* for failing to recognize the brilliance of Walsh's stories. Mary and her husband Lawrence had both worked previously for the paper.

At CBS, the luster of the Columbia/duPont Silver Award had dimmed.

CHAPTER 26

Brothers in Blood

My center is giving way, my right is in retreat; situation excellent. I shall attack.

—GENERAL FERDINAND FOCH, 1851–1929

A group of twelve mujahaddin belonging to Khalis' party were traveling in the far western province of Nimruz in early June of 1987. They were headed for a war zone near Shindand, a major Soviet base for air operations in western Afghanistan. Shindand was in Farah Province, another stronghold of the Khalis party.

The group was in two jeeps traveling north on a road adjacent to the Iranian border. They were bringing nine Stinger missiles to use against aircraft departing Shindand air base. At a point where they had previously forded a river, they encountered heavy run-off water and, forced to detour to the west, unintentionally crossed the border into Iran. Within an hour they were accosted by a patrol of the Revolutionary Guards who demanded to search their vehicles. The Afghans refused. A firefight ensued causing casualties on both sides. The Iranians called for reinforcements and overcame the small band of Afghans.

The Revolutionary Guards confiscated the Stinger missiles and held one Afghan hostage but allowed the rest to return to Afghanistan. The Khalis subcommander immediately reported the incident to Din Mohammad, deputy leader of the Khalis party.

Din Mohammad went to Islamabad personally and notified the CIA station chief and Ambassador Arnie Raphel. American

Intelligence accepted the story, and later said they had corroborating evidence to support Din Mohammad's report.

The Americans immediately prevailed upon Pakistan's ISI to negotiate with Iran to seek the return of the missiles. The Iranians said they would discuss the possibility, but demanded that Younas Khalis go to Teheran in person. Khalis had hostile relations with the Shiia mullahs, who controlled the Iranian government, and refused.[1]

Months later a report was printed in Switzerland under the byline of Beat Kraetlli, a Swiss journalist, that accused the Khalis group of selling Stinger missiles to Iran. The story, reprinted in a British newspaper, was written this time by Saira Shah. Saira Shah and Kraetlli lived together in Peshawar in 1987 and 1988. Their report charged that Khalis commander Fakir Mommad received $1 million for the missiles.

Fakir Mommad and the Khalis high command were indignant. They held a news conference, attended by Saira Shah and Kraetlli, and gave their version of the story. The story received some play in the European press, but died down—until October 8.

On that day U.S. navy helicopters fired upon and destroyed an Iranian patrol boat in the Persian Gulf. The navy pilots said the boat had fired on them with machine guns. In the wreckage of the patrol boat they found what was described as spare parts and batteries from U.S. Stinger missiles. The *New York Times* reported on October 17 that the missile parts belonged to those captured from the Afghans earlier in the year.

I was in Kunar Province with Din Mohammad when this story was reported on a Voice of America newscast. Din Mohammad told me this was not possible since the missiles captured from his men were still in a warehouse in Teheran. Negotiations were going on with the Iranians for the return of the weapons, and he was partaking in them. Din Mohammad said he had been told by the Pakistanis that the missile parts found on the patrol boat had come from a shipment sent to the Greek military.

In November, Zalmy Khalilzad, working for the State Department, held a briefing in the home of Richard Hoagland, USIS director in Peshawar. A dozen journalists attended. I asked Khalilzad directly, "Does the United States government know, from the serial numbers involved, that the Stinger missile batteries found on the Iranian patrol boat did *not* come from any supplied to the Afghan mujahaddin?" Khalilzad answered, "That is correct." Where did they originate? Khalilzad would not answer directly, but said, "This is still being assessed."

Two years later a major Afghan commander told me he had pieced together what he thought had actually happened. He said they had received information that some high-ranking Pakistani military officers had indeed sold Stinger missiles to Iran from Afghan supplies. In order to cover up the sale they had set up Fakir Mommad. Fakir Mommad, the commander went on, had been given instructions by an ISI officer to travel a designated route during a heavy rainy period. The ISI officer told him of an area inside Iran where it would be safe to cross the river. No problem. Within an hour of crossing the border Fakir Mommad found the Iranian military waiting for him.

While I was in Kunar with Din Mohammad we received a radio message that Abdul Haq had been badly wounded outside of Kabul, perhaps killed. The two of us left immediately to meet him as he was being brought back to Pakistan. Din Mohammad is Abdul Haq's older brother; Abdul had become my brother. The first reports said he had stepped on a mine and was bleeding to death. As we left a camp high in the Hindu Kush overlooking the garrison town of Barikot, it began to snow. What should have been a ten-to-twelve hour trip to the Pakistani border took over two days, struggling and fighting the elements.

At the border Din Mohammad received word that Abdul Haq would be transported directly to Peshawar. When we arrived at their family home, we walked in on what appeared to be a wake. Hundreds of people were gathered outside the walls of the house. Inside women were wailing and the children, usually loud and playful, were subdued. Abdul was lying on a bed in a room filled with over a dozen male relatives. He was as pale as the sheet wrapped around him. His foot was heavily bandaged, and someone, a cousin, was unaccountably massaging it.

Abdul Haq had been leading an attack on a garrison in Paghman when he slipped in the mud on a hillside and slid straight into an antipersonnel mine. He watched as his right foot flew into the air and away. In shock, and bleeding profusely, he climbed on his horse—who seemed to understand he needed help—and rode off. He was only alive because of the angle at which his body hit the mine. He had slid into it much as a baseball player slides into third base.

His men took him by horseback twenty-five miles to a medical clinic in Ghazni where a Hungarian doctor gave him first aid and temporarily sewed the remnants of his heel together. The doctor hated the Soviets and had moved to Afghanistan to help in the only way he knew how. His battlefield surgery, without benefit of anesthesia, saved Abdul Haq's life.

I immediately called Ambassador Raphel at the U.S. Embassy and told him the situation, and he made arrangements to have Abdul evacuated to Pittsburgh's Shadyside Hospital. The next morning I drove Abdul, who was taking nothing but aspirin, to Islamabad where the ambassador and Ed Abington of the political section met us. He was placed on a Pakistani airliner to New York.

Within three months Abdul Haq was back in Afghanistan leading his troops.

The incident affected me profoundly. Abdul Haq had become my closest friend. I was accused of championing him blindly. Most journalists covering Afghanistan became close to one commander or group to the exclusion of others and received the same criticism. I did cover the others and, when I thought warranted, I took issue with Abdul, but I don't deny that he was very dear to me. Kipling described the relationship as well as words are able. Most people are familiar with his line: "Oh, East is East, and West is West, and never the twain shall meet." But they don't remember its context. Kipling was describing the relationship between the son of a British officer and an Afghan tribal warrior. The poem continues:

They have looked each other between the eyes, and
there they found no fault.
They have taken the Oath of the Brother-in-Blood
on leavened bread and salt:
They have taken the Oath of the Brother-in-Blood
on fire and fresh-cut sod,
On the hilt and half of the Khyber knife, and the
Wondrous Names of God
There is neither East nor West, Border, nor Breed
nor Birth,
When two strong men stand face to face, though
they come from the ends of the earth!

Abdul Haq had one of the most analytical minds I have ever encountered. As a brilliant military commander, he drove the Soviet army berserk; as a gifted political planner he was a major force in making the mujahaddin what they were. He loves his country and his people, and wants to help them join the twentieth century. He will be a significant figure in shaping the future of his nation. He is not alone.

The war continued despite the wounding of Abdul Haq. He was lucky; he returned to his battlefields. The year 1987 had been crucial for the Afghan Resistance. On the battlefield, they had accomplished a great deal. Politically, the turmoil developing within the Soviet Union began to change the complexion of the war.

The year ended with a major Soviet attempt to relieve the siege of the city of Khost in Paktia Province. Commander Jalaladin Haqani had effectively cut off the garrison town from all but air-dropped supplies.

In early December, General Boris Gromov launched a campaign to relieve the city. The only land route from Kabul to Khost was southeast to Gardez and south through the Sarto Kandow pass to the city. Haqani had effectively blocked the narrow pass. His fighters were positioned throughout the mountains on both sides of the pass, and he had hundreds of rockets and heavy weapons. Behind these front line defenses he had six captured Soviet tanks.

The Soviet operation began with saturation bombing of the mountains concealing the mujahaddin. For over two weeks, dozens of aircraft dropped antipersonnel cluster bombs, rockets, and napalm. Haqani's men stood firm.

At Gardez, meanwhile, the Soviets assembled several battalions of infantry and armored columns for an assault on Sarto Kandow. I arrived several days before Christmas, the eighth anniversary of the Soviet invasion. Soviet television was showing actual reports from the battlefield. It became a "battle the Soviets must win." The main Soviet assault began December 23. I filmed the attack from the southwestern side of the pass, which CBS News later ran as a feature story interspersed with Soviet TV reports from the northeastern position. It was probably the first battle of a major war using footage from both sides of the battling forces. It was great television.

The Soviet story showed Deputy Foreign Minister Genady Garasimov giving daily reports on the battle. It was reminiscent of the daily battle reports given by the American command in Saigon during the height of the Vietnam War. It was given so much publicity that it became a "battle the Soviets must win."

The Soviets failed in their first real attempt to break through the pass to the beleaguered city of Khost. It was a big propaganda loss for them and their regime, precisely because it received such worldwide attention, a situation the Soviets had brought upon themselves by heavily covering the battle.

During the siege of Khost, the Soviets announced that they had killed an American advisor near Gardez. Afghan regime General Nabi Azimi gave a briefing saying such an American had been killed. In Washington, State Department spokeswoman Phyllis Oakley stated: "There are no American advisors in Afghanistan." The story was never clarified.

Haqani's siege held until late January when a Soviet tank battalion finally broke through his defense. But after delivering supplies, they had to fight their way out as viciously as they had fought their way in, and the siege by Haqani's mujahaddin clamped down once again. The Soviets never returned.

Retreat from Jalalabad

I have discovered the art of fooling diplomats; I speak the truth and they never believe me.

—CAMILLO DI CAVOUR, 1810–1861

The diplomatic efforts to reach accord on Afghanistan were given top priority in early 1988. The Soviets had announced that the only stumbling block was the timetable for their withdrawal. On January 5, Under Secretary of State Michael Armacost and Robert Oakley, then Middle East director of the National Security Council staff, arrived in Islamabad and met with Pakistani officials, including President Zia ul-Haq and Prime Minister Mohammed Khan Junejo.[1] Armacost led off with the Afghan situation and the next round of UN talks in Geneva scheduled for February.

At this same time, Soviet Foreign Minister Eduard Shevardnaze arrived in Kabul for an unannounced meeting with Najib. The simultaneous visits fueled speculation that a deal was in the works and a new proposal would be presented in Geneva.

The next day a Soviet deputy foreign minister, Anatoly Adamishin, was quoted in New Delhi as saying the "USSR wants the next scheduled round of talks on Afghanistan to be the last and to end in agreement." He told a selected group of Indian journalists that Moscow had "taken a strong decision to withdraw troops in 12 months—it could be even earlier."[2]

At the end of the week, Secretary of State George Shultz said the withdrawal of Soviet troops from Afghanistan seemed "close at hand" but the United States would "continue to send weapons to anti-Communist rebels until the insurgents' objective of a self-governing and neutral nation has been assured." Shultz denied an insinuation by Shevardnaze that the United States would end its military assistance before the Soviets began their withdrawal.[3] But the State Department, two years earlier, had agreed to just such a proposal.

The agreement to stop U.S. aid was reportedly made by Michael Armacost. The State Department said it had been cleared with Donald Fortier, head of the political-military affairs section of the National Security Council. Fortier made a convenient scapegoat, given that he had died the previous August. It was later reported by the *New York Times* (February 10) that President Reagan was surprised at news of the deal.[4]

For the next two weeks the mujahaddin offices were abuzz with talk of a deal between the Americans and the Soviets. Although matters seemed right on the surface, they didn't believe that such a deal would be in their best interests. They began to feel they were being treated like pawns instead of like the rightful leaders of the future Afghanistan.

In mid-January, the Pakistani Foreign Ministry announced its new demand: that a broad-based government *including* the regime be in place in Afghanistan before any agreement was implemented regarding the Soviet withdrawal. The State Department immediately said that Washington had "no intention of promoting such a government or pressing the guerrillas into accepting one." And a senior administration official was quoted in the *New York Times* as saying, "There is no interest in Washington of trying to propose or construct an interim government in Kabul."[5] The U.S. seemed, once again, to be standing side-by-side with the mujahaddin.

The Pakistani move had apparently thrown a monkey wrench in the drive for a settlement by the U.S. and the USSR. Now, with a pullout imminent, the State Department had either to back-track and dump the mujahaddin, or to impose stringent demands on the Soviets.

For the next several weeks there was an increase in the diplo-matic maneuvering that led up to what was going to be a most significant round of talks.

On January 20, 1988, Khan Abdul Gaffar Khan died in Peshawar. Khan, an adherent of Mohandas Ghandi's politics—an end to British rule in India and the partitioning of the subcontinent—was a Pushtoon tribesman from the old north-west frontier of British India. He and his followers, known as the "red shirts," had founded the left-wing Awami National party in Pakistan. He was a leader of the separatist movement for Push-toonistan in the 1960s and distinctly pro-Indian.

Once, upon his release from a British jail, Khan was quoted as saying, "With love you can persuade a Pushtoon to go to hell, but by force you cannot take him even to heaven." But he failed to support the Pushtoon uprising against the foreign Soviet in-vaders and backed the communist regime in Kabul.

Peshawar became a scene of frenzy upon Gaffar Khan's death. Hundreds of thousands of mourners paraded through the city, and his body was laid out in a public square for all to view—a distinctly un-Muslim thing to do.

Early the next morning I received a phone call from Ikramullah Jan, director of the Peshawar office of the Pakistan Information Ministry. "Go directly to the military gate at the Peshawar airport," he said. "Rajiv Ghandi is arriving in twenty minutes to pay his respects," and he hung up.

I couldn't believe it. Rajiv Ghandi, president of India, and Zia ul-Haq had no love for each other. Ghandi had never been to Pakistan, and he was not welcome. Nevertheless, I quickly loaded my camera and drove off.

As I arrived, the air force guard opened the gate with no questions and directed me to drive onto the tarmac of the airport. As I did, I saw an Indian air force plane, clearly marked, taxiing towards the VIP reception area. I grabbed my camera in time to tape the arrival of Rajiv and Sonia Ghandi and their two children—the second time in history an Indian leader had set foot in Pakistan. For South Asia it was a monumental event. I was allowed into Ghandi's caravan and watched as he paid his respects to Gaffar Khan's seventy-five-year-old son Wali Khan before praying at the bier. It was eerie watching the Hindu Ghandi offer Hindu prayers in one of the most Islamic cities on earth. Rajiv Ghandi's visit to Pakistan, from the time his plane landed until the wheels of his plane lifted off, was exactly sixty minutes.

Gaffar Khan had asked to be buried in Jalalabad, Afghanistan, his hometown. The Kabul regime complied and also allowed thousands of his followers to travel by road to Jalalabad for the funeral. Zia's government agreed, not wanting to inflame the hundreds of thousands of distraught mourners. At the bier with Rajiv Ghandi, Wali Khan asked me to come to the funeral and videotape it for American audiences. I told him the Afghan government had frequently refused to issue me a visa because I was a well-known journalist covering the mujahaddin. But he told me to go to the Afghan consulate in Peshawar and bring my friends. "It is all arranged, you will have a visa."

Along with my friend Steve Masty, I went to the consulate. On arrival, I was greeted by a regime functionary with a hearty, "Welcome Mr. Lohbeck." It was unsettling, but he stamped our visas allowing us to enter the "Democratic Republic of Afghanistan." Pakistan and Afghanistan did not exchange ambassadors, but they kept consular offices in the respective countries in order to maintain some channel of communication.

That afternoon I received a second phone call from Ikramullah Jan. This would lead me into real trouble and teach me a valuable lesson. "We have just received information, Mr. Kurt, that there will be very, very big dignitaries at the funeral of the late Mr. Khan. Mr. Mikhail Gorbachev, Colonel Mumammar Khadafi, and Chairman Yassir Arafat will also be attending the services in Jalalabad."

"It couldn't be true!"

"No, this is very, very true, and our government has been informed," he insisted.

I couldn't believe that Gorbachev, Khadafi, and Arafat would travel to the middle of an Afghanistan surrounded by warring mujahaddin. But then I hadn't believed that Rajiv Ghandi would travel unannounced to Peshawar either.

I telephoned Brigadier Muinuddin, deputy to General Aktar of ISI. "I have been told that Gorbachev, Khadafi, and Arafat are going to attend the funeral in Jalalabad." I asked a man I knew to be truthful. The brigadier said, "Yes, we have that same information. We are alerting the mujahaddin to honor a two-day ceasefire." I had two good government sources. I called CBS Radio and reported the story.

Upon hearing my CBS Radio story, ABC and NBC news desks began to move crews from Moscow to Jalalabad to cover the story. Within hours the Soviet Foreign Ministry was denying that Gorbachev would travel to Afghanistan and the CBS foreign desk began heating up my telex line with orders to verify my story. I called both my sources, they stuck to their story, but CBS Radio stopped running it.

The story, I later learned, had started when Wali Khan told the governor of the NWFP that Gorbachev, Khadafi, and Arafat *should* attend the funeral. The governor told Ikramullah they *would* attend. Ikramullah reported this to his superiors in Islamabad, who told President Zia, who told General Aktar, who told Brigadier Muinuddin, who told me. So much for the journalists' rule of two sources for a story. I had egg all over my network news face—but the next day I didn't much care; I had a bigger problem.

The caravan of hundreds of vehicles was scheduled to leave Peshawar at 5:00 A.M. on the morning of January 22. The night before several journalists were drinking at the American Club and decided to make the trip. Among them was Richard Weintraub of the *Washington Post*, Joe Gaal, a Canadian photographer and good friend, and a British photographer. An aid worker, Harriet Sandys, also wanted to go, claiming she had an assignment from a British newspaper. Having agreed to take them along, I realized my jeep wouldn't hold all of us and my camera equipment. Abdul Haq's younger brother Daud told me not to worry, he had a nine-seat van I could use. We joined the strange parade at 5:00 A.M.

The parade of honking, cheering, shouting, wailing mourners barreled down the road towards the tribal territory and the Khyber Pass like drunken stock-car racers in a free-for-all dog race. The cars, buses, vans, and motorcycles tore up the winding switchbacks of the Khyber Pass at breakneck speed, a "Far Side" cartoon come to life.

On the northern side of the pass the menagerie was stopped at the Afghan border. Each car was searched, the occupants examined, and the mourners allowed to proceed. As I was about to drive on, Whitney Azoy, an American friend, opened the side door of the van and pushed a young woman in. "Kurt, I've decided not to go please take my friend," he shouted as he disappeared into the crowd. I now had a sixth passenger.

The Sarandoi border guards waved us to the side of the road after we were twenty yards across. The Brit had no visa. They took him down from the van and ordered us all into their guard office. I became queazy thinking that some border guard might decide to collect the regime's price on my head. But after reexamining our visas, the guard allowed us to proceed, except for the Brit who was ordered to walk back to Pakistan.

Three hours later we reached the city of Jalalabad. Throughout the trip I had pointed out to Steve and Richard Weintraub those areas where I had been with the muj attacking various military installations—a strange sensation. In Jalalabad we were directed to a large walled complex of houses not far from the main gate of the Soviet 66th Division headquarters. As we approached, we passed the theater on the state farm. It was blackened, with all the windows blown out, a shell. I remembered the day of the attack with Qadir and Alain Guillo.

We parked the van about ten feet from the entrance to the Soviet military installation and began to walk across an open field to the burial site. After a moment or so, I decided I needed another camera battery as a backup, so I walked back to pick up a spare. With battery in hand, I ran to catch up with the rest of our group. When I was twenty yards away from the parking area, a huge explosion shook the ground. I spun around and saw vehicles in the air, bodies and parts of bodies thrown about. My van was lifted straight up several feet and slammed back down. People were screaming all around. There was nothing to do but proceed to the funeral site.

Approaching the wall was a cordon of security guards, Afghan and Soviet. The Soviets were in plain clothes and looked like thugs from a "B" movie. Inside the wall, a small crowd was packed up against a makeshift platform stage. On the stage were Najib, Sultan Ali Keshtmand, Suliman Laiq, the Soviet ambassador, and Wali Khan, along with various other communist dignitaries. I began videotaping.

After capturing the spectacle on tape, I went over to the side of the stage. Najib was descending the steps, surrounded by East German bodyguards carrying Uzi submachine guns. I walked towards him and asked, "What was that explosion?"

"That is just a celebration," he answered in passable English.

"People have been killed!"

"Gulbaddin must have done it." He smiled as he walked away.

After the burial, we worked our way warily through the now tense crowd of thousands to the parking area. Our van had the twisted look of a pretzel. The windows were blown out and the interior was a mixed mass of plastic, metal, and leather. I had no idea how we would return to Pakistan. The afternoon sun was dipping on the horizon. This would not be a pleasant place to be after dark. By this time, the masses of people realized what had happened. The explosion had destroyed dozens of vehicles, several buses were blown apart, and seventeen people were dead, their body parts lying around and draped in the branches of trees. It was a gruesome, surreal scene.

For some reason, I climbed through the twisted carcass of the vehicle and tried the ignition. It started. Not stopping to question miracles, we contorted ourselves, climbed aboard, and left. We chugged along on a nightmare trip, with rocket trails streaking across the sky. This time we wondered if we would be on the receiving end of mujahaddin attacks. The road was constantly patrolled by Soviet tanks and APCs. It took us eight hours to reach the Pakistani border.

Driving on the dusty road at night with no windshield was horrible. The bitter cold of the January night froze my face and made visibility near zero. When we arrived at the border checkpoint the Sarandoi guards doubled over with laughter at the sight of us. On the Pakistani side, the tone was more serious; hundreds of people huddled in groups. News of the explosion had reached Pakistan, and these people waited, searching, hoping, for a returning relative.

When we reached the city limits of Peshawar the engine on the van died. It was fatal; it never started again. The next day Daud shook his head sadly when he viewed the remains. He said it was poetic justice—the van belonged to mujahaddin leader Younas Khalis. Daud had borrowed it from him. My jaw dropped. "You mean I took Khalis' van to Jalalabad to see Najib?" I gibbered.

Later in the day the regime accused the Khalis mujahaddin of planting the bomb. Although Khalis' party was in control of the area around Jalalabad it would have been almost impossible to plant such a high-powered explosive less than ten yards from the gate of the Soviet infantry headquarters. Khalis immediately accused the Soviets and the regime of causing the explosion themselves in order to place blame for it on the mujahaddin. Qadir swore he had not been responsible for the bomb. "We are Muslims, we don't attack funerals," he told me.

The deadly funeral incident marked the beginning of a subtle change in the relationship between the Pakistani locals and the Afghan refugees. For years the Pakistanis had treated the refugees as "fellow Muslims," supporting their struggle. But now, the Pakistanis began openly carping about the millions of "invaders" from Afghanistan. Friction began to develop between the Afghans and local police. And for the first time, the Pakistani government confined Afghans to the refugee camps upon certain occasions, such as religious days of celebration or on days when Pakistani political rallies were scheduled in Peshawar.

The growing anti-Afghan feeling was more pronounced in

regions far from the Afghan border. The political marches that took place in Lahore, Rawalpindi, and Karachi had a distinct anti-Afghan feel, and news stories appeared quoting Pakistani citizens and shopkeepers as wishing the "guests" would go home. The change was understandable. With bombings, violence, and terror increasing in their own country, the Pakistani were feeling less secure. If the Afghans would leave, so would the problems.

On February 12, a tragedy occurred in Peshawar. Professor Burhanuddin Majrooh was assassinated at his front door. The gunman had cut the elderly man down with an automatic machine gun. Nobody was ever charged with the murder that saddened most Afghans and the entire Western community. Majrooh had recently published a poll showing widespread support for the return of Zahir Shah, the former king. Spokesmen for Gulbaddin warned Afghan refugees that those who supported Zahir Shah would share Professor Majrooh's fate.[6]

With this as a backdrop, diplomatic efforts in April 1988 not only got on the fast track but on greased rails. On April 5, the Soviets stated an agreement was near. Senator Gordon Humphrey warned, in Islamabad, that the United States and its allies might be "falling into a trap." He said he thought the U.S. was "being too optimistic in estimating that the Kabul regime will fall in a matter of weeks after a settlement is negotiated. I think it will take months, maybe more than a year."[7] That was the crux of mujahaddin discontent—an Afghanistan still under communist rule or influence, an Afghan still prisoner to an alien philosophy.

Three days later, the Soviets and Afghan regime announced simultaneously that the last barriers to a negotiated settlement had been eliminated. Translated, Eduard Shevardnaze had twisted Najib's arm into accepting the Soviet position, which included the time frame for troop withdrawal, whether to leave Soviet advisors in place, and so on.[8]

The next day, April 9, UN mediator Diego Cordovez stated in Geneva that a full agreement had been reached on a treaty under which the Soviet Union would withdraw its 115,000 soldiers from Afghanistan. Cordovez said the agreement called for the safe return of the refugees which would be guaranteed by the United States and the Soviet Union. "The documents are now finalized and ready for signature," said Cordovez at a news conference. Officially, the treaty would be signed by Afghanistan and Pakistan. In addition, the U.S. and USSR would sign the documents.

In Tashkent, following a meeting with Najib, Mikhail Gorbachev said the accords should not be "viewed as a present to President Reagan on the eve of his visit to the USSR."[9] Translated: the accords were not a presummit ploy; they were for real.

In Geneva on April 14, the treaty was signed by Pakistan Acting Foreign Minister Zain Noorani, Afghan Foreign Minister Abdul Wakil, Soviet Foreign Minister Eduard Shevardnaze, and Secretary of State George Shultz. The agreements called for Soviet troops to begin withdrawing by May 15, 1988. At least half of the Soviet troops were to be out of the country in three months and the withdrawal completed in nine months. Nothing on the mujahaddin.

Following the ceremony, U.S. officials said Shultz had planned to announce the American position on further aid to the mujahaddin but was given no opportunity to do so.[10] The mujahaddin alliance office in Peshawar said they rejected the Geneva accords outright and vowed to ignore them—they had not been party to them, and the accords did not specify their future role in governing their country. White House spokesman Marlin Fitzwater tried to pour diplomatic oil on the situation by assuring that the United States "will support the mujahaddin as the Soviets support the Kabul government." He added, "President Reagan has encouraged the rebels to fight on if the opposition remains, if the fight is there to maintain."[11]

President Zia was not pleased with the Geneva accords. He had wanted to hold out for a provision requiring that an interim government be in place during the time of transition. He felt he had been unfairly pressured by the U.S. State Department, through Ambassador Raphel, to acquiesce to the accords. But Prime Minister Junejo, who wanted to sign the agreements, had ordered Zain Noorani to do so.

Junejo was fired shortly thereafter. The primary reason was his insistence in pursuing an investigation of the ammunition dump explosion. Zia, however, was also displeased at being pressured from within his own government to accept a flawed agreement on Afghanistan.

Soon after the accords were signed, UN Secretary General Javier Perez de Cuellar was pushed by the Reagan administration to name a coordinator to cut the bureaucratic red tape and stop the infighting between rival agencies involved in the Afghan relief efforts. De Cuellar named Pakistan Prince Sadruddin Aga Khan to coordinate all international resettlement efforts and to distribute assistance impartially to the communist government in Kabul and the political leaders of the mujahaddin.[12] Sadruddin was uncle to Karim Aga Khan, spiritual leader of the Ismaili Muslim sect.

With American assistance, Sadruddin organized several programs—Saalam One, Saalam Two, and so on—to deliver humanitarian aid inside of Afghanistan and to encourage refugees to return. One such program attempted to pay refugees in rice, wheat, and cash to leave Pakistan and return home. Many refugees took the goodies and stayed put, reluctant to go back until peace and security could be assured. Which it couldn't— the military activity increased during the opening phases of the Soviet withdrawal.

Sadruddin and his UN office were in frequent contact with the regime in Kabul, and for that reason were never really accepted by the mujahaddin, particularly by the commanders in the field. Besides, the mujahaddin had denounced the Geneva accords as a sellout of their struggle, and they were not going to cooperate with anything that resulted from the accords.

On April 22, Din Mohammad sent me word that the mujahaddin were about to capture the garrison and town of Barikot in Kunar

Province. Din Mohammad was preparing to leave for Barikot and I was welcome to film and report what would become "the first liberated town in Afghanistan." I grabbed my equipment and left.

Din Mohammad and I flew in an old Pakistani Fokker twin prop airplane to Chitral on the far northeastern border of Afghanistan. The flight was harrowing—the mountains shot up beyond twenty thousand feet but the airplane only made it to twelve thousand. We flew along the highest ridge lines of the Hindu Kush under the dominating K-2, the second highest mountain in the world with the wondrously beautiful snow-capped peaks.

At the airport several mujahaddin jeeps were waiting for us. We were quickly loaded aboard and took off at breakneck speed on a dirt road to the border village of Arandu. Barikot was two miles from the border. We crossed the Kunar river, which marked the frontier, over hastily constructed log bridges by foot. We could hear gunfire ahead. The crisp and clear mountain air was suddenly filled with the sweet but heavy odor of cordite—a distinct coffee-like aroma that never fails to awaken a sixth sense of alertness.

We walked into the edge of the town in a single-file troop, about twenty-five men. Our tension was shattered by a sharp explosion immediately in front of us—about ten yards. A mine had exploded and cut a young muj in half. He was dead by the time we got to him. In that town, the mujahaddin had just forced the last of the Afghan army defenders to board the helicopters that were standing by to evacuate them and the few Soviet advisors. As mementos, they had littered the entire area with a new and deadly device—sonic mines. The mines implanted on stakes were geared to explode when the ground around them vibrated. Before the day was over four men shared the fate of the first booby-trapped muj.

Inside, the town was jubilant. Hundreds of young men were ripping through what had been a Soviet garrison, tossing and tearing red booklets with pictures of Lenin on the cover—a fitting contrast to the dead tanks hunkered along the sides of the streets. I filmed a group of men tearing down the Red army flag and closed in as they replaced it with the white flag of the mujahaddin.

We spent the night in the Soviet officers barracks. The next morning a surprising sight greeted the mujahaddin as they were performing their early morning prayers. Hundreds of people— old men, women, children—were walking up the road to Barikot. Refugees who had fled years before were not going to wait one single day before returning to their homes. (Din Mohammad quickly organized a mine-clearing operation to avert a further tragedy.) I saw a sight I would never have imagined possible in this strict Muslim society: women, without veils, ran up to the nearest mujahaddin warriors and hugged them. Men with tears still streaming down their faces went to nearby fields and began clearing them of shells and junk, restoring them for farming. The land was once more theirs.

Din Mohammed assembled his command of several hundred mujahaddin, and they prayed a prayer of thanksgiving. Din Mohammed told them they were now standing on the first piece of ground of "a Free Afghanistan," but they must continue their struggle until the entire country was free.

The first of the Soviet units to withdraw from Afghanistan left in early May 1988. Ronald Reagan was scheduled to visit Moscow on May 29. In Kabul, General Boris Gromov declared that by August 15 Soviet troops "will have pulled out of 11 of 18 garrisons and 170 posts" and that the departing troops would leave behind $1 billion-worth of equipment and supplies for the Afghan army. This marked the beginning of the Soviet "Afghanization" of the war. Gromov estimated that within nine months the Afghan army would be ready to take over.[13]

On the morning of Gromov's news conference a huge truck bomb went off in downtown Kabul. The preceding week, mujahaddin rocket and bomb attacks had increased significantly in the city. Abdul Haq and other commanders in the region were intent on advising the regime and the residents of Kabul that they would be under siege once the Soviets were gone. Najib began to complain that the mujahaddin were setting up obstacles to the Soviet "peaceful march homeward."

Gromov and Najib then piously declared that all mine fields laid by the Soviet army would be removed before the Soviet soldiers left. Four years later the United Nations estimated that up to 30 million land mines remained in Afghanistan—one of the greatest humanitarian hazards in the world.

A few days before President Reagan landed in Moscow, General Aleksei Lizichev of the Soviet Defense Ministry ended the long news blackout on Soviet casualties in Afghanistan. Lizichev's figures showed 13,310 soldiers had been killed, 35,478 were wounded, and 311 were missing.[14]

CHAPTER 28

The War on Drugs

The authorities were at their wits end, nor had it taken them long to get there.

—DESMOND MACCARTHY, 1877–1952

The opium poppy thrives in an area called the Golden Crescent, which stretches across northern Iran, through southwestern Afghanistan, and across northern Pakistan. All the elements combine to produce flower bulbs which are rich in the narcotic paste that is Asia's contribution to the drug culture.

Farmers in these agrarian societies have for centuries used about a kanal (approximately $^1/_8$ acre) of their land to grow opium poppy. The cultivated paste was used in medicinal teas, smoked by the mountain people to strengthen their stamina, and, mixed with a type of chewing tobacco, used as a mild stimulant. Derivatives of opium paste—morphine and heroin— were discovered by Arab and European physicians and used extensively as pain killers. Around the turn of the century, the extremely addictive heroin hit the drug culture.

Prior to the fall of the shah of Iran in 1978 most illegally grown opium came from Iran and Turkey. The paste was shipped to France to be refined into morphine and heroin and from there sent to the United States. Because of the political changes and some successful actions against the processing laboratories, the underworld drug business sought other sources of supply.

242

The extreme poverty of the tribal peoples of Pakistan and the political upheaval in Afghanistan were ideal for the purpose. The local tribes already had knowledge of the poppy, and the new flow of money fueled an increase in supply. Farmers whose average annual income was less than $300 were offered $1,000 for a single kanal's worth of opium paste.

By the mid- to late-1980s the amounts of heroin being smuggled out of Pakistan and into the United States and Europe reached alarming proportions. The United States Drug Enforcement Agency (DEA) opened offices in 1986 at the embassy in Islamabad and in Peshawar to assist the Pakistanis to eliminate the cultivation of poppy in Pakistan. The task was not only difficult, it was nearly impossible. The government of Pakistan has no police authority over the country's tribal areas, which are politically autonomous.

Next, a crop substitution program was attempted. Backed by the DEA, the Pakistani Narcotics Control Board (PNCB) offered to purchase onions if they were planted instead of poppy. Many farmers complied; they planted a lot of onions. They also moved their poppy crops deeper into the mountain valleys where they were inaccessible to PNCB inspectors. The Pakistanis subsequently failed to buy all of the onions and many thousands of tons of onions were thrown by the disgusted tribesmen to rot on the road.

By the spring harvest season in 1987, several back mountain areas of northern Pakistan were carpeted with the sweet-smelling flowers of the opium poppy. The farmers who were receiving thousands of dollars for their crop became the nouveau riche of the Pakistani Pushtoon tribesmen.

Rumors were rife that top Pakistani political figures were involved in the drug business. Several DEA agents in Peshawar were convinced that then-Governor General Fasle Haq was a major protector of the drug dealers. The son of his predecessor, Governor Hoti, was arrested in the United States with a large supply of heroin. The DEA asked the ambassador to pressure President Zia to bring a case against Fasle Haq. But Fasle Haq had been a close ally of Zia during his coup against Ali Bhutto and was considered safe from such charges. Fasle Haq was also a strong supporter of Gulbaddin Hekmatyar's Hezb-i-Islami. In their book *False Profits*, Peter Truell and Larry Gurwin quote an expert on the heroin trade as saying that the mujahaddin took opium "across the border and then sold it to Pakistani heroin refiners who operated under the protection of General Fasle Haq." Fasle Haq and the future Pakistani president Ishaq Khan had extensive connections to the BCCI bank as well. After Benazir Bhutto became prime minister in late 1988, several high-ranking military officers were arrested for involvement in the drug trade.

In addition, there was an explosion in the cultivation of poppies in Afghanistan during the war, and the mujahaddin were accused of financing their forces through drug profits. Some commanders undoubtedly did. But there was never any slightest evidence that the mujahaddin parties or top leaders had any connection with the criminal enterprise. Most of them, in any case, were fundamental religious leaders and thus opposed to such dealings.

In early 1987 I was surprised to see in Logar Province an area of about fifty acres in blooming poppies surrounded by a litter of shrapnel and dotted with bomb craters. Everything in the area with the exception of the opium had been bombed by the regime. I mentioned this to a DEA agent, but he adamantly denied that the Soviets were involved in the heroin trade. Yet, just two months later, a Soviet freighter was boarded in Rotterdam, Netherlands, by customs inspectors who discovered that several dozen containers of Afghan raisins had bottoms filled with twenty kilos of heroin. The containers had been loaded in Kabul, transported across the Soviet Union to Kiev, and then shipped to Rotterdam. It would have been impossible for such a significant shipment to have made the journey without the knowledge of Soviet authorities.

A similar incident occurred in London in 1988 when three-and-a-half tons of Afghan hashish were seized. British Home Office Minister Peter Lilley said at a news conference that the drugs had been trucked from Afghanistan to the Soviet Union where they went by rail to Leningrad and thence by sea to London's Tilbury docks.[1]

The antidrug campaign became an American priority in 1987. Phyllis Oakley, wife of Ambassador Robert Oakley and former spokesperson for Secretary of State George Shultz, was put in charge of a program aimed at stopping the cultivation of opium in areas of Afghanistan controlled by the mujahaddin. The program not only flopped; it stimulated growth. When the program paid some farmers not to grow opium, many who had not previously planted the narcotic now did so in order to be paid to stop.

The Shinwari tribe is located in Nangahar Province adjacent to the Pakistani border. Almost all the Shinwari people were living in refugee camps in Pakistan, but because the border was so close, the older men would work their fields inside Afghanistan and return to the Pakistani camps at night for safety from the constant air bombardment in Nangahar. Many of these people grew poppy because it required little tending and only a small plot of land.

All of the resources of Qadir, the major commander in Nangahar, were devoted to the siege of Jalalabad. He offered to destroy all of the opium in Nangahar if the Americans would provide him with an adequate supply of weapons and munitions for his operations. The offer was rejected because the Americans thought Qadir should be more concerned with American drug habits than with the bombs dropping daily on his head.

The American-sponsored programs showed ignorance in all kinds of ways. The aid workers, for example, would circumvent the tribal hierarchy and the commanders and go directly to individual farmers, not understanding that the culture wasn't geared to such methods. Another flop.

I was having lunch at the Peshawar American Club one day when Jim Grafineous of the DEA's Peshawar office introduced me to his boss who headed the DEA at the embassy. The DEA chief, whom I'll call "Charlie," pulled me out to the veranda for a private request. "Charlie" said he knew I made frequent trips into

Afghanistan, and had I seen any locations that might be heroin laboratories? I told him of one occasion in Nangahar when the mujahaddin had pointed to the ruins of a village with only two or three dwellings intact and claimed this was an Afridi tribe heroin laboratory. "Charlie" then asked if on my next trip I would pinpoint the exact location on a map he would supply. The DEA, he said, would make a commando raid on the place and "take it out." I pointed out that the buildings were in Afghanistan which was at the time occupied by the Soviets. Was he suggesting an American paramilitary raid into Afghanistan? That was exactly what he was suggesting. "I'm not concerned with the politics, I just want to hit the drug factories." He promised I could go along on the raid and film it for CBS News.

When I later asked Jim and Ernie Mertens, also of DEA, if "Charlie" was serious, their eyes widened. In the collective opinion of the DEA, "Charlie" was nuttier than a fruitcake.

With antidrug stories coming into vogue in the United States during the late 1980s Richard Wagner and Derrick Williams came to Peshawar from the CBS Hong Kong bureau and we set out to report the drug scene in Pakistan. April and May are the only months when opium growing offers any visuals for television. In these months the beautiful fields of bright red, purple, and white poppies are a delight to the eye.

We contacted the Peshawar deputy chief of the PNCB and asked where he advised we go to film poppy and talk with growers. Saifullah Khan not only offered advice but agreed to take us to "our very own Mafia right here in Pakistan." Having no idea what we were in for, we accepted and headed for the mountains of the tribal areas in Swat.

We worked our way over trails that were more cow tracks than roads into one of the most isolated mountain valleys on earth, a hidden principality in the upper ranges of the Himalayas. Once hailed as the potential "Switzerland of Asia," Swat had become isolated and somewhat dilapidated since its partition from India. The "Wali of Swat," celebrated in song as the Sultan of Swat, was an old man, revered by his people, who spent most of his time in political exile in Lahore. The tribes of the area recognized no government other than the Wali's, and Zia thought it wise to permit him one annual visit only to his homeland.

Saifullah drove us past miles of terraced farmland, happily pointing out a kanal of blooming poppies here, and see over there, and another just off to the left. After several hours driving through a valley untouched by the smoke and machines of modern man we came to a big complex of houses within a great wall. Saifullah beeped and beeped until an armed guard peered through a small door in the gate. On recognizing the Pakistani narcotics agent, he swung open the huge steel gates to the villa.

After a few minutes he returned with a smile so wide it seemed to split his Groucho Marx moustache. "We are pleased and grateful to be the guests of the sahib and his brothers," he exclaimed.

We were greeted by three men straight out of a Francis Ford Coppola movie on the mob. They were wearing sport jackets over their *shalwar kameezes*, highly polished Gucci shoes, and a cosmopolitan air far removed from these mountains.

"These are the drug lords of Swat," Saifullah proudly proclaimed. We shook hands and followed them to an English garden where servants were preparing to serve tea.

Over the next two hours the men spoke frankly of their control of thousands of acres of opium poppy. "This is the only way the poor and starving people of this area can survive," one of the brothers reeled off. They explained the economics of opium. One kilo of paste will bring the farmer $1,000. Ten kilos of opium will refine to one kilo of heroin. One kilo of heroin will fetch $200,000 to smugglers who transport it to New York and Los Angeles. In America that same kilo will be cut perhaps fifty times with various ingredients and bring from $2 to $5 million on the streets.

The trio said they worked with communist officials in Afghanistan to bring raw opium to Pakistan and to cut deals with the authorities there. And they talked freely about how they arranged with the government of Pakistan to allow PNCB agents to destroy opium acreage in the Gadoon area in exchange for overlooking Swat. "Next year we will probably let them destroy the crop in Swat and leave us alone in some other region. You must understand these people are politicians, we are business-men. It is better for business if we allow the politicians to have such successes, and it is better for them to allow us a considerable profit." He smiled—politics and business as usual.

The next day we arranged with the Pakistani air force to ac-company them in helicopters as they sprayed chemicals on pop-pies in Gadoon. Derrick strapped himself onto the side of a helicopter as we swept low over miles of opium during the operation. In one village where we landed, the people com-plained that the government had destroyed their livelihood. We didn't tell them that next year they would probably be left in peace. Saifullah was rather proud that Pakistan had risen to the top of the list of heroin-producing nations. It made him that much more important. "Please tell my chief that I have been on the famous CBS News," he said as we thanked him for the tour.

One day an officer of the Pakistan Customs Department drove to my house and handed me a personal invitation. The Customs Division and the U.S. DEA would be holding a joint session to destroy narcotics seized from criminals in a field on the Isla-mabad highway outside of Peshawar. The two agencies would burn two thousand tons of hashish and three tons of heroin.

I picked up Steve Masty and we drove to the open field thirty miles east of Peshawar where a huge tent was set up with chairs for dignitaries and tables laden with food. Before the tent in a vacant lot about an acre and-a-half in size, were twenty or so large mounds of drugs, each mound nearly eight feet high and about six feet in diameter, spaced five yards apart.

Assembled in the tent were the top officials of the Northwest Frontier Customs Department and about ten Americans from the DEA. After several congratulatory speeches, several men went from mound to mound sprinkling kerosene and then touching each mound with torches. I filmed the entire operation—two thousand tons of hashish and three tons of heroin make a very large display. Billowing smoke began to spew into the sky, and as I filmed away, the wind shifted and began to blow the thick brown smoke directly over me and into the open front of the tent. The flames got higher, the smoke got thicker, and the wind held course.

Within minutes everyone was coughing and choking and looking for somewhere to hide. There was nowhere. We wrapped a kerchief or blanket or whatever around our faces to avoid the smoke until, finally, the wind shifted and the flames died down. Everyone was laughing. Actually, everyone was giggling.

We were also hungry, and most of us began to wolf down food as we continued to giggle. At this point in the ceremonies, each agency was scheduled to present the other with fancy plaques commemorating the event. But we were all so stoned that not one of us could stand up straight.

After some time—whatever that meant, minutes, hours—Steve and I left for Islamabad where I planned to send the videotape by satellite to London. But I couldn't define a straight line, much less drive one. What should have taken two hours became a six-hour odyssey.

On the trip back, Steve and I hooted with laughter at one particular Customs official. Realizing everybody was higher than a kite, including all of the DEA agents, he boasted of the "great quality of hashish and heroin we produce in Pakistan." If we thought this was wonderful, we should stop by his office any time; he had more than enough to go around. Solving the drug problem of the Golden Crescent was not to be in our lifetime.

CHAPTER 29

Whodunit

Assassination is the extreme form of censorship.

—GEORGE BERNARD SHAW, 1856–1950

As the Soviet withdrawal began in earnest the mujahaddin in several areas of the country repeatedly attacked the retreating Soviet convoys, inflicting heavy casualties. General Gromov sent a delegation to strike a deal with Commander Masood. The Soviets would allow the Tajik commander to take control of the Salang Pass to the north if he in turn undertook not to attack the retreating Soviet forces. When Masood accepted the deal he was embraced by the press in the Soviet Union.

Artyom Borovak wrote in *Ogoniok*, the Soviet magazine, that Masood "was a good person to negotiate with" and offered the information that Masood's high command included an unusually high proportion of graduates from Moscow's Frunze Military Academy. He added, "There is a rumor that Masood himself studied at the academy under an assumed name."[1]

The mujahaddin attacks inside the city of Kabul were also more pronounced. Car bombs went off at government installations killing several ranking KhAD or military personnel; unfortunately, but inevitably, some missed their military targets and killed civilians.

In early August 1988, I was with Abdul Haq outside Kabul as he launched attacks against new Afghan army posts and the retreating Soviets. One afternoon he was in an unusually upbeat mood. "The finance officer of KhAD Directorate Five has defected," he told me. He sent me along with two of his men to a small group of tents hidden under an overhang in a narrow mountain valley where I met a big imposing man with a shaved head.

The man's name was Waseel, and he told me on videotape that he had been in charge of disbursing payments to KhAD agents and employees for various operations outside Afghanistan. The most significant was in early 1988 when he delivered money to a small group of Turi tribesmen in Pakistan. The men were paid to assassinate a prominent Shiia mullah in Peshawar named Arif Husseini. The murder created violent civil strife for Zia's government—tens of thousands of Shiias took to the streets to protest. Zia confidante and former NWFP governor, Fasle Haq, was accused by the Shiias of the murder, arrested, and temporarily charged with the crime. Waseel told me that the assassination was part of a continuing KhAD campaign to disrupt the social and political order in Pakistan.

President Zia fought back then and fought back now. In June and July, the ISI gave orders to several mujahaddin groups to target political figures in Kabul. One truck bomb near the Afghan Defense Ministry just missed killing Najib who had left the building only moments before.

The problem escalated. The Soviets entered the scene. The Soviet ambassador to Pakistan publicly complained about Zia's continued heavy supply of weapons to the Resistance. But they were deterred from making loud public complaints about the United States' role in the arms pipeline because Secretary of State George Shultz had stated at the signing of the Geneva accords that the United States would continue to supply the mujahaddin "as long as the Soviets continued to supply the Kabul regime." Still, Zia was a different matter. Tension intensified between Islamabad and Moscow.[2]

In the first week of August the Soviets announced they were suspending their withdrawal effective August 15. They said the action was in direct response to Zia's alleged violations of the

Geneva accords and charged Zia with sabotage campaigns in Kabul.[3]

American ambassador to Moscow, Jack Matlock, was summoned to the Foreign Ministry and told the Soviets intended "to teach Zia a lesson."[4] The pressure on Zia continued—from another quarter and on a different subject, but it was part of the whole. Indian Prime Minister Rajiv Ghandi informed Pakistan on August 15 that it would "have cause to regret its behavior" in providing arms to the Sikh separatists in the Punjab region of northern India.[5] Sikh gunmen had assassinated his mother, Indira, two years before, and in recent months had begun to attack several Indian government installations.

On August 17, President Zia and ISI chief Acktar flew to a military base in Bahawalpur, Pakistan. The top two leaders of the country traveled with nine of the army's top generals to witness a demonstration of a U.S. army M-1 tank. Following the military show, Zia and Acktar invited U.S. Ambassador Arnold Raphel and U.S. military attaché Brigadier General Herbert Wassom to return to Islamabad with them. Raphel and Wassom had been scheduled to return on a U.S. Embassy aircraft after picking up Raphel's wife due in after a visit to the States.

Pakistan's deputy chief of army staff Lieutenant General Aslam Beg left the party of generals and took another plane to attend a meeting elsewhere. The other eight generals boarded President Zia's airplane, a C-130 Hercules dubbed "Pak One."

The C-130 was equipped with a capsule passenger compartment which had been loaded into the transport plane and bolted down. The capsule was divided into three parts. The front section, a plush cabin with several comfortable chairs and tables, held Zia, Acktar, Raphel, and Wassom. The middle section held the eight generals on bench-like seating. The remainder of attendants, junior officers and flight crews in the last section, brought the total number of passengers to thirty-four. The VIP capsule was separated from the flight deck by a door and a staircase leading down to the cockpit.

On that afternoon, August 17, I was having lunch with Abdul

Haq at his military *markaz* in Jalrez. His guest for lunch was an Afghan general who had traveled from Kabul in a civilian automobile. It was not the only such contact he had made during the course of the war. With the Soviet army withdrawing, the regime's military leaders were looking to their own future. Their conversation was in Farsi. I sat quietly and ate. Abdul told me the general had said that their KGB counterparts never sat down to eat with Afghan officers. He thought the American visitor with Abdul Haq must be his CIA counterpart. Abdul saw no reason to disillusion the man. "It is better that he think Americans are surrounding Kabul in the mountains," he laughed.

That evening we listened to a radio newscast on the Voice of America. The lead story: a plane crash near Bahawalpur, Pakistan, that had killed President Zia, General Acktar, Ambassador Raphel, and the top military command of Pakistan. Abdul Haq's face grew tense, but he told me in English not to show anything in front of his men. He did not want them to realize the importance of the death of Zia. It was difficult; I was shocked at the news. Further reports on the BBC and Radio Moscow added little other than that the plane had apparently lost radio contact almost immediately after taking off.

Later that night, when we were alone, Abdul Haq spoke of his fears of the consequence of Zia's death on the cause of the mujahaddin. He thought Zia's hard line for a broad-based mujahaddin government might be softened by his successors—that they would betray the mujahaddin. He took it for granted the crash had been sabotage and began to theorize about those responsible for it.

"A lot of people wanted Zia out of the way: Benazir Bhutto and her PPP [Pakistan People's party] followers, the government of India, the KGB, the CIA, and, perhaps even his own army high command," he speculated. He then ticked them off one by one: the PPP opposition would have been unable to penetrate Zia's presidential security, and India's RAW intelligence did not have the know-how for the sophisticated method employed. Closer to home, although somewhat reluctantly, he eliminated the other

Pakistani army generals: all but one of the top leadership was on the plane, and Zia had done a great deal for the generals under his command.

That left two agencies with access to the proper sophisticated sabotage devices and the capability to penetrate the security of the president—the KGB and the CIA. (When I asked Abdul if KhAD could have been involved, he said, "That's the same as the KGB, they can't do anything like that on their own.")

But surely the CIA would not do such a thing in light of the investigations of the organization in recent years, I protested. Besides, the American ambassador had also been killed. Abdul Haq raised his eyebrows, his "maybe yes maybe no" look.

Two days later we heard that Secretary of State Shultz was coming to Zia's funeral in Islamabad, accompanied by the newly appointed ambassador Robert Oakley. Abdul gave me a note of greeting to Oakley, and I left for Pakistan.

Bob Oakley immediately took charge of the Afghan operations. He met with each of the seven party leaders and several of the more significant commanders. A major item on Oakley's agenda was to hammer into the different Afghan factions the need to unite, to form an alliance.

The tragic deaths of Zia and Acktar also caused the Pakistani high command to be restructured. Gulham Ishaq Khan, head of Agha Hasan Abedi's BCCI Foundation and past president pro tempore of the Pakistani Senate, became president of Pakistan. Lieutenant General Hamid Gul assumed the directorship of ISI.

The death of Zia created political turmoil within Pakistan. Zulfikar Ali Bhutto's daughter Benazir was quoted as saying, "The death of Zia was by divine intervention; it was an act of God."[6]

Perhaps. But it was not divine intervention that laid roadblocks in the path of a serious inquiry into the plane crash. The counterterrorism section of the FBI was to send a team to Pakistan to investigate the crash. The FBI has the authority to investigate suspicious air crashes that involve U.S. citizens—an American ambassador and an army general unquestionably fall into that category. But before their departure Secretary of State George

Shultz recommended the FBI not go because of "delicate political problems." Thus an American air force team headed by Colonel Daniel Sowada went instead, but only to assist Pakistan's official board of inquiry. Shultz later defended his decision saying he wanted to avoid myriad political problems should the FBI discover that any of the prime political suspects was, in fact, responsible for the murders.

The State Department went even further. Stories were leaked to the media, and printed in the *New York Times* on October 14, 1988, that the crash was an "accident" due to a malfunction on the aircraft—notwithstanding that the Pakistani inquiry, fully supported by the U.S. air force investigators, concluded that "sabotage was the only possible cause of the crash consistent with known facts."

In the most thorough investigation published on the crash, Edward Epstein examined every malfunction which could conceivably occur on a C-130 and logically eliminated them one by one. He concluded that a complete investigation would have to be conducted to pin responsibility on the culprit. The only Pakistani agency with such capability was the ISI. In an interview with General Hamid Gul, Epstein was told that the "government had called off the ISI inquiry and transferred responsibility for the probe to a civilian panel." Hamid Gul implied that he did not expect any resolution of the case.

In his report, Epstein said that a chemical analysis of the wreckage discovered "traces of pentaerythritol tetranitrate (PETN), an explosive commonly used by saboteurs." Chemical experts were quoted by Epstein in an article in *Vanity Fair* (June 1989) saying such a chemical, used by the Soviets in Afghanistan, had paralyzed mujahaddin while still holding their rifles and that death had apparently ensued in less than thirty seconds. This chemical agent, manufactured in the Soviet Union, could have been placed in a container the size of a soda can, put in the air vents of the aircraft, and set to explode when pressurized air was pumped in.

Other experts were quoted as saying the American-manufactured VX nerve gas was odorless, easily transportable in liquid form, and that a tiny quantity would have been sufficient to kill the flight crew and cause the crash. The *Vanity Fair* article said the residue would have been phosphorus. Debris from the cockpit showed heavy traces of phosphorus.

But official demands for an inquiry quickly dissipated in the political upheaval in Pakistan following Zia's death. The truth was never revealed. The American air force inquiry and the testimony of officers involved, which was demanded by Congress, was classified. In November 1988, Benazir Bhutto was elected prime minister of Pakistan. She was content with Zia's death. Revealing his murderer was not in her political interests. She did not want Zia to be a martyr.

Epstein and others, including myself, who investigated the crash came up with one identical conclusion: because witnesses at the Bahawalpur airport were never interrogated but transferred; because autopsies which would have revealed chemicals in the bodies of the victims were not allowed; and because of the amount of disinformation about the crash; therefore, a well-organized and well-executed coverup had taken place. And, as Epstein reported, "If this is so, then the crash of Pak One has to have been an inside job." He added, "The KGB might have had the motive, and even the means, to bring down the plane, but not the ability to stop planned autopsies at a military hospital in Pakistan, stifle interrogations, or, for that matter, keep the FBI out of the picture. The same is true of anti-Zia undergrounds."

Regardless of who killed Zia, the assassination did have a profound impact upon the mujahaddin. The immediate effect was to intensify the factionalism between the different groups. This would become their greatest problem since the Soviets invaded their country.

CHAPTER 30

History Begins to Repeat Itself

A populace never rebels from passion for attack, but from impatience of suffering.

—EDMUND BURKE, 1729–1797

With Zia and Aktar out of the picture and the significantly more liberal Benazir coming to power in Pakistan, the Soviets moved to take advantage of the situation, most notably by introducing SCUD missiles in Afghanistan.[1] The missiles had a range of about two hundred miles and the explosive power of several thousand-pound bombs. But they were highly inaccurate, missing their targets by ten kilometers or more. This in itself was dangerous to the mujahaddin, particularly in a large open valley area like that surrounding the city of Jalalabad where the men were scattered across the flat terrain.

Up to ten SCUDs were fired into the Nangahar plains surrounding Jalalabad every day. They had a much larger psychological than military effect. One afternoon while I was filming operations of the mujahaddin laying siege to Jalalabad three SCUDs exploded within the range of my camera. The clouds of dust and shrapnel were terrifying.

The SCUDs also created concern in Pakistan, because the Northwest Frontier of Pakistan was now within range of destructive weapons fired from Kabul. The U.S. State Department issued a briefing paper which surmised that the Soviets' main purpose in deploying them in Afghanistan was to intimidate Pakistan, still the sole conduit for the delivery of weapons to the mujahaddin.

While the change in government following Zia's death was taking place in Islamabad, George Bush was elected to succeed Ronald Reagan in Washington. A test of wills between the two new governments surfaced in regards to Afghanistan shortly after the election. In the eyes of the Pakistani, President-elect Bush sent a mixed signal to the Soviets.[2] While the new administration would resolutely hold the Soviets to the schedule of withdrawal called for in the Geneva accords, he emphasized his eagerness to build good will between the superpowers.

At about this time, State Department officials were taken aback by an action taken by outgoing President Reagan. Professor Rabbani, who now headed the mujahaddin alliance, visited Washington and was warmly received by the president. Reagan not only told Rabbani that he would pressure the Soviets to withdraw as promised, but went one step further. The president promised American solidarity with the mujahaddin themselves. And George Shultz repeated the pledge in a meeting with Rabbani the next day.[3]

In short, the Soviets and Americans were positioning their respective allies in the best manner possible in anticipation of a complete Soviet withdrawal. The Soviets were arming and escalating the military capacity of the Kabul regime, and the Americans were shoring up political support for the Resistance.

Situation reports issued by Abdul Haq described life in Kabul as increasingly anxious. The general population feared a future without the Soviet military defense. In Kabul, American chargé John Glassman did nothing to allay the alarm. On the diplomatic cocktail circuit he was heard to say, "We want to teach the Russians their Vietnam lesson and get out."[4] In fluent Russian, he would ask Soviet and Eastern European envoys if they had adequate plans for evacuation following the Soviet withdrawal. I myself was in a group at a party at the American Consulate in Peshawar when he said he'd told the Soviets nobody could prevent the mujahaddin from spreading their *Jihad* into the Central Soviet Republics.

This diplomatic social banter worked both ways, of course. The communist representatives compared Gulbaddin Hekmatyar to a scourge. "If you liked Khomeini in Iran," they would tell the Westerners, "you'll love Hekmatyar."

Soviet KGB chief in Kabul, Victor Polyanichko, was among the first of the Soviet high command to leave Kabul. But he did not leave Afghanistan. He just moved his base of operations to the northern city of Mazar-i-Sharif.

To the mujahaddin commanders in late 1988 it seemed as if the CIA, through ISI, was taking more operational control over the war. Until then, the Resistance strategy consisted in hit-and-run attacks on targets of opportunity. But now, coordinated sieges, urban guerrilla warfare, and sustained campaigns were being forced upon them by ISI control officers, who obviously received their directions from the U.S. Embassy. If the commanders did not agree with the orders, they were unable to do much but offer their reason for opposition. The ISI controlled the flow of weapons and money and, thereby, the operations. The biggest disaster would come in Jalalabad several months later. But in 1988, mujahaddin commanders, with guerrilla warfare in their genes, were frequently heard to say, "Why should a country which has never won a war [Pakistan] advise a people who have never lost one [Afghanistan]?"

The political pressure from the embassy was also intense. Oakley and his assistants tried to force a working coalition among the seven different parties, parties which in any case had been created originally by the CIA/ISI to serve their practical needs. Ed McWilliams was appointed "special envoy" to the mujahaddin. McWilliams had been stationed at the embassy in Kabul and was recommended by the late Ambassador Raphel and Undersecretary of State Michael Armacost.[5] McWilliams was led to believe by a small group of Western-educated Afghans and those he had met in Kabul that tribalism was becoming obsolete in Afghanistan. While the political parties of the Afghan mujahaddin were not devised along tribal lines, the social and military structures inside

the country definitely were. For this and other reasons, Mc-
Williams was soon replaced. Peter Thompson, former deputy
chief of mission at the U.S. Embassy in Beijing, was appointed
envoy in 1990 with the rank of ambassador.

When it became apparent that the Soviets were actually leaving Afghanistan, several countries jumped into the political end
game. Iran pushed to have the small Shiia groups of mujahaddin
included in the Peshawar-based alliance—and thus in any future
government. And the British stepped up their meetings with the
Afghan leadership, as did the French. One of the more interesting of the late bloomers was the West German ambassador. The
Germans began to meet frequently with top commanders and
politicians to help a postcommunist country get on its feet.

The Germans had an interesting relationship with the Afghans
dating back to World War II. Immediately after the war the
victorious Allies requested that the large official German delegation in Kabul be turned over to them as detainees of war. King
Zahir Shah refused. He told the British and Americans that Afghanistan had been officially neutral and the Germans were
therefore their "guests." Under *Pushtoonwali*, the code of the
Pushtoons, "guests" were protected and defended. The Germans
were given official sanctuary in Afghanistan.

I remembered this special German/Afghan relationship one
day when I arrived at Abdul Haq's office as the German ambassador was leaving. He was a tall gruff-looking man with a distinct
military bearing. He was a younger version of an old man I had
met two years earlier . . .

Steve Masty and I were Asian bazaar pack rats. We would spend
hours rummaging through the shops and stalls throughout the
Northwest Frontier and in the tribal areas looking for interesting
items and collectibles. One day I found a strange medallion. It was
minted with milled edges and had the quality workmanship of a
coin. Made of silver and nickel it had the profile of Adolf Hitler on
one side with the dates: "1889–1945." On the reverse was the
German eagle clutching a swaztika with the phrase "Ein Volk-Ein

Reich-Ein Führer" stamped around the emblem. The shopkeeper sold the medallion to me for twenty rupees, about $1.50.

A medallion with the picture of Hitler and the death date meant it had been minted *after* Hitler's death—when he must have been the most despised person on earth. Who could have made this medallion?

Many months later I was traveling with Mir Zaman and the mujahaddin. On the border of Kunar Province we stopped for tea in a small village set high on a mountainside overlooking the Kunar river. Our host, an Afghan friend of Mir Zaman, told me that an old man from the West lived alone outside the village. I asked to meet him and was taken about half a mile to a small stone house off the main trail.

I was introduced to an elderly man who, though not an Afghan, looked as weatherbeaten as one. He spoke English with a heavy German gutteral accent. When he asked about my name, Kurt, I explained my German ancestry and he smiled and offered tea. When I in turn asked him how he came to live among the Afghans in one of the most remote sections of the country, he launched into a long story.

During the war he had been with the German government legation in Kabul. Round about 1945, he wasn't sure of the date, he decided to stay in his beloved Afghanistan and had spent many years in the upper reaches of the Hindu Kush in Nooristan before moving to his present location.

Then I remembered the medallion, which I carried in my wallet. I showed it to him and asked if he knew what it was. He sat up straight and bellowed, "Where did you get this?" I told him the story. He relaxed and was quiet for a time. He walked to his teapot, poured more tea, and explained.

The coin, he said, was an identification medallion for members of ODESSA, a Nazi organization created to smuggle members of the SS into countries where they would take on new identities. Many were routed through Afghanistan, where the German Embassy had functioned into the immediate postwar years, and the medallions were used by members of the supersecret organization as identity badges.

The old man laughed when he said, "In Afghanistan we worked very closely with the Zionist organizations who were smuggling Jews out of Stalin's Soviet Union." He added that the two sides, despite their bitter mutual hatred, had come to an agreement whereby they would both use Afghan territory to smuggle their own to safety. I thanked the man for the tea and left. I kept the medallion as a memento of another terrible episode in history.

The United Nations and USAID began to show great concern over the 15 to 30 million land mines (according to a UN study) left behind in Afghanistan by the retreating Soviet soldiers. Dangerous minefields such as those I'd encountered in Barikot were being widely reported.[6] Prince Sadruddin Aga Khan instituted "Operation Salaam" to teach Afghans the techniques of mine clearing, and several countries contributed military units trained in demining to instruct Afghans in such clean-up operations.

The fighting took an ugly turn as the Soviet withdrawal continued. While the mujahaddin attacked the Soviets, the communist regime started to entrench itself and build strong defense belts around Kabul, Kandahar, Jalalabad, and other cities.

But the mujahaddin were weakened because the groups began vying for control. Different commanders in various parts of the country started staking out their own turf. In nearly every case of heavy fighting among the mujahaddin, the parties of Gulbaddin and Rabbani were involved. In one meeting Mojadidi and Gulbaddin drew pistols and threatened to shoot each other until guards calmed them down. In short, the groups were falling into helpless disarray as they anticipated a post-Soviet Afghanistan. The political alliance of the seven parties was a sham.

The mujahaddin were created by a culture to combat a foreign invader. In this respect, they were never a separate entity from the general population, but rather an expression of the people and their culture. As a military force, they relied on their age-old methods of combating foreigners. But as a cohesive political organization, they failed miserably. The two facts were not contradictory. The lack of regimentation and centralization in their military commands was precisely what allowed them to face a superpower army. Had they been a centralized and disciplined force, the Soviets would have been able to sweep them away in short order.

Afghanistan, moreover, had never had a strong central political structure. The government in Kabul was historically viewed with mistrust in the countryside. The Pushtoon tribes with their history of blood feuds and territorial disputes were not disposed to any rigid political structure, and the minority Tajiks and Uzbeks in the north had survived in the Pushtoon-dominated culture by maintaining autonomous political institutions. The country was a coalition of tribes and ethnic groups, not a political entity. Many Afghan observers stated they hoped "the mujahaddin could win the war so the Afghans could get back to normalcy—organized chaos and anarchy."

Despite the pressures from CIA and ISI to control their war, the mujahaddin had never knuckled under. They fought their own war, provided their own motivation, and sought their own solutions. They were not in a position totally to refuse the advice of helpful foreigners, but they maintained their identity and independence.

Now, however, realizing the Soviet withdrawal would inevitably lead to the collapse of the Kabul regime, the mujahaddin commanders were faced with a serious problem. Their violent infighting prevented an interim government from being in place to replace the communists. Yet they had not fought and died for a decade only to have the country descend into anarchy, and that was what lay before them.

The Americans were pushing the politicians to form a broad-based coalition government comprised of all the parties and ethnic groups, including the puppet regime (with the exception of some top figures). But since the ISI continued to promote Gulbaddin as a major power, this pressure simply broadened the schisms between them. They felt that no matter what they did, Gulbaddin would come out on top.

Finally, Abdul Haq called a council of ten major commanders from various parts of the country. The prime attendees were, in addition to himself: Jalaluddin Haqani of Paktia; Qazi Amin

Wardak of Wardak; Mullah Malang of Kandahar; Qari Baba of
Ghazni; Engineer Maqmood and Abdul Qadir of Nangahar; Anwar of Logar; Sayed Jaglan of Bamyan; and Ramatullah Safi of
Mahaz. Their council formed the *Shoora of Afghan Mujahaddin
Commanders*, which became known as the "Commanders' Council." Their aim was to convene a large council of over three
hundred big and small commanders representing all regions of
the country, all ethnic groups, and all religious groups, regardless
of political party membership.

Letters and radio messages fanned out across Afghanistan. The
response was overwhelming. But the remoteness of many commands put great time barriers in the way. In some cases, it could
take up to a month to receive responses from commanders or
regional leaders. The council nevertheless plodded along in its
attempt to find a political solution for the future.

Abdul Haq and his fellow commanders' formula for stability
called for the inclusion of each major section of Afghan culture.
The tribal leaders were invited to join their council, as well as
religious leaders and advisors, both Sunni and Shiia, and the
technocrats and intelligentsia, most of whom were in exile in
Europe or America. With their participation, the commanders
would be able to provide conditions that would allow a true
peace to settle on the nation.

This formula was given to G. I. Picco, assistant to United Nations Secretary General Perez de Cuellar. He enthusiastically
endorsed it, and it eventually became the basis for a peace plan
that was presented by the UN. But it was not until nearly a year
after the Soviet withdrawal that Masood and other significant
leaders from the north finally agreed to join the Commanders'
Council. When they all did finally meet, two years later, the
ethnic and religious divisions being promoted by outside
forces—Iranians, Americans, Russians, and Pakistanis—prevented this one serious attempt at cohesion from taking hold.
The plan was ignored by the Americans, Russians, and Pakistanis. Instead, the Americans and Pakistanis forced a meeting of
Afghan delegates comprised entirely of the seven political parties
based in Peshawar to hammer out an interim government.

CHAPTER 31

Goliath Goes Down

Even victors are by victories undone.

—JOHN DRYDEN, 1631–1700

A convention of Afghans was held at the Islamic Center in Islamabad in the first week of February 1989. Delegates came from all around the world. The grounds of the center were ringed with hundreds of armed mujahaddin from each of the seven Pakistan-based parties. Inside, I watched as nearly four hundred delegates from the seven parties, as well as prominent Afghans from Europe and the United States, crammed into a room the size of a high school basketball court. They were there to form an interim government for Afghanistan following the Soviet departure.

Seated at the head table were the seven party leaders: Sayed Ahmed Gailani, Burhanuddin Rabbani, Sibgratullah Mojadidi, Maulvi Younas Khalis, Mohammad Nabi Mohammadi, Abdul Rasul Sayyaf, and Gulbaddin Hekmatyar.

The meeting was chaotic. Delegates demanding to voice their opinions shouted at the top of their lungs, only to be drowned out by others doing the same thing. International journalists were kept outside and only allowed into the hall during recesses in the proceedings. Several remained until they were caught and unceremoniously escorted out.

On the second day, some semblance of sanity appeared to take hold. A movement gathered steam to pick an interim government formed of individuals who were not from the seven party leadership—an artificial grouping imposed by non-Afghans—but the leadership was able to postpone a vote until the next day. Overnight, ISI representatives went to work bribing and pressuring delegates until the idea of a truly independent government was dead. As a result, on the third day, the Interim Government of the Islamic Republic of Afghanistan was announced without anybody having voted for it. The de facto government was carved up into seven equal sections with each of the party leaders holding a major cabinet post. Their deputy party leaders filled the remaining slots. Representatives of tribes and other groups left in complete disgust.

The hundreds of journalists scurried off to be on hand on February 15 when the Soviets were to complete their withdrawal from Afghanistan. They bombarded the mujahaddin offices demanding escorts to Jalalabad, the nearest Afghan city to Peshawar, just one hundred miles on the other side of the famed Khyber Pass. ISI, for its part, was pressuring the mujahaddin to ignore them, for their own safety, and because the ISI had a more important agenda.

Qadir's mujahaddin had for months maintained a near total blockade of Jalalabad: the regime had been reduced to supplying the city by night-flying helicopters. But now the ISI pressured mujahaddin from other parties into the Nangahar plains to storm the city. Gulbaddin was given truckloads of armaments and urged to move towards Jalalabad, an area where he had practically no popular support.

Qadir and Maqmood, the top commanders in Nangahar, were furious. Qadir contended that a forced operation to storm the city would result in the deaths of thousands on both sides, whereas the blockade would eventually force the collapse of the defense from lack of adequate supplies. Moreover, Gulbaddin and others would loot the city and murder innocent people. But Pakistan and its American backers wanted a swift victory.

The ISI won out: there was an all-out frontal assault. In a quick trip to Qadir's position near Samarkhel I saw a jeep carrying three American intelligence agents—the first time ever, to my knowledge, inside of Afghanistan. Their jeep was leaving the only position occupied by Gulbaddin's forces.

The assault was a complete disaster. After the regime had mounted the heaviest bombing campaign of the war in the region surrounding the city, its forces counterattacked and retook territory lost over the previous year. The defenders enlarged their security perimeter and gained a tremendous propaganda weapon. With hundreds of journalists in Peshawar, and several in the area itself, the story of a great mujahaddin defeat soon spread through the airwaves. It could and should have been otherwise.

Kabul was the heart of Afghanistan and the center of Najib's government. With the Soviets all but gone, the deciding battles of the war would occur right there. I went to Paghman, a suburb of Kabul, with Abdul Haq and a full CBS crew. Correspondent Anthony Mason, producer Joe Halderman, and cameraman Jonathan Partridge left with me in two four-wheel drive trucks on February 10. We traversed Paktia Province, now completely under the control of Jalaluddin Haqani, skirted Gardez, still held by the regime, and drove into Logar Province.

Stopping one night at the home of a local commander, we were roughly awakened early in the morning by a rocket shell exploding at the door of our room—the compound was under heavy rocket attack from a regime post located on a hill overlooking the entire area. Running to a nearby river embankment we crouched down among large rocks on the banks, where we were pinned down by mortar and machine gun fire. For a time we thought we weren't going to escape to tell the story. Our escort decided we had to leave our position before heavier artillery destroyed us, and one by one we ran across an open field to a group of ruins fifty yards away with mortars exploding all around us.

We continued our journey by foot into the mountains that ringed Kabul Province and reached Jalrez, the main camp of Abdul Haq's Kabul Front mujahaddin. And it began to snow. It snowed into the evening and all that night and the next day and the next night. Thirty-six hours later, we were surrounded by four feet of snow with drifts well over our heads.

The third day we left on horseback headed to Paghman. The bitter cold and deep snow made our progress slow and miserable; we were soon frozen and beyond feeling. The snow reached the chests of our horses and at times we would dismount so they could move through the drifts. After over ten hours of creeping progress we reached the last mountainside to the west of Paghman, which descended about four miles into the former resort center of Afghanistan.

As we began pushing through the snow and down the mountain, we lost the trail. The entire mountain was littered with mines and only the deep snow prevented us from being blown apart. Halfway down, tank fire began spraying our position, and as huge explosions erupted all around us, we realized our dark figures were standing out starkly against the snow, presenting tempting targets for artillery and tanks at the bottom of the mountain.

Anthony Mason was walking through a trough in the snow that had been carved out by the men plodding through in front of him and I followed him, leading my horse through the heavy drifts. Then, with a high singing wheeze, a shell zipped over our heads and exploded with a deafening roar. We lurched and fell. It hit my horse, directly, just three feet behind me. The brutally contrasting color was horrifying. We ran, or attempted to run, through the snow up to our waists and made it to a clump of trees at the bottom of the mountain. It was the most difficult and dangerous trip I had made in the six years I had been covering the war. And we still didn't know how we were going to get out.

Finally, we reached a camp located in a group of bombed-out ruins in the town of Paghman—exhausted, frozen, and afraid. Green tea and a warm fire helped. But there would be no major mujahaddin assault on Kabul in this weather.

The next morning Gul Mir, Abdul's subcommander for Paghman, took us to a rise outside the town which overlooked Kabul. From there, we saw a placid scene—a stunningly beautiful city ringed by towering mountains. The deep blanket of white disguised all evidence of the military security belts that also girded the city. The history of this place was almost tangible. Here the armies of Ghengis Khan, Tamerlane, Cyrus, the British, and now the Soviets had tried—and failed—to swallow up the capital of Afghanistan.

*   *   *

Fifteen months later, I stood on that same rise as the same mujahaddin attacked a major base just below. As I ducked behind and alongside a two-foot high adobe wall to change cassettes in my camera, everything went black—a tank just one hundred yards away had fired a shell into the adobe wall. My life did not pass before my eyes, only a microsecond thought that this was death—and what was next?

I was buried underneath a pile of rubble and the men, who were certain I was dead, radioed the news to Abdul Haq. Nearly a half hour passed before they saw my arm move and they dragged me out from under the pile of adobe and dirt. But I couldn't hear. I felt explosions from the shells nearby, but I couldn't hear them. With blood flowing down my face, the men carried me down the rise and into Paghman where I was cleaned up a bit and put on a horse that took me to Abdul Haq's base camp in Jalrez where I could receive some medical assistance.

Early the next morning Abdul Haq came tearing up to my room. "You stupid son-of-a-bitch, why were you so close?" he bellowed. I could barely hear his voice, but I knew what he said. Later Hamid Jaglan asked Abdul why he greeted me so roughly when he had almost broken his neck to reach me, speaking on the way of our deep friendship, vowing that he, Abdul, would go to Albuquerque to inform my father of my death. "I just don't want him to get too proud," my best friend explained.

I was driven to Peshawar and med-evaced to San Diego's Scripps Memorial Hospital where both of my eardrums were replaced and the larger pieces of shrapnel removed from my face. Because of the danger of the operation, one piece was left in my eye. My hearing was partially restored. And I returned to Afghanistan, grateful to Dr. Mammud Mahoavi for his surgical skills.

But on this cold day in February 1989 there was no heavy fighting, only more heavy snowing. We packed up and returned to Peshawar on February 15.

In Paktia and Kunar provinces the mujahaddin had completely overrun all regime positions. But Jalalabad had not fallen, and Kabul was not only still under the regime's control, but strengthened by Najib's new defenses and new resolve. Yet everyone knew it was only a matter of time. The events taking place on the northern border of Afghanistan that very day had cemented Najib's future. It was February 15.

A final line of tanks, with a company of Spetznaz soldiers in their distinctive blue-and-white striped shirts marching behind, crossed the bridge from Hairitan in Konduz Province in Afghanistan, over the Amu Darya/Oxus river, and into Termez in the Soviet Union. A band played on the Soviet side.

Watching on the Afghan side was General Boris Gromov, supreme commander of all Soviet forces in Afghanistan. They had come ten years before to "do their international duty." Reports leaking out of Kabul claimed that one of Gromov's international duties was to secrete boxes of the famed Bactrian gold, discovered by archaeologists in Afghanistan in 1978,[1] to his private vaults in Moscow. Another report, with some confirmation, said that Gromov had viewed a treasure of Afghanistan at the Chilsatoon Palace—a ninety-meter-long carpet over three hundred years old—ordered it cut into nine pieces, and sent a section to each of several friends in Russia.[2]

But this afternoon Gromov was not reflecting on stolen gold or carpets. Or on the 1.5 million martyred Afghans. Or on the 6.5 million people his forces had uprooted from their homeland. This day his thoughts were concentrated on the last contingent of Soviet troops as they marched across the bridge at Termez.

Then he came to attention. He saluted the Red flag of the Soviet Union and began his own march across the bridge—the last uniformed Soviet to leave. Halfway across the bridge his fourteen-year-old son ran to meet him carrying a bouquet of flowers. Gromov took the flowers in his left hand and his son's hand in his right. He walked the final twenty-five yards across the bridge. He did not look back as he left the country—another would-be conqueror—without the banner of Afghanistan on his lance.

Bittersweet Victory

War is only a cowardly escape from the problems of peace.

—THOMAS MANN, 1875–1955

The Soviet national daily *Pravda* (Truth) quoted Mikhail Gorbachev in 1986 as saying, "Our international solidarity with the Afghan people is as exclusively and equally important as the security of the Soviet Union."

Two years after the Soviets were forced to withdraw from Afghanistan, the Soviet Union itself collapsed into the trash bin of history. But in 1986, not a single political prognosticator, not one anti-Marxist activist, not one intelligence analyst inside the labyrinthine headquarters of the Central Intelligence Agency had predicted the total disintegration of the communist empire.

When the Soviets invaded Afghanistan, the people fought back. Not a symbolic throwing of rocks at tanks, as in Hungary in 1956. Not a spring uprising soon smothered by superior strength, as in Czechoslovakia in 1965. But a hard revolt dedicated to fighting until "only one Afghan is left—and then they can have desert."

The ferocity of the Afghan Resistance became the first chisel driven into the totalitarian wall of the Soviet Union. Without it *Die Mauer*, the Berlin Wall, might still be standing today, dividing two separate countries. Vaclav Havel might still be in a Prague prison rather than a recent inhabitant of the Presidential Residence. Lech Walesa might still be toiling in a Gdansk shipyard. And some might still give a damn when Fidel Castro opens his mouth. The world can thank the ornery and unruly Afghan mountain people for its collective sigh of relief.

But this same world walked away from the Afghans soon after the Soviet soldiers did. The Soviet supporters of the Kabul regime left SCUD missiles, heavy armaments, tanks, jet bombers, advisors, and KGB agents. The American supporters of the mujahaddin left heavy armaments, Iranian agents, Pakistani advisors, CIA agents, and fractious infighting.

Following the departure of the Red Army, the Soviets began airlifting military supplies into Kabul, up to forty Antonov transport planes a day. The Americans and Pakistanis stopped supplying the mujahaddin—with the exception of Gulbaddin—for the remainder of 1989. The result was a stalemate inside the country. Najib and his paid militias, headed by the Dostham group of brigands, strengthened the defenses of Kabul, Mazar-i-Shariff, and Jalalabad. Herat lay in ruins and Kandahar was at the mercy of rival factions of militia and mujahaddin.

Gulbaddin began moving forces into Logar Province outside Kabul. But he was prevented from expanding his area of control by Abdul Haq and Qadir who took all of Nangahar with the exception of Jalalabad, and captured Sorobi. And by Masood, whose forces moved from the Panjsher to the northern and eastern outskirts of the city. By the end of 1989, Masood and Gulbaddin were locked in fierce combat across the north of Afghanistan.

In Peshawar the interim government, which included each of the seven parties, was a sham. Ministries run by the different parties did not communicate with each other, and the acting president, Sibgratullah Mojadidi, had no authority to exercise and therefore didn't.

The United States, through the embassy, the CIA, and USAID, attempted to force its version of the American Civil Rights Act upon the Afghan mujahaddin by requiring quotas of Afghan ethnic minorities to participate in all aid programs as well as in the interim government. This caused turmoil when the eight

Shiia parties (smaller combined than the smallest of the Peshawar-based organizations) demanded equal participation, supplies, and money.

Meanwhile, it was only a question of time before the Najib regime would collapse. In early 1990 the communist defense minister Shahnawaz Tanai defected to Gulbaddin. By warmly embracing Tanai, Gulbaddin lost his luster with a majority of the Muslim population. The U.S. Embassy, however, praised the merger of Gulbaddin and Tanai as "a step towards peace in Afghanistan."

The new American envoy to the mujahaddin, Peter Thompson, tried unsuccessfully to close the deepening divisions among the various factions. It was a futile effort since his mission worked at cross-purposes with the covert actions of the CIA and ISI, which were supplying Masood and Gulbaddin and pushing them to attack Kabul—just as the feud between the two erupted into open, deadly warfare. The infighting broadened the gulf between the political leaders and all the commanders.

At this time, the Commanders' Council, begun by ten men in 1989, took on new life. By the summer of 1991, over three hundred commanders of all parties, religious groups, and ethnic minorities had joined. Masood reluctantly agreed to meet with them—the first time since the war started that he left the north of Afghanistan.

The meeting was held at Garam Shashmah near Chitral. For two days Pushtoon, Tajik, and Uzbek commanders discussed the future of the country. Shiias and Sunnis sat down together. Only Gulbaddin's command was absent. Before they left, they had agreed to work out all disputes within the council. Their next step was to invite exiled technocrats and scholars, the *Ulema* (religious leadership), and tribal leaders to a grand council to decide the future of the country.

But Masood had meanwhile created his own council comprised of Tajik commanders in the far north. When he returned from the meeting, he opted for his council and withdrew from the Commanders' Council.

The Commanders' Council meeting was attacked from the

moment it ended. Party leaders decried it as an assault upon the party system; Gulbaddin claimed the meeting was anti-Islamic without saying why; and the Pakistanis scoffed at its inexperience. The rapid flow of events in the mountains further doomed the promise the council had held.

In the spring of 1992, many of the commanders who had attended the council meeting were working in concert. As a result, they were able to tighten the sieges on Kabul and Kandahar, and Qadir broke through the defenses of Jalalabad and captured the city.

Qadir's first concern was to secure Jalalabad and prevent widespread looting. He established an administrative system and general defense for the city. Peace was on the horizon in Nangahar.

On April 5, 1992, a massive helter-skelter assault on Kabul began. Masood attacked from the north, and Abdul Haq's forces moved from the west and south. The Dostam militia, Najib's last line of defense, cut a deal with Masood and invited him into the city. But several hundred of Gulbaddin's soldiers had slipped into the city and a bloody free-for-all ensued.

Meanwhile, the United Nations had prepared a plan for an interim government for the country. It would include each segment of Afghan society and avoid the party bickering. As part of the plan, Najib would resign the presidency and a council representing each mujahaddin faction, along with some government functionaries, would take temporary control.

UN Representative Benon Sevon was in Kabul attempting to put the plan into operation when the assault began. Najib resigned and was at the Kabul airport when Dostam, Masood, and Gulbaddin revoked their tentative agreement to support the UN plan. The plane designated to evacuate Najib was sabotaged. Afghans described this action with an old Pushtoon adage, "They each had to stick a knife in the dragon after it was dead. Then each would claim they had killed it." Najib took refuge with the UN in Kabul—just another Afghan refugee, no longer a dragon.

Sevon and others complained that the U.S. and Pakistan deliberately undermined the broad-based interim government plan in order to allow Masood to consolidate control in the city. But the fervor unleashed by the downfall of Najib made consolidation by anybody impossible.

The party leaders descended upon Kabul. They arrived as victors looking for spoils.

Mojadidi was chosen interim president for a period of three months; Masood demanded and was named defense minister; Abdul Haq was installed as commander of the national police; and Pir Gailani became foreign minister. The remaining ministries were divided among the leadership of each of the seven parties. The political chaos of the seven party alliance was shifted from Peshawar to Kabul.

Within weeks it was obvious the real power in the streets of Kabul belonged to General Dostam's militia—the same force that had controlled the city under Najib's rule following the Soviet departure. Dostam's Kabul office was filled with KGB agents, now representing the new Russian Republic. Gromov himself was the military commander of the St. Petersburg (formerly Leningrad) District of Russia. In Russia and in Afghanistan the *déjà vu* of all times was taking place.

Dostam and Masood combined forces and drove Gulbaddin's men out of the city over the summer of 1992. Gulbaddin returned to his fortress in the mountains of Logar and began to launch long-range rockets indiscriminately on the city. Many hundreds of civilians were killed.

After ninety days Mojadidi was replaced by Jamiat leader Burhanuddin Rabbani, and he and Masood moved to take over completely. This power grab by the Tajiks set off ethnic fighting unlike anything Afghanistan had seen in centuries of internecine warfare.

Throughout this period Iran had been supplying the Shiia groups which had joined in an organization called *Hezb-i-Wahdat*. While the Dostam/Masood faction was occupied fighting Gulbaddin, Shiia militias moved into the city and took control of the northwestern quadrant. Kabul was becoming the nightmare pessimists had dreaded—another Beirut.

The Dostam/Masood alliance only lasted three months, but by the end of 1992 the city was fractured with various groups holding different areas amidst daily firefights. The city was being destroyed.

Not to be left out, Pakistan's ISI moved into Kabul as conquerors, treating the Afghans like lackeys. And Pakistani Prime Minister Nawaz Sharif began to revive the old Zia/Aktar dream of a confederation of Pakistan, Iran, Afghanistan, and Turkey.

The original group of commanders who had formed the Commanders' Council complained vigorously to the Americans and the Pakistanis. The seven parties of the mujahaddin, they said, were a creation of CIA/ISI—not a natural political evolution of Afghans. They had been formed to distribute material and keep control over the Resistance. But now the fanatics that had sprung from them were preventing peace. Their complaints fell upon deaf ears.

Kabul turned into a fireball, its flames fanned by outsiders with interests other than a return to peace and stability in Afghanistan. By the spring of 1993, 75 percent of the ancient capital had been destroyed.

Iran's deepening involvement with the Shiia factions caused the CIA to turn a blind eye to the situation. As one ranking intelligence official told me, "It is better for Iran to be concerned with Afghanistan to the east than to frighten the Arabs to the west."

A minister of the interim government put it more broadly. Lamenting what outsiders were doing to his country, he said, "The Americans, Russians, and Pakistanis do not want stability in Afghanistan. They are afraid of a cohesive alliance of non-Arab countries in central Asia. And they need a bogeyman in foreign affairs. At this time, Islam is that bogeyman. If they understood the Afghan they would leave us alone." The Afghans held no threat of a return to the days of the Ottoman Empire. They are tribal, independent, uncohesive.

The one bright spot in the country was Jalalabad, now firmly under Qadir's control. A governing council of elected representatives from each district and village was installed, with Qadir elected governor of Nangahar. Refugees from Kabul streamed into Jalalabad, over 200,000 people in the first three months.

Qadir reopened the schools, university, and medical schools as coeducational institutions in direct defiance of the fanaticism of Gulbaddin and Masood. By contrast, in Kabul, Rabbani and Masood imposed strict fundamentalist edicts upon the population while anarchy reigned in the streets.

Abdul Haq refused to participate in the chaos, resigned as head of the national police, and left the city. Mojadidi and Gailani, prevented from having a real share in the government, went to London. Rahim Wardak was already there. He later returned to Kabul as chief of staff of the army for a period.

Robert Oakley was replaced as U.S. ambassador to Pakistan and soon retired, only to be recalled as special presidential envoy to Somalia.

Yuri Vorontzov, Soviet Premier Yuri Andropov's first special envoy to Kabul in 1984, became Boris Yeltsin's ambassador to the United Nations.

Vladimir Posner, Radio Moscow's man who had so often praised the Soviet rape of Afghanistan, moved to New York where he has a talk show with Phil Donohue.

Afghan refugees from areas in the country other than Kabul returned in droves to their homeland, despite the continued fighting and the millions of land mines.

The international journalists left Pakistan and Afghanistan for Saudi Arabia during Desert Storm and then went on to Somalia for the landing of the Marines.

Most of the humanitarian aid groups ran out of money and went home to England, Sweden, Germany, France, and the United States.

Across Afghanistan thousands upon thousands mounds of earth are marked with small flat stones stuck into the ground. On each mound, tall wooden stakes with tattered colored rags or scarfs blow in the wind. They are grave sites. Well over one million of them.

When they placed their bodies and their blood in the path of

Soviet expansionism, the world noticed and watched in awe. And gave them tools to kill the common enemy.

Then the Soviet Union fragmented—and the world looked elsewhere. In the New World Order, there isn't much room for the Afghans. After all, they are only crazy mountain people constantly fighting among themselves.

But Afghanistan will recover. The people will become fed up with the fighting and killing of the Masoods, Gulbaddins, and Dosthams. Outside influences will be rejected. The people will demand a traditional *Loya Jirga*, a grand council of tribal elders, religious leaders, and prominent people. The *Loya Jirga* will settle the country and install peace and security. And it will enter the twenty-first century as a new nation, built along the lines of Abdul Haq's dreams of technology, enterprise, production, and freedom.

The Free World, and indeed the former captive nations of Europe, owe a tremendous debt of gratitude to the people of Afghanistan and their mujahaddin. The mujahaddin who triumphed with the battle cry, *Allah Akhbar—Afghanistan Zindabad* (God is Great—Long Live Afghanistan) have gone home once again to become farmers, shopkeepers, teachers, builders, and businesspeople. The mujahaddin no longer exist in Afghanistan, and they won't—until the next time their country needs them.

Glossary

Chai tea

Chaikhana teahouse, or waystop on mountain trail

CIA U.S. Central Intelligence Agency

Commander term applied to all mujahaddin military commanders of whatever rank—with no military structure the term describes generals down to sergeants

DIA U.S. Defense Intelligence Agency

Haji person who has made the pilgrimage to Mecca

INR Intelligence and Research Division of the State Department

Ikhwan or Ikhwan al-Muslami Muslim Brotherhood

ISI Pakistan's Inter-Service Intelligence Agency

SIS British Secret Intelligence Service (formerly MI-6)

Jihad Holy War

Karez system of underground irrigation canals used in the mountain areas of Afghanistan—the ancient system has been in effect for centuries

KGB Soviet Intelligence Service

KhAD Farsi acronym for the Afghan Secret Police and intelligence service, modeled after the KGB

Khalq Farsi word for "masses or people," Khalq is also the second communist faction of the PDPA

Madrassa Islamic religious school

Loya Jirga Grand Assembly or Council—the *Loya Jirga* has for centuries been the Afghan traditional method of choosing leaders or solving national problems—the system has been misused by the communists and by factions of the Resistance in recent years when they called councils of their own supporters and claimed they were nationwide representative assemblies

Markaz military camp hidden in the mountains

Maulvi Islamic religious scholar

Mujahaddin holy warrior for Islam—*Muj* is a slang term adopted by Western journalists and aid workers

Mujahid singular of mujahaddin

NSC National Security Council (a White House agency)

Parcham Farsi word for "flag"—the two factions of the Afghan PDPA or Communist party drew their respective names from the titles of their newspapers

PDPA Peoples Democratic party of Afghanistan (the Communist party)

Pushtoon the dominant ethnic population of Afghanistan—the British referred to them as "Pathans," which was the accepted term until the 1980s when it was obvious they referred to themselves as Pushtoon

Ramazan the Islamic holy month of fasting—the Islamic calendar is lunar-based rather than solar-based—as a result the months do not occur at the same time each year as in Western calendars

RAW Indian Intelligence Service

Shaheed martyr, the plural is *shaheedan*

Shoora council

Tajik ethnic Afghans from the northern regions of Afghanistan, they comprise between 15 to 20 percent of the population

Ulema religious leadership of the country collectively

Uzbeg or Uzbek ethnic Afghans believed to be directly descended from the invading Mongols in the 1500s—they make up approximately 10 percent of the population—many are Shiia Muslims

The Seven Parties of the Mujahaddin

HEZB-I-ISLAMI HEKMATYAR (Party of Islam): A fanatic and radical party dedicated to promoting the Pan-Islamic movement. Affiliated with the *Ikhwan* (Muslim Brotherhood) it is led by Gulbaddin Hekmatyar. Heavily favored by U.S. and Pakistani covert agencies, this party received far more weaponry and money than its constituency or battlefield prowess warranted.

HEZB-I-ISLAMI KHALIS (Party of Islam): Led by Maulvi Younas Khalis, an Islamic scholar, former teacher, and journalist, and administered primarily by Haji Din Mohammed. Described as "fundamentalist," it is tribally based and much more moderate than Hekmatyar. This party led the military actions against the Soviet army. Major military commanders: Abdul Haq, Jalaluddin Haqani, Abdul Qadir, Qazi Amin Wardak, and Mullah Malang.

JAMIAT-I-ISLAMI (Islamic Society): Led by Professor Burhanuddin Rabbani, a former professor and theologian at Kabul University, the party consists primarily of ethnic Tajiks from the north of the country. It is also dominated by Pan-Islamists and members of the *Ikhwan*. Its two significant commanders: Ahmed Shah Masood and Ismael Khan.

ITTEHAD ISLAMI (Islamic Unity): Headed by former university professor Abdul Rasul Sayyaf, it became closely aligned with Gulbaddin in the last year of the war. Sayyaf received most of his support from radical elements in Saudi Arabia, Iraq, and other Muslim countries.

MAHAZ-I-MILLI ISLAMI (National Islamic Front of Afghanistan, or

NIFA): Led by Pir Sayed Ahmed Gailani, leader of a powerful Sufi sect, Mahaz has strength in the Kandahar area of the country and is noted for being strongly promonarch. Its military command was headed by Rahim Wardak, Sharooq Gran, and the late Haji Abdel Latif.

JABHA-I-NIJAT-MILLI (Afghan National Liberation Front): Led by Sibgratullah Mojadidi, a religous leader from Kabul, it is also a royalist party. It had no significant military command. Mojadidi was highly respected and frequently chosen as a compromise leader to ward off clashes among other groups. He was the first interim president of Afghanistan following the collapse of the communist regime in 1992.

HARAKAT-I-INQILAB-I-ISLAMI (Islamic Revolutionary Forces): Led by a moderate member of the Islamic clergy, Mohammad Nabi Mohammadi, it was involved in several important military operations. Harakat is the only one of the seven parties that existed as a political operation before the communist coup in 1978. Its membership is derived from intellectuals and the more moderate clergy.

Afghan Mujahaddin Commanders

ABDUL HAQ Born in Surkh Rud, Nangahar Province, son of Mohammed Amman. Became active in the Resistance at age sixteen. Formed the Kabul Front in 1981. Affiliated with Younas Khalis's Hezb-i-Islami, although the Kabul Front maintained almost total independence of party politics.

DIN MOHAMMAD Deputy leader of Khalis's Hezb-i-Islami, runs day-to-day party activities. A religious scholar, he is highly respected by all factions of the mujahaddin. Fundamentalist but not fanatic. He has been at odds with Gulbaddin frequently. Led several military operations in Nangahar and Kunar provinces.

ABDUL QADIR Overall commander of Khalis mujahaddin in Nangahar Province. Elected governor following fall of Jalalabad to his forces. Affiliated with Khalis and considered to be among the most moderate of mujahaddin commanders and leaders.

AHMED SHAH MASOOD Tajik commander of the Panjsher region of northern Afghanistan. Formed Council of the North which administered large regions of the northern tier of provinces. Bitter enemy of Gulbaddin and affilitated with Rabbani's Jamiat-i-Islami. Masood became defense minister in Kabul following fall of the communist regime.

ISMAEL KHAN Jamiat commander for Herat. Successfully fought

Soviet and regime attempts to control northwestern areas around Herat.

JALALUDDIN HAQANI Primary commander in Paktia Province. Maintained continual sieges of Khost and Gardez. Commanded major battle with Soviet forces at Sarto Kandow pass in December 1988. An original organizer of the Commanders' Council.

RAHIM WARDAK Top military commander for Gailani's MAHAZ or NIFA party. Moderate with a Western education, Wardak was defense attaché in New Delhi at the time of the Soviet invasion.

QAZI AMIN WARDAK Not closely related to Rahim Wardak, Amin was regional commander of Wardak Province and area around Ghazni. Originally affiliated with MAHAZ, he later joined Khalis. Considered an independent in party politics he was an organizing member of the Commanders' Council. A moderate, he has visited several Western countries.

SHAROOQ GRAN A medical doctor by profession he was a leader in Gailani's MAHAZ and commander in Nangahar and Paktia provinces. A moderate, he was educated in England and the United States.

MULLAH MALANG Commander of Khalis forces in region from Kandahar to Zabol. A chain-smoking moderate, he never carried a weapon, but earned respect for desert fighting in the flat gypsum plains of southwestern Afghanistan. His name, a nom-de-guerre, means "Crazy Mullah."

SAYED JAGLAN An independent Shiia commander in the Hazarajat region of central Afghanistan. Distanced himself from the more radical Shiia groups controlled by Iran. A member of the Commanders' Council and considered a moderate. He was a major in the precommunist army.

SHEIKH ASSIF MOSENI Leader of the Shiia party Harakat-i-Islami in the Hazarajat. Closely affialiated with Iran and supplied by the leftist Revolutionary Guards.

RAMATULLAH SAFI A brigadier in the precommunist army, Safi was originally a top military leader of MAHAZ. He later joined the Commanders' Council and became closely associated with Jalaluddin Haqani. Educated in England, he received military training in the U.S. and USSR. He is moderate and Western in outlook. He ran training camps for the mujahaddin during the Soviet occupation.

MOHAMMED ANWAR A Jamiat commander in Jagdelak. Anwar was an early member of the Commanders' Council.

There were hundreds of mujahaddin commanders over the course of the war. Some were military commanders who led thousands of troops. Others were smaller but wielded authority in specific areas. Those listed here are relevant to this book, but this is not to suggest that many others were not also important. The commanders of the mujahaddin can be compared to the men at Lexington during the American Revolution. They were average citizens from all walks of life who took up arms when their way of life was threatened. It is interesting to note that Afghanis do not use surnames as we know them; they go by first names alone.

U.S. Statement on Signing of Geneva Accords

The Geneva Accords on Afghanistan were signed on April 13, 1988. They called for a phased withdrawal of Soviet troops to begin on May 15 and to be 50 percent completed by August 15. The remainder of foreign troops were to be out of the country nine months later.

The accords further called for the safe return of Afghan refugees to their homeland.

Pakistan and Afghanistan agreed not to interfere in each others' internal affairs.

These agreements were also signed by the Soviet Union and the United States of America as guarantors of the accords.

The following U.S. Statement was attached to the accords by the United States:

The United States has agreed to act as a guarantor of the political settlement of the situation relating to Afghanistan. We believe this settlement is a major step forward in restoring peace to Afghanistan, in ending the bloodshed in that unfortunate country, and in enabling millions of Afghan refugees to return to their homes.

In agreeing to act as a guarantor, the United States states the following:

(1) The troop withdrawal obligations set out in paragraphs 5 and 6 of the Instrument on Interrelationships are central to the entire settlement. Compliance with those obligations is essential to achievement of the settlement's purposes, namely, the ending of foreign intervention in Afghanistan and the restoration of the rights of the Afghan people through the exercise of self-determination as called for by the United Nations Charter and the United Nations General Assembly resolutions on Afghanistan.

(2) The obligations undertaken by the guarantors are symmetrical. In this regard, **the United States has advised the Soviet Union that, if the USSR undertakes, as consistent with its obligations as guarantor, to provide military assistance to parties in Afghanistan, the U.S. retains the right, as consistent with its own obligations as guarantor, likewise effectively to provide such assistance.**

(3) By acting as a guarantor of the settlement, the United States does not intend to imply in any respect recognition of the present regime in Kabul as the lawful Government of Afghanistan.

NOTES

CHAPTER TWO

1 Michael Malinowski, conversation with author, Fall 1988.
2 Haji Din Mohammad, conversation with author, November 1987.
3 Malinowski, conversation with author, Fall 1988.
4 President Zia ul-Haq, conversation with author, 1986.
5 Majid Mangal, interview with author, 1985.
6 Kuldip Nayar, *Report on Afghanistan* (New Delhi: Allied, 1981), pp.78–81; Christopher Andrew and Oleg Gordievsky, *KGB: The Inside Story* (New York, N.Y: Harper-Collins, 1990), p. 575. A variety of stories purport to tell how Hafizullah Amin was killed, including a story that he and several bodyguards fought it out with guns for several hours with the KGB attackers. Having heard this version from several sources in Kabul at the time, the author has settled on it as the most accurate.
7 Abdul Haq, conversations with the author, 1983–1993.
8 Interview by author of one of the three participants.
9 Radio Moscow broadcast, London, December 26, 1979.
10 ABC Television News, "Voice of America," December 27, 1979.
11 Interviews by author of various members of the royal family at various times.
12 In-depth briefings by Gen. Abdul Acktar and interviews with royal family members.
13 Zbigniew Brzezinski, conversation with the author, 1986.

CHAPTER THREE

1 From Soviet military books captured by mujahaddin.
2 Conversation with Afghan historian Louis Dupree.
3 Don Lohbeck, *Patrick J. Hurley* (Chicago, Ill.: Regnery, 1956), pp. 226–228.

4 Ibid.

5 Conversations with numerous Afghan and American officials.

6 To this day, the former U.S. AID complex is called Little America.

7 Conversations with the three sons: Din Mohammad, Abdul Qadir, and Abdul Haq.

8 *Afghanistan, The Great Game Revisited*, edited by Rosanne Klass (New York, N.Y.: Freedom House, 1987), p. 41.

9 General Abdul Wali, conversation with the author, July 1987.

10 Louis Dupree, *Afghanistan* (Princeton, N.J.: Princeton University Press, 1973), p. 47.

11 Allen Dulles, director of the CIA, had attempted to install U.S. observation installations on the Afghan-Soviet border but was rebuffed by the Afghan government. Neither of the Dulles brothers—Allen or John Foster, secretary of state—notified Afghanistan of the U-2 spy flights over Afghan territory en route to the Soviet Union. These flights from Peshawar, Pakistan, stopped after Khrushchev brandished the wreckage of Powers' plane before an embarrassed Eisenhower.

12 Dupree, *Afghanistan*, p. 53.

13 Anahita Ratebzad was Babrak's mistress and the only woman among the founders of the PDPA; she was later a minister in Babrak's government.

14 Majid Mangal, interview with the author, 1985.

15 Known as Ikhwan-i-Muslimi, the Afghan organization was never, and is not today, as radical and fanatical as the Ikhwan in other Islamic countries.

16 Conversations between each of them—Gulbaddin Hekmatyar, Din Mohammad, Ahmed Shah Masood, and Qazi Amin—and the author.

17 The Shola-i-Jawid was also active at Kabul University, particularly among the more educated elite. Many of these self-described "intellectuals" moved to Pakistan after the Soviet invasion. While they ostensibly supported the Resistance against the Soviets, they actively worked to discredit the mujahaddin party leaders. Many of them worked for Western aid organizations or received financial support from Western donors, both public and private.

CHAPTER FOUR

1 Conversation between participants and author, Fall 1988.

2 Abdul Wali, interview with author, Rome, July 1987.

3 Interviews by author with each of the three leaders, Daoud, Rabbani, and Khalis, Summer 1988.
4 Din Mohammad, several conversations with author during 1988–1990.

CHAPTER FIVE

1 Michael Dobbs, "Vance Praises SALT Pact," *New York Times*, April 11, 1978.
2 Monthly reports on war published by Burhanuddin Majrooh quoting interviews with defectors.
3 Magid Mangal, Afghan chargé d'affaires to Moscow, who was present at signing ceremonies, interview with author, July 1984.
4 *Afghanistan: The Great Game Revisited*, edited by Rosanne Klass (New York, N.Y.: Freedom House, 1987), p. 56.
5 Malinowski, in an interview with the author (Fall 1988), said the events took place so rapidly that it was impossible to assess what had happened. He remembers pleading with the KGB officials to negotiate with the kidnappers, but to no avail.
6 Edward Lutwak, PBS "American Interests," May 1979.
7 Oleg Gordievsky, *The KGB: The Inside Story* (New York, N.Y.: Harper Collins, 1992), pp. 573–574.
8 Ibid.
9 Assessment of Pakistan's President Zia ul-Haq who regularly conversed by telephone with Amin during this period.
10 Louis Dupree, *Afghanistan* (Princeton, N.J.: Princeton University Press, 1973), p. 388.

CHAPTER SIX

1 This statement was widely quoted in January 1980.
2 Cliff Moore, DIA, interview with author, March 1985.
3 Jody Powell, White House news briefing, December 29, 1979.
4 ABC TV, "President's Address to the Nation," December 29, 1979.
5 Ibid.
6 *Afghanistan: The Great Game Revisited*, edited by Rosanne Klass (New York, N.Y.: Freedom House, 1987), pp. 60–61.
7 Pakistan had lost three wars against India's superior military since the Partition in 1947.

CHAPTER SEVEN

1 Joseph Persico, *William Casey* (New York, N.Y.: Viking, 1990), p. 203.
2 William Casey, conversation with author, September 1985.
3 Interviews between CIA personnel in Pakistan and author, Fall 1988; also reported in Bob Woodward's book *Veil* (New York, N.Y.: Simon & Shuster, 1987).
4 CBS News interview with Wilson, 1987.
5 Cost figures supplied by Brigadier Said Azar, Pakistan's director of Refugee Commission.

CHAPTER TWELVE

1 Richard Peck, interview with CBS News, March 1986.
2 Gleaned by the author from numerous conversations over the years at the American Club in Peshawar.
3 Martin Barber also blamed the U.S. for the ongoing problems in Cambodia and Laos in an interview in Peshawar, 1989.
4 Eiva distributed a regular newsletter decrying MacMahon's positions.
5 I saw two such dossiers, one from Aziz of the secret phone number, and another from a major general in Pakistan's military intelligence (MI) section.

CHAPTER THIRTEEN

1 Wardak told me he had been taken to a CIA installation in the United States where Soviet-type weaponry was being manufactured.

CHAPTER TWENTY

1 Assistant director of NSC, interview with author, 1989.
2 Interviews by author of various participants over the years, including: Robert Peck, Morton Abramowitz, Gerald Helman, and Robert Oakley at State; Lt. Gen. William Odom, Lt. Cliff Moore, and others at Defense; Ken Degraffenred and Walt Raymond at NSC; several officials at CIA.
3 General Mohammed Yousaf, *The Bear Trap, ISI* (Islamabad, Pakistan: Institute of Strategic Studies, 1992), excerpts reprinted in *Pakistan Times*, December 12, 1992, confirmed in several conversations with Gen. Abdul Acktar Rahman.

4 Frequent conversations between author and many of these officials.
5 Interviews by author with Maitre, Walt Raymond, and employees of AMRC, Spring 1989.
6 Statements made frequently by a number of major commanders.

CHAPTER TWENTY-ONE

1 Extensive conversations with Haji Din Mohammad, Izatullah Mojadidi, and others.
2 Although a Pushtoon, Gulbaddin came from a Tajik-dominated area in northern Konduz Province. His family had been "exiled" out of the Pushtoon tribal areas of the south nearly a century before over a blood feud dispute. Gulbaddin therefore had no tribal base for his politics. His oratorical ability drew followers when he attended Kabul University in the 1960s.
3 While both Saddam Hussein and Khadafi are viewed as more secular than the fanatic Ikhwan, they both have a history of assisting them for political purposes within the Islamic world.
4 Interviews by author with Hasan Nouri and Izatullah Mojadidi, attendees at the meeting, July 1992.

CHAPTER TWENTY-TWO

1 News releases and briefings by Masood Khalili, Masood's Peshawar spokesman, 1983–89.
2 Interviews by author of several journalists upon their return from the Panjsher Valley, 1985–89.
3 The British newspaper *The Telegram* and the French magazine *Paris Match* continually referred to Masood as the "Supreme Commander of the Moujahedeen."

CHAPTER TWENTY-THREE

1 Interviews with pertinent U.S. and Pakistani personnel. Also, reports in *Afghanistan, The Great Game Revisited*, edited by Roseanne Klass (New York: N.Y., Freedom House, 1987), pp. 61–63; Joseph Persico, *William Casey* (New York, N.Y.: Viking, 1989); Bob Woodward, *Veil* (New York, N.Y.: Simon & Shuster, 1987); and hundreds of newspaper reports.
2 Report to the Senate Committee on Foreign Relations, Senators Robert Kerrey and Hank Brown, September 30, 1992.
3 Conversations with member of House Intelligence Committee and Khashoggi representative Shahan. A GAO report requested in

March 1987 by Chairman William Grey indicated heavy use of BCCI accounts as did the Senate Report on the BCCI affair. Also, Elaine Sciolino, "Afghan Guerrilla War: Was U.S. Aid Diverted?" *New York Times,* March 24, 1987.

4 Peter Truell & Larry Gurwin, *False Profits* (New York, N.Y.: Houghton Mifflin, 1992), p. 133.

5 Mohammed Yousaf, *The Bear Trap* (Islamabad, Pakistan: Institute of Strategic Studies, 1992), excerpts reprinted in *Pakistan Times,* December 12, 1992.

6 Interviews with representative of Khashoggi and member of House Intelligence Committee.

7 Conversations with Mahasal Khan, official of Bank of Oman in Pakistan.

8 Pakistan's Bank of Oman offices had close relationship and even interlocking management with the United Bank of Pakistan, headed by Hasan Abedi prior to his forming BCCI.

9 Truell & Gurwin, *False Profits,* pp. 132–133.

10 Conversation with agent who had been to all three locales; also reports of congressional members of the committees involved.

11 Interviews with commanders; also reported in Mohammed Yousaf, *The Bear Trap.*

12 Mohammed Yousaf, *The Bear Trap,* excerpt reprinted in *Pakistan Times,* December 12, 1992.

CHAPTER TWENTY-FOUR

1 Elaine Sciolino, "Pakistan, Citing Rise in Air Raids, Seeks to Lease U.S. Radar Planes," *New York Times* April 28, 1987.

2 Steven R. Weisman, "Afghans Down Pakistani F-16, Saying Fighter Jet Crossed Border," *New York Times,* May 2, 1987.

3 Steven R. Weisman, "Afghans Use Plane as Anti-U.S. Exhibit," *New York Times,* May 8, 1987.

4 "Former Afghan Chief is Said to be Arrested," Associated Press, Beijing, May 3, 1987.

5 Steven R. Weisman, "Afghan Agreement Moving Closer," *New York Times,* March 11, 1987.

6 In-depth interview with Yaqub Khan in 1990.

CHAPTER TWENTY-FIVE

1 This regime offer was openly promoted in Afghanistan and in Pakistani bazaars.

CHAPTER TWENTY-SIX

1 The story did not become public until October 17, 1987, when it appeared in a *New York Times* story by Stephen Engelbert with Bernard E. Trainor, "Iranians Captured Stinger Missiles From Afghan Fighters, U.S. Says." The chain of events was reported to me by Fakir Mohmad, Din Mohammad, the ISI, and U.S. government officials.

2 I had this Kipling poem taped to my desk in Peshawar for several years.

CHAPTER TWENTY-SEVEN

1 "U.S. Soviet Diplomats Step Up Afghan Moves," *Los Angeles Times*, January 5, 1988.

2 Reuters, New Delhi, January 7, 1988.

3 Associated Press, Moscow, January 7, 1988.

4 David K. Shipler, "Reagan Didn't Know of Afghan Deal," *New York Times*, February 10, 1988.

5 David K. Shipler, "Pakistan's Afghan Moves Perplex U.S.," *New York Times*, January 15, 1988.

6 Henry Kamm, "Key Afghan Rebel Faction Chief Vows War," *New York Times*, March 18, 1988.

7 Rone Tempest, "Senator Warns of 'Trap' in Afghan Talks," *Los Angeles Times*, April 5, 1988.

8 Associated Press, Moscow, April 8, 1988.

9 Ibid.

10 Norman Kempster, "4 Nations Sign Afghan Pact," *Los Angeles Times*, April 15, 1988.

11 Ibid.

12 Paul Lewis, "U.N. Picks Official To Run Afghan Aid," *New York Times*, May 11, 1988.

13 Rone Tempest, "Soviets Link Troop Pullout Rate, Summit," *Los Angeles Times*, May 15, 1988.

14 Philip Taubman, "Toll in the Afghan War: Soviet Lists 13,310 Dead," *New York Times*, May 25, 1988.

CHAPTER TWENTY-EIGHT

1 "Anglo-Soviet Team Seizes 3 $1/2$ Tons of Hashish in London," Associated Press, London, April 30, 1988.

CHAPTER TWENTY-NINE

1 Borovik is also quoted in Paul Quinn-Judge, "Soviets to embrace Afghan foe?" *Christian Science Monitor*, October 19, 1988.
2 Edward Cody, "Soviet Aide Accuses U.S., Pakistan of Imperiling Afghan Accord," *Washington Post*, March 11, 1988.
3 Associated Press, Moscow, August 3, 1988.
4 Edward Epstein, "How General Zia Went Down," *Vanity Fair*, June 1989.
5 Ibid.
6 Interview with Benazir in Peshawar August 30, 1988, "CBS News."
7 Epstein's investigation as printed in the June 1989 *Vanity Fair* was the most thorough and logical of the many articles written about the plane crash. After talking with many of Epstein's sources, I have accepted his version and rely heavily on his published articles for this chapter.

CHAPTER THIRTY

1 Robert Pear, "Soviets are Said to Deploy Missiles in Kabul that Can Hit Pakistan," *New York Times*, November 1, 1988.
2 Elaine Sciolino, "President-Elect Sends the Soviets A Dual Message," *New York Times*, November 10, 1988.
3 Evans and Novak column, November 28, 1988.
4 Rone Tempest, "Propaganda, Rumor Fuel Intrigue in Jittery Kabul," *Los Angeles Times*, May 31, 1988.
5 "U.S. names special envoy to advise Afghanistan's major guerrilla groups," New York Times News Service, September 25, 1988.
6 Edward Girardet, "Land Mines: Soviets leave dangerous legacy behind in Afghanistan," *Christian Science Monitor*, June 22, 1988.

CHAPTER THIRTY-ONE

1 The collection of 20,000 pieces includes crafted crowns, solid gold bowls, and intricate jewelry. *Le Monde* and other sources reported it was taken from the country.
2 Author was told this story by a caretaker at the palace who defected and escaped in early 1988.

Index